Cross-Cultural Social Work: Local and global

Edited by
Ling How Kee
Jennifer Martin
Rosaleen Ow

palgrave
macmillan

First published 2014 by
PALGRAVE MACMILLAN
15–19 Claremont Street, South Yarra 3141

Visit our website at www.palgravemacmillan.com.au

Associated companies and representatives throughout the world.

National Library of Australia
Cataloguing-in-Publication entry

Title: Cross-cultural social work: local and global/edited by How Kee Ling,
            Jennifer Martin and Rosaleen Ow.
ISBN: 9781420256802 (paperback)
Notes: Includes index.
Subjects: Social service.
            Cross-cultural studies.
Other authors/contributors:
            Ling, How Kee, editor.
            Martin, Jennifer, editor.
            Ow, Rosaleen, editor.
Dewey number: 361.32

Publisher: Elizabeth Vella
Project editor: Ingrid Bond
Editor: Gill Smith
Cover designer: Dimitrios Frangoulis
Text designer: Patrick Cannon
Permissions clearance: Sarah Johnson
Typeset in Bembo/11 pt by diacriTech, Chennai
Cover image: Shutterstock/Ozerina Anna
Indexer: Fay Donlevy

Printed in Malaysia

Internet addresses
At the time of printing, the internet addresses appearing in this book were correct. Owing to the dynamic nature of the internet, however, we cannot guarantee that all these addresses will remain correct.

Contents

About the contributors

Editors

Ling How Kee is a social work educator with a deep interest in culture and diversity, and Indigenous knowledge. Having joined academia after practising as a social worker in the State Social Welfare Department of Sarawak, Malaysia, for 13 years, her teaching and research reflect her longstanding commitment to cultural diversity and community development in marginalised groups. She has given many seminars and written numerous publications on culturally appropriate social work practice and education, both locally and internationally. Her professional and personal involvement spans across women's issues, disabilities and ageing. Currently she is Associate Professor of Social Work and Director of the Centre of Excellence for Disability Studies at Universiti Malaysia Sarawak in Malaysia.

Jennifer Martin is Associate Professor of Social Work at RMIT University in Melbourne, Australia. She has considerable cross-cultural social work experience and is a leader in this field, both locally and internationally. She has written over 50 scholarly texts and articles on social work in both local and global contexts, focusing on cross-cultural social work practice with refugees and asylum seekers, and in disaster recovery, conflict management, mental health and wellbeing, and education and technology. She is a passionate advocate for social justice and social work practices to develop sustainable multicultural communities that are responsive to, and respectful of, all cultural groups—particularly new and emerging minority groups. In her own community she is the vice-president of a local association, the Chinese from the North, a group that promotes racial harmony and celebrates Chinese and all world cultures.

Rosaleen Ow is currently Head of the Department of Social Work at the National University of Singapore. Her teaching and research interests are in social work practice with low-income families, single-parent families and children of divorce, and social work in health care, especially in end-of-life issues from a multicultural perspective. Her current projects include a book on child welfare services in Singapore, advance care planning, intergenerational issues related to dysfunction and families of divorce. She sits on a number of advisory boards in local non-government organisations and government committees on research and service delivery. She is engaged with the regional Consortium of Institutes on Family in the Asian Region (CIFA) as a council member and is the current chair of the Scientific Committee for the 2016 International Conference on Social Work in Health and Mental Health.

Contributors

Nirmala Abraham's Master of Social Work research thesis was driven by her working knowledge of elderly members of the Assyrian Chaldean and Somali communities, and the need for advocating on their behalf for appropriate services. Her commitment and passion to complete her thesis was strengthened by her journey of migration and the challenges of starting a new life in a new country. She hopes that her audience, through reflecting on her discussions and recommendations, come to realise that the barriers and challenges for newly arrived migrants, when English is not their first language, can be very complex and frustrating.

Ann Joselynn Baltra-Ulloa, 'Jos', is a Chilean Mapuche woman, social work lecturer and PhD candidate in the Social Work program at the University of Tasmania, in Australia, where she teaches intercultural social work in the Bachelor and Master of Social Work programs. She has worked with migrant and refugee communities in Australia for many years. Her research interests are refugee resettlement, decolonised social work practice and 'whiteness' in social work. Her PhD explores social work encounters with people from refugee backgrounds. Her dream is to forge connections with Latin American and Asian scholars to contribute to international dialogue, action and change on issues of forced migration, the treatment of refugees and asylum seekers in resettlement countries and the rights of First Nation peoples across the globe.

Anaru Eketone belongs to the Ngāti Maniapoto and Waikato tribes of the North Island of New Zealand. He is a qualified social worker and senior lecturer in Social Work at the University of Otago. He has 20 years' experience working in Māori communities in South Auckland and his hometown Dunedin as a youth worker, social worker and health promotion advisor.

Christine Fejo-King is an Aboriginal woman from the Northern Territory of Australia. Her father was a Larrakia man from Darwin and her mother a Warumungu woman from Tennant Creek. She has been a social worker for 34 years and, over that time, has worked in the areas of mental health, substance misuse, palliative care, child protection, juvenile justice, family and individual counselling, mentoring, course development, teaching, community development and reconciliation. Christine has presented at social work conferences nationally and internationally, and has published a number of journal articles and co-authored chapters in various social work texts. In 2011 she completed a PhD at the Australian Catholic University titled 'How understanding the Aboriginal kinship system can inform better policy and practice: social work research with the Larrakia and Warumungu peoples of the Northern Territory'.

Gai Harrison is a senior lecturer in the School of Social Work and Human Services at the University of Queensland in Brisbane, Australia. Her research interests span language identity and the politics of language use, cross-cultural practice, inclusive higher education, and professional identity and education in the social welfare professions. She has taught social work in both the United Kingdom and Australia, and has also worked in Japan as an English teacher and trainer for women's services. In addition to her work in higher education, Gai has 16 years' practice experience as a social worker in a variety of fields, including community health, adult sexual assault, child sexual assault, domestic violence, HIV/AIDS counselling, and local government community work.

Peter J Mataira is from Aotearoa New Zealand and is of Māori descent. His tribal affiliations are to the Ngāti Porou and Kahungunu on the eastern coast of the North Island. He earned his PhD in Social Policy and Social Work from Massey University in Auckland, New Zealand. His doctoral research focused on Māori entrepreneurial leadership in the context of growing antagonism between tribal social obligation and economic imperatives towards shareholder profit. Currently he is an Assistant Professor and the Director of Indigenous Affairs at the Myron B Thompson School of Social Work, University of Hawaii. Peter has extensive community mental health and clinical psychiatric social work experience and has served on a number of health-related community boards and advisory committees. He teaches courses in community organising, human behaviour and the social environment, knowledge development and generalist practice, and has, over the years, lectured in areas of Indigenous evaluation research, social entrepreneurship and international social work. He publishes in Indigenous research and economic development and continues to work with Indigenous people throughout Asia and the Pacific region on social enterprise building. He is currently working on two culturally based evaluation projects in Hawaii and serves as a program accreditation consultant and social innovation adviser in Aotearoa.

Jayashree Mohanty is Assistant Professor in the Department of Social Work, National University of Singapore, and previously worked for five years in a child welfare agency in India. Her research interest includes the mental health of immigrant children and adolescents; specifically, the psychosocial adjustment of internationally adopted children, children in multicultural families and foreign-born young people. Her articles have been published in social work professional journals including *Research in Social Work Practice, Children and Youth Services Review, Journal of Ethnic and Cultural Diversity in Social Work, Families in Societies, Family Issues* and *Journal of Adolescence*. Her teaching areas include research methods, program evaluation and working with children and youth. She is an invited reviewer for several academic journals including *Adoption Quarterly, Cultural Diversity and Ethnic Minority Psychology, Asia Pacific Journal of Social Work and Development*, and *International Journal of Population Research*.

Supriya Pattanayak has qualifications from the Tata Institute of Social Sciences (MA) and the National Institute of Mental Health and Neurosciences (MPhil) in India and RMIT University in Melbourne, Australia (PhD). She has extensive teaching, research and policy experience, and her research interest is in the field of gender and development issues, and social work pedagogy in different contexts. She has worked with non-government organisations, multilateral and bilateral agencies, and federal and state governments and universities in India and Australia. In her present role as State Representative (Odisha), Department for International Development India (British High Commission), she works collaboratively with various development partners to pursue harmonisation of development efforts and achievement of the Millennium Development Goals.

Shayne Walker is of Kai Tahu, Ngāti Kahungunu, Scottish and English heritage. He is a senior lecturer at the University of Otago in New Zealand, where he has worked since 1996. Together with his wife Helen he has fostered approximately 200 children. They have three daughters and several *whangai* (foster children cared for long term). He has a background in Māori community organisations, child protection and youth work. His current research examines the links between resiliency and child protection within an Indigenous foster care model (that is, *Maatua Whangai*).

Acknowledgments

Author acknowledgments

The idea for this book originated in 2009 when How Kee from the Universiti Malaysia Sarawak (UNIMAS) was on sabbatical leave in Australia at RMIT University and the University of Queensland. From discussions with social work colleagues in Malaysia, Australia and Singapore it soon became apparent that a book on cross-cultural social work would fill a major gap in the literature by providing a much-needed focus on cross-cultural and Indigenous issues in the Asia–Pacific region. Sincere thanks to the many people who have supported us along the journey in writing this book and, in particular, all of the contributing authors for their unwavering commitment. Thanks to our reviewers Linda Briskman, Leon Fulcher, Donna McDonald, Gill Raja and Colin Smith for their thoughtful and candid feedback. We are appreciative of the enthusiasm and support for the idea of the book from our three universities (UNIMAS, RMIT and the National University of Singapore), and Elizabeth Vella from Palgrave who has encouraged and guided us throughout the writing process. We are grateful for the skillful editorial assistance provided by Gillian Smith and Ingrid Bond, and the formatting of the draft manuscript by Russell Tien.

Publisher acknowledgments

Copyright © 1987, 1999, 2007, 2012 by Gloria Anzaldúa. Reprinted by permission of Aunt Lute Books, <www.auntlute.com>, **87**; Extracts from *Puao-Te-Ata-Tu: The Report of the Ministerial Advisory Committee on a Māori Perspective*, from Ministerial Advisory Committee 1986, for the Department of Social Welfare, <http://www.msd.govt.nz/documents/about-msd-and-our-work/publications-resources/archive/1988-puaoteatatu.pdf>, **69–70**; Extracts from the 'Harvard Project on American Indian Economic Development', About the Harvard Project Overview, 2010, <http://hpaied.org>, **140**; Extracts from 'Definition of social work', International Federation of Social Workers (IFSW), 2012, <http://ifsw.org/policies/definition-of-social-work>, **123**, **132**; Extract from 'Policies: Health', International Federation of Social Workers (IFSW), 2012, <http://ifsw.org/policies/health>, **155**; Extract from personal communication with the author (How Kee Ling) by Jayl Langub, 2012, **17**; Extract from 'Forget cultural competence: Ask for an autobiography' by D, Hollinsworth, *Social Work Education: The International Journal*, 1, 2012, **13**; Extracts from *Opening New Worlds: Stories from Fields of Bicultural and Cross-cultural Practice* by Susan Young, Department of Community and Family Studies, University of Otago, 2003, **74–5**.

The author and publisher would like to acknowledge the following:

Extract from 'UNHCR Projected Global Resettlement Needs 2013', United Nations High Commissioner for Refugees, <www.unhcr.org/refworld/docid/4ff149472.html>, **156**; Extract from 'Text of the Convention Relating to the Status of Refugees', United Nations High Commissioner for Refugees 1951, <http://www.unhcr.org/3b66c2aa10.html>, **156**.

Foreword

The themes of cross-cultural social work practice, research and curriculum policy are central and enduring facets of social work debate on a global level. No matter what the country context, the issues associated with formulating sound methodologies of practice and an appropriate response to cultural diversity are firmly on the agenda. While acknowledgment of this fact is undisputed, what is more contested are the very formulas, discourses, models and methods proposed at different times and in different places. Yet the strength of this debate is itself a strength of social work. The profession's willingness to debate, cogitate, critique, propose and draw from emergent theory in practice signals not simply the complexities of the terrain it seeks to navigate but also the ongoing development of theory and practice.

Cross-Cultural Social Work: Local and global makes a significant contribution to this endeavour. The range and depth of the theoretical debate, the international reach of the dialogue and the number of practice fields drawn upon to illustrate various dimensions of this debate together make this text both unique and important. The contributions span the Asia–Pacific region and accordingly reflect some of the live issues in this context, including indigeneity and indigenous knowledges, social entrepreneurship, migrant settlement, international adoption, and culturally sensitive palliative care. This text is, however, wholly global in as much as these issues are engaged with in order to provide lessons for places elsewhere. Theories and perspectives on working with cultural diversity are critically evaluated, reconceptualised and applied in interesting and illustrative ways using case studies and worked examples. The underlying principle that culture is not static, that it is historically and socially contextualised and that it is subject to the intersectionalities of age, gender, socioeconomic status, time and other factors is sustained throughout the text to its credit.

Perhaps the strongest thematic thread of the book, however, is in terms of what it demands of the profession itself. This is a text that speaks to students, to educators, to practitioners and to those involved in the delivery of services, challenging them to reorient their focus away from the dominant paradigm of 'us' (dominant majority) working with 'them' (minority cultures) to one in which they are able to enter into the fluidity of this terrain and grapple with competing knowledges, engage with and celebrate diversity, and critically reflect on their own positioning within this dialectic.

This text brings together the distinguished and authoritative voice of scholars in the region and makes a unique contribution to a literature that has hitherto been dominated by North America, the UK and Europe. It provides a rich picture of the complexities of practice and lays down usable knowledges for students, practitioners and those who teach about service delivery.

PROFESSOR CHARLOTTE WILLIAMS OBE
DISCIPLINE HEAD AND CHAIR OF SOCIAL WORK, RMIT UNIVERSITY

Charlotte Williams is Professor and Head of Social Work at RMIT University in Melbourne, Australia. In 2007 she was made an Officer of the Order of the British Empire for services to ethnic minorities and equal opportunities. Her engagement with minoritised groups is aimed at capacity release and sustainability. She is a member of the TiSSA International Steering Committee, an international network of universities that seeks to enhance and promote international scientific and professional discourse about social work.

Introducing cross-cultural social work: local and global

Ling How Kee, Jennifer Martin and Rosaleen Ow

Social work is now a global profession. The International Federation of Social Workers (IFSW) has member organisations from 90 countries across the globe. However, despite increased interdependence and globalisation, the questions of appropriate models and methods of social work practice continue to confront practitioners and educators worldwide.

In a similar way, cultural diversity is at the forefront of social work practice within and across countries. Increasingly, social workers in different countries have to relate to multicultural societies and develop culturally relevant and appropriate practices with individuals, families, groups and communities. In addition, social workers are working more across different national boundaries or with issues that emanate from forces both within and beyond the countries they are from. Social work education therefore has to prepare graduates to work in varying cultural and socioeconomic contexts locally and globally.

Cross-cultural Social Work: Local and global is intended to meet the growing needs of social work students, practitioners and educators in a variety of contexts in the arena of international social work practice and in cross-cultural social work. Chapters are included on social work in non-Western countries; social work with immigrants and ethnic minorities from non-Western backgrounds residing in Western countries; social work with Indigenous communities; and issues for social workers working with people from a culture different from their own. The countries represented in this book are in the Asia–Pacific region: Australia, India, Malaysia, Singapore, New Zealand and Hawaii. The writings are, however, from a global perspective and yet, at other times, are distinctively local.

Social work education curriculum in many countries in the Asia–Pacific region, including Australia, has to incorporate in its content cross-cultural practice as well as standards of practice with minority communities, as stipulated by professional accreditation bodies such as the Australian Association of Social Workers. However, teaching materials in this topic area have not moved in tandem with this new development. Much of the existing literature is from United Kingdom and North America. This book endeavours to contribute to the knowledge and skills much needed in this region.

This book places culture on the centre stage of social work practice; in doing so, it engages the reader to critically reflect on cultural underpinnings of dominant social work theories and methods and to challenge the way we think about culture and cross-cultural practice. It differs from other competing titles in that it offers a rethinking of cross-cultural practice beyond adapting practices by social workers from dominant cultures when working with minority cultures, to orientating social workers to be able to think and work in the many cultures of the world.

Each chapter provides a critical understanding of the complex issues and themes related to cross-cultural social work practice. Combining theoretical discussions and practical knowledge-building materials, interspersed with illustrative case examples from different practice settings and countries, each chapter aims to facilitate the development of cultural competency in social work students and educators, practitioners and researchers.

A distinctive feature of this book is that much of the writings are drawn from the insightful knowledge and recent research of social work educators and practitioners who themselves have lived experiences of grappling with being in different cultures in which their majority or minority position is fluid: in one culture, they may be in the majority, but in another they are part of a minority. This offers the reader refreshing recounts of lessons learned from the field, while at the same time addresses profound issues confronting social workers in different practice areas in which culture cannot be ignored.

A main theme throughout the book is the celebration of different understandings within and between cultures. This acknowledges the fluidity of culture in terms of factors that impact upon individual experiences such as age, gender, socioeconomic status, time and reasons for migration, and so forth. The contributions of different cultures to the fabric of society are highlighted and suggestions are provided for how service needs can be best met by collaboration between mainstream health and ethno-specific health and welfare service providers. It is acknowledged that there remains a place for ethno-specific services and the importance of tailoring all services to cultural needs.

Structure of the book

The book is divided into two parts. Part 1 discusses the theories and perspectives of culturally appropriate social work theory and practice, as well as education and research. Chapter 2 explores major discourses on developing culturally appropriate practice theory and approaches in various countries or cultures in the past few decades. It identifies authentisation, Indigenous social work, cultural knowledge, cultural awareness and power analysis as complementary approaches to social work engaging with cultural diversity. The second part of the chapter takes the reader through a critical discussion of the much taken-for-granted concept of culture and explores how differing understandings of the concept may have impacted on the way culturally appropriate social work practice is conceptualised and developed. We then recast our gaze at social work itself as a culture, and in so doing, pull together the salient issues for further reflection on social work across cultures. Key themes and ideas in this chapter are taken up in the later chapters.

Chapter 3 critically analyses the idea of cultural competence in terms of it being an influential discourse in both policy and practice, and how it is variously defined and understood in the national and international literature. The chapter discusses how cultural competence can be conceptualised not only at the individual and professional levels, but also at the systemic and organisational levels. Cultural competence therefore can be considered as a participatory approach to working with people that operates at the micro (individual), meso (institutional) and macro (community) levels. In this way, cultural competence is concerned with addressing system-wide barriers to responsive care that equally impact on a social worker's capacity to work effectively at the interpersonal level.

The issue of white privilege and associated power relations has not received adequate attention in cross-cultural social work practice and education. In Chapter 4, Ann Joselynn Baltra-Ulloa explores her attempts in an Australian university classroom to introduce students of social work to the concept of 'whiteness' in social work's efforts to recognise diversity and work for social justice and social change. She presents an alternative pedagogy in which teaching diversity-focused social work becomes less about promoting the crossing of cultures via competent and sensitive practices and more about turning the gaze inwards and towards social work to reveal the *why* of what we do as social workers.

Chapter 5 explores the concept of biculturalism in the New Zealand context following the Treaty of Waitangi, the nation's founding agreement between Māori and the settlers who emigrated to New Zealand. This chapter looks at how and why social work students are prepared to work biculturally in the first instance and from there to a multicultural approach. The focus is on the local southern New Zealand context, but also includes a critical analysis of the New Zealand approach, considering the Social Workers Registration Board's requirement to assess cross-cultural competency.

In Chapter 6, Supriya Pattanayak explores social work practice and education in India noting that the underlying theoretical framework is very much a Western import and does not take into account the extensive diversity in the Indian context. Speaking from a critical theory and postcolonial perspective, she proposes the integration of Indigenous theory and practice principles incorporating Gandhian principles of *satyagraha* (non-cooperation), non-violence, self-reliance and self-governance, which have exerted great influence in the everyday lives of people and communities. The discussion of *epistemic violence*—a term used by postcolonial writers to describe the dominance of Western thoughts and systems over non-Western knowledge and ways of knowing—on social work education in India is echoed in Chapter 7, entitled 'Developing culturally based methods of research'.

This chapter, jointly authored by Ling How Kee and Christine Fejo-King, maintains that professional imperialism prevails in research and knowledge development of culturally appropriate social work practice. Writing in a personal style, they narrate their personal experience of conducting research, first within a Western-centric research paradigm and then breaking free from it, with insights on culturally based methods of research. The chapter discusses different ways of decolonising research before concluding with some recommendations for new reflexive research practice.

Part 2 of this book focuses on specific perspectives of or approaches to working with culturally diverse groups or in areas of practice in which culture needs to be at the core of attention. Chapter 8, entitled 'Working with marginalised Indigenous communities', situates cultural differences within the socioeconomic context of Indigenous communities and within the larger context of dominant social relations. Using a number of case studies from Australia, the chapter highlights the prevalence of whiteness and wilful blindness in social work and government policy, which serves to further marginalise and disempower these communities.

Chapter 9 explores social entrepreneurship as a critical adaptive tool for establishing a more comprehensive understanding of the nature of cross-cultural practice within a global capitalist context. Peter Mataira argues that social work, and by implication social work training and education, needs to reinvent itself in ways that respond purposefully to fiscal, technological, political and social innovations and change. Social work skills and knowledge must be based on an understanding of market forces and business practice, and how these might best serve the needs of marginalised individuals, families and communities. It is argued that social entrepreneurship should be taught as a macro practice course within social work, with examples of social entrepreneurial activities being undertaken by Indigenous social workers in the Asia–Pacific region.

Moving on to Chapter 10, the lens of cultural safety is used to explore the resettlement experiences of new and emerging communities in Australia. For many new and emerging communities the initial settlement experience is very challenging and is further complicated due to their limited skills in English, loss of networks, financial difficulties, lack of confidence, experiences of loss and trauma, and shame. This chapter explores the experiences of older Somalis and Assyrian Chaldeans and, in particular, the barriers they face in accessing appropriate health and welfare services. This chapter highlights the importance of a strengths approach, embedded within the theory of cultural safety, challenging social workers to move beyond conceptions of migrants and refugees as social problems to develop culturally appropriate health and welfare service models.

Chapter 11 explores a neglected topic area in social work: end-of-life issues from a multicultural perspective. It examines the contribution of the cultural component in holistic care planning, including concepts of a 'good death', perceptions of pain management, and the role of different sub-systems in the patient's environment in decision-making. The chapter identifies the discourse on end-of-life issues as guided by three main questions: First, what is a 'good death' (is there one)? Second, what is 'good' palliative care? Third, what is 'good' caregiving among formal and informal carers? Illustrative examples are drawn from different societies in Asia, Australia, the United States and Europe.

Chapter 12 explores the issues and challenges related to international adoption. It describes the practice of international adoption and adoption triad members in Singapore and the United States. Key issues discussed are the importance of ethnic and racial socialisation experiences of international adoptees and ethnic identity development, parental cultural competence and biological mothers' rights in international adoption. The author, based on her experience of conducting studies in the United States and Singapore, makes recommendations for social workers working in international adoption.

In the final chapter, Jennifer Martin examines key factors relevant to building and maintaining a culturally diverse human services workforce. Issues of cultural appropriateness and quality are explored in relation to staff recruitment and retention strategies. Non-traditional recruitment strategies to source broad language and cultural representation are discussed, alongside strategies for staff retention and continuing professional development. A case study highlights workforce issues for social work practice with older members of a Vietnamese community in the northwest of Melbourne, Australia. The chapter concludes with a model for building a culturally diverse aged-care workforce.

PART 1

Theories and perspectives: culturally appropriate practice, education and research

2

Social work across cultures: contexts and contestations

Ling How Kee

Introduction

Social work in diverse cultures

In the quest to develop social work practice appropriate for their own country, Egyptian social work scholars Ragab (1990) and Walton and Abo-El-Nasr (1988) coined the term 'authentisation' (or 'authenticisation'), incorporating the Arabic concept *Ta'seel* meaning 'to go back to one's roots to seek direction' (Ragab 1990, p. 43). They are among a number of social work writers who urge social workers in non-Western countries to recast their focus away from indigenisation—adapting Western-originated theory and knowledge to fit local needs—to that of authentisation—generating practice theory by grounding social work in the local culture (Ling 2003, 2004; Osei-Hwedie 1993). The idea of 'indigenisation', which began in the early 1970s and continued to the late 1990s, is said to be an outmoded concept (Gray & Coates 2008).

The question of the transferability and applicability to non-Western countries of social work practice models that originated in the West has been a recurring debate among academics and practitioners. This debate has been fielded by writers from across the Asian and African continents, where social welfare services and schools of social work have been established in the post-independence era, and also in the newly established democracies such as China and Vietnam (Fulcher 2003a; Tsang & Yang 2001; Yao 1995; Yip 2001; Yuen-Tsang & Wang 2002). Midgley (1981) described this unilateral transfer from 'the west to the rest' as 'professional imperialism', and his view has been supported by others as 'cultural imperialism' (Ngan 1993; Prager 1985). These writers have argued that the nature of social problems in non-Western developing countries is substantially different from that of Western developed countries, so entails different fields of practice and different roles for social workers. Further, the values and philosophical foundations of social work that are rooted firmly in liberal democratic values espousing individualism, self-reliance, equality and freedom are considered to be at odds with Asian and African cultural values that emphasise respect for elders and those in authority, interdependence, communal responsibility and social cohesion (Bar-On 1999; Canda, Shin & Canda 1993; Chow 1987, 1996; Goldstein 1986; Silavwe 1995). Also, the community-oriented social structures of many non-Western societies render the Western individualised casework approach irrelevant (Bose 1992; Rao 1990).

In unison with the above, First Nation and Indigenous social workers in Australia, Canada, New Zealand and the United States have been developing practice models from the core values, beliefs and approaches of Indigenous helping practices or Indigenous cultures (Hart 2002, 2006; Morrissette, McKenzie & Morrissette 1993; Ruwhiu et al. 1999; Watson 1988; Weaver 1998, 1999; Webber-Dreadon 1999; Wikaira et al. 1999). Parallel to this has been an increasing recognition of the need for culturally sensitive or ethno-specific practice with immigrants and minority ethnic groups or with 'people of color' (Henderson 1994) in the United States, United Kingdom and Australia (Cox 1989; Devore & Schlesinger 1999; Herberg 1993; Okun, Fried & Okun 1999). This is reflected in the plethora of writings in social work and other human services professions on cultural awareness (Green 1999), multicultural social work (Ewalt 1999; Sue 2005), bicultural social work (Foster 2000; see Chapter 5), culturally relevant practice (Gray, Coates & Yellow Bird 2008) and anti-racist social work (Bhatti-Sinclair 2011; Dominelli 1988). Since the 1990s, the term 'cultural competence' has begun to gain common usage in the field of human services and health care (Fong & Furuto 2000; see Chapter 3 for a fuller discussion). Yet another term which has emerged since the 1980s is 'cultural safety' (Fulcher 2002a, 2002b, 2003b; see also Chapter 10).

The key questions raised in these parallel discourses are:

- How can social work be applicable across diverse cultures and contexts?
- What models of social work will be relevant when working with people of diverse cultures and in differing countries or contexts?
- Can the methods and skills of social work be universally applied?

The central theme of all these questions is culture, or rather cultural differences between social work practice theory and method and the people that social work practitioners work with.

This chapter explores these major discourses about developing appropriate practice theory and approaches in various countries or cultures. In critiquing these positions and approaches, the much taken-for-granted concept of culture, as used in social work discourse, is 'interrogated'. The concept of culture beyond ethnicity is explored. Also discussed is culture as a site of differences and power differentials and as relational and dynamic, and the way these impact on social work practice. We then cast our gaze at social work itself as a culture and in so doing pull together the salient issues for further reflection on social work across cultures. The chapter concludes with a call for creating a metaphorical cultural space for open dialogue and mutual exchanges towards a greater understanding of developing culturally appropriate social work practice both locally and internationally.

Contested approaches for culturally appropriate practice

This section explores various positions and approaches that have been proposed or developed for culturally appropriate practice in specific society or contexts. Throughout this chapter, the term 'culturally appropriate practice' is used in a general way to mean approaches that are considered appropriate, rather than referring to a particular approach.

Authentisation and Indigenous social work

Authentisation of social work arises from the position that there are distinctive differences between the cultures of non-Western and Indigenous peoples and the values and world views of Western-originated social work practice theories and methods. The proponents of this position therefore argue that social work needs to be grounded in the world views and cultures of the people. Indigenous social work, and the development of a culturally appropriate practice model for, with and by Indigenous peoples, is premised on this position. First Nation peoples in Australia, New Zealand, Canada and the United States have developed some noteworthy examples of Indigenous and culturally appropriate social work practice based on the principles of reclamation of their cultural identities, decolonisation, spiritual liberation and community synergy and revitalisation (Hart 2002, 2006; Hazlehurst 1994; Morrissette, McKenzie & Morrissette 1993; Ruwhiu et al. 1999; Watson 1988; Webber-Dreadon 1999; Wikaira et al. 1999). Hart (2002, 2006), a First Nation Canadian, developed an Aboriginal approach to helping based on the concept of the 'medicine wheel', which generally symbolises wholeness, harmony and balance, nurturing relationships and healing.

Outside Western contexts, Ow (1990a, 1990b, 1990c) in Singapore and Ling (2003, 2007) in Malaysia have observed discrepancies between clients and the professional in defining problems and problem resolution. Values such as group-centredness, harmony, respect for elders, conflict avoidance and belief in the supernatural influence clients' perception and definition of problems and their problem-resolution strategies. Studies by Ling (2003) in Sarawak, Malaysia, further observed that local traditional helpers, rather than the social workers, appeal to help-seekers because of the mutuality between the underlying cultural themes of help-giving and help-seeking. The local helpers reinforce the help-seekers' cultural imperatives of maintaining interconnection, interdependency and harmonious relationships among significant others, and between human and nature, as well as between human and 'super-nature'. Ow and Ling suggest that social work practice in the region needs to incorporate culturally based or client-oriented criteria of problem resolution; for example, cultural principles concerning fate, family roles and cultural precedents for handling personal problems may be utilised in an intervention approach.

In a similar vein, O'Collins (1997), based on her experience in Papua New Guinea, argues for culturally appropriate approaches that deliberately seek to build on traditional methods rather than ignoring or taking away the role of the local helpers. In Israel, Al-Krenawi and Graham (1996, 1999) have included the use of traditional healing rituals among the Bedouin of the Negev in which the utilisation of community resources and the strengthening of natural support systems and helping networks serve as a part of the helping process.

In the past two decades, there has been an interest in developing Islamic-based social work. Noting the incongruence between the dominant world views of social work and Islamic world views, Barise (2005) proposes an Islam-based social work practice model incorporating Islamic values of family ties, community support and spiritually based methods of problem solving. A fundamental difference between the concept of 'helping' in Islam and in social work is that the help-seeker would 'see God as the ultimate source of help and helpers as means only' (p. 5). Crabtree, Husain and Spalek (2008) also discuss how Islamic principles inform and influence the lives of Muslim populations in the United Kingdom and illustrate how these principles can be translated into professional practice (see also Graham, Bradshaw & Trew 2009).

Many of the proponents of the authentisation and Indigenous social work approaches are insiders of the cultures and therefore have personal experience of the misfit between social work approaches and 'Indigenous ways of knowing, doing and being' (Weaver 2008, p. 71). In spite of this, Weaver (2008), a Native American social work academic, expresses her dilemma in using the term 'Indigenous social work' and raises several pertinent questions. For example, social work in one Indigenous context may not be 'Indigenous' in another Indigenous context, even among the different Indigenous communities in the United States. Further, 'the terms social work and social workers are associated with a profession that many Indigenous peoples experience as oppressive' (Weaver 2008, p. 72), and therefore even when Indigenous social workers are working with Indigenous clients and communities, they may be reluctant to term their practice 'social work'. The most incisive question she raises is 'whether helping practices truly guided by Indigenous principles, values, beliefs and ways of life could appropriately be called social work' (p. 72). This also raises the question of whether some traditional ways of helping or the values embedded in the helping practices may contravene broader human rights values enshrined in social work (Wakefield 1995). Still others challenge the claim of the universality of the definition of human rights as another form of Western imposition, and argue that human rights need to be defined in different cultural contexts (Ife 1997, 2000, 2008).

Another pertinent question is whether the world view and culture of the people in a country or among an ethnic or cultural group is homogenous. The presence of multiplicity of world views within and between varying cultural groups is not adequately addressed, nor is the changing and dynamic nature of culture taken into consideration. The People's Republic of China is a good example. Scholars of Chinese descent have written about the development of social work in China grounded in Chinese cultural tradition and values, particularly Confucianism (Chan 2006; Cheung & Liu 2004) and the predominance of benevolence over rights in Chinese society (Chow 1987; Tsang & Yan 2001; Yao 1995). Others have critiqued this position. Huang and Zhang (2008) maintain that the Chinese social work discourse has overstated the differences between China and the West and understates the differences within China. Sin (2008) went one step further, posing the question 'who and what is Chinese?' Through a review of 98 articles on Chinese populations, communities and cultures, Sin (2008) observed that the 'majority of the authors of the selected texts were scholars of Chinese descent living and teaching in Hong Kong' and 'ten authors writing from the Chinese diaspora in Australia, New Zealand, Canada and the United States' (p. 175). Sin's questions cut right through the 'politics of representation' (Mohanty 1999; Smith 1999) as to whether Hong Kong scholars are 'qualified' to represent the interest of the people in mainland China.

The cultural knowledge approach

Arising from recognition of the need to adapt practice approaches when working with people from a different culture, the 'cultural knowledge' approach necessitates acquiring knowledge of substantial ethnographic cultural characteristics of diverse ethnic or cultural groups. The ethnic-sensitive social work practice model from mainly North America is inclined towards this approach (see, for example, Devore & Schlesinger 1999; Lynch & Hanson 1992). The cultural knowledge approach details cultural characteristics of varying cultural groups and imparts culturally specific techniques to help social workers from dominant Anglo-Saxon backgrounds to work sensitively and competently with people from a minority culture.

While this approach may provide useful background knowledge about clients from a different culture, it is not without limitations. The assumption that the people from one ethnic group are homogenous runs the risk of cultural stereotyping (Rogers 1995). For example, some social work writings discuss cultural differences by focusing on varying communication styles of people from different cultures. This draws on cross-cultural communication theory, which generally views culture as differentiated by high- and low-context cultures. Low-context cultures concentrate on verbal expressiveness (generalised as Western style) and high-context cultures are more attuned to nonverbal cues and messages relying more on shared experiences. Based on this understanding, some cross-cultural communication guidebooks designed to promote Westerners' understanding of non-Western styles of communication contain simplistic, shallow understandings and consequently condescending views of people of non-Western backgrounds (see, for example, Brislin et al. 1986).

Arguably, cross-cultural training material such as this may not be in use today; however, the observation made by Hollinsworth as recently as 2012 in Australia suggests that:

> It is common for health and social care and educational services to provide training or resources that ignores or misrepresents the diversity, complexity and sometimes even the very existence of ethnic or social categories ... Generic statements are made about the 'Burmese' when there are dozens of minority communities that are not 'Burman' and who are over-represented as refugees in countries such as Australia. Even more ridiculous characterizations would include Africans, Indians or Chinese (2012, p. 3).

This essentialist definition of culture based on the assumption that people can be slotted into primordially determined characteristics not only disregards the heterogeneity within an ethnic group, but further the approach can, at its worst, lend itself to be used in a racist way (Dominelli 1988; Fong & Mokuau 1994; Gross 1995). As Hollinsworth (2012, p. 3) notes, 'The homogenization of cultural and religious groupings to which we do not belong is one of the starkest manifestations of cultural racism and should not be reproduced in cultural competency curriculum education or service delivery'.

The cultural awareness approach

Proponents of the cultural awareness approach argue that one cannot be expected to know all the different cultures, but the cornerstone to culturally competent practice is to be aware of cultural differences and one's own cultural biases. In this approach, knowledge of a culture is less emphasised; instead, the focus is on developing social workers' self-awareness of their own attitudes and values towards cultural differences (Bender, Negi & Fowler 2010; Green 1999; Lum 2003; Rogers 1995). The cultural awareness approach challenges the way a person views the norms and values of their own culture as absolute and uses them as a standard against which to judge and measure all other cultures. It challenges ethnocentrism—the belief that one's own culture is superior—and promotes the view that each culture should be respected in its own right.

Training for cultural awareness often entails social workers going through a process of becoming deeply aware of their own personal cultural assumptions and biases in order to be open to other cultural points of view. An example is the inclusionary cultural model proposed by Nakanishi and Rittner (1992), who offer an experiential way of approaching cross-cultural teaching and learning.

Yan and Wong (2005) critique the underlying assumptions of this cultural awareness approach: that 'workers are presumed to have professional commitments, organizational control, and a level of autonomy that can transcend the limits of cultural influence, all of which enable them to help their clients in a way that culturally fits the clients' needs' (p. 185) is untenable. This assumes that that 'social workers are subjects capable of becoming neutral and impartial culture free agents' (p. 181), while on the other hand the client is assumed to be passive, without the capability to react, adjust or modify their cultural limits in relation to the worker undermining the agency of the individual person.

Both cultural knowledge and cultural awareness approaches posit culture as an entity—that it is a knowable and measurable thing—and the dynamic and relational nature of culture is not taken into consideration. As Jayasuriya (1990a) cautions, knowledge of varying communication styles needs to be accompanied by an understanding of how these differing styles operate across a variety of contexts and social interactions. Social workers who apply this knowledge rigidly without an understanding of the dynamic nature of communication will be limited in their ability to foster meaningful cross-cultural interactions (Jayasuriya 1990a, 1990b). The cultural awareness model and cultural knowledge model also overlook the unequal power relations between various ethnic groups in a society. As Jamrozik, Boland and Urquhart (1995) highlight, encounters between people from different cultures, which entail unequal power relationships, are likely to be conducted on the terms of the dominant culture.

The power analysis approach

The power analysis approach does not focus on culture or cultural differences; rather it emphasises social workers having an understanding of the issue of unequal power relations that marginalise minority groups in society. The anti-racist approach (Dominelli, 1988) and anti-discriminatory and anti-oppressive approach (Dominelli 2002; Thompson 2006) developed in the United Kingdom are exemplary in forging a power analysis approach that extends beyond ethnicity to women, people with disabilities and older persons. One of the key tenets of the approach is that the origins of the problems faced by clients lie in social structures and therefore social workers need to address the structural disadvantage faced by minority groups in society.

The power analysis approach highlights a pertinent issue, as stated in the International Federation of Social Workers (IFSW) definition of social work: 'human rights and social justice are fundamental to social work' (2012). Yet we practise in an unjust society (Jordan 1990) and are confronted with the need to challenge policy and procedural processes at the organisational and institutional level. For example, a glaring example in the context of Malaysia is the provision of health care, housing and education, which subjects ethnic minority groups in the rural regions and migrant workers to disadvantage. Accessibility (physical and financial) and social inclusion are two important considerations in addressing the issues faced by the minority. On the other hand, anti-racist social work writers such as Dominelli (1988) and Dixon and Scheurell (1995) remind us that social work itself can be used as an instrument to perpetuate oppression and marginalisation in society.

Aligned with the theme of acknowledging unequal power relationships is the cultural safety approach, which has its underpinnings in critical social theory (Fulcher 2003b; see also Chapter 10). The focus of cultural safety moves beyond cultural practices to the political, economic and social context impacting upon the individual's lived experience and social status. More recently, the gaze has turned to social workers themselves in the burgeoning writing on 'whiteness studies', a standpoint that interrogates the privileges and power of the dominant racial and cultural group. Ignoring white privilege, and adopting a colour-blind social work, is said to perpetuate racist approaches (see chapters 4 and 8).

The above discussion on contrasting approaches shows a parallel and interrelated discourse in social work in non-Western countries and with non-Western people and Indigenous peoples in Western countries. Within this discourse, social work is seen as historically part of colonisation and now part of globalisation in which, as some have argued, Western social work still assumes dominance (Cox & Pawar 2006). Embedded in these approaches for developing culturally appropriate practice is the concept of culture, which is examined in the next section.

Culture in social work

Culture is a highly contested concept in everyday and academic discourses. An interesting contrast between the everyday discourses of culture in Malaysia and those in Western academic literature, including social work literature, is noted. Culture is often seen as a source of pride in a people's heritage, as reflected in statements like 'We Chinese have more than four thousand years of culture'. Culture is also used to denote a people's superiority; for example, 'These people have no culture, unlike us'. Culture is used to differentiate 'us' from 'them', as in statements like 'We have a different culture from …' Conversely in Western literature and in social work literature, culture is what 'the others' have. As anthropologist Renato Rosaldo (1993) describes, 'the more power one has, the less culture one enjoys, and the more culture one has, the less power one wields' (p. 202). The concept of culture used in social work discourse is further explored below.

Culture to denote differences

The assumption that there is a set of practices that differentiates one cultural group from others permeates discourse on cross-cultural social work. In other words, there exist varying cultures—entire ways of life, activities, beliefs and customs of a people, groups or societies. While this has been associated with race and ethnicity, as in books such as *Race and Social Work* (Coombe & Little 1992) or *Ethnic-sensitive Social Work Practice* (Devore & Schlesinger 1999), recent discussion has shifted away from race and ethnicity to the concept of culture. This is evident from the statement in the Australian Association of Social Workers' (AASW) Education and Accreditation Standards document, which states that cross-cultural practice refers to practice where there is a diversity of tradition and intergenerational issues; ideologies, belief and religion; and race and ethnicities (AASW 2009, p. 66).

In the field of multicultural counselling, particularly in the United States, cultural diversity encompasses gender and sexual orientation, age, religion and so on (Fong & Furuto 2001). This shift reflects a view of culture as extending to groups within society 'who spend much of their time in unique contexts that foster and reward remarkably distinctive assumptions, values, beliefs and rules for behaviour' (Koegel 1992, p. 1). Again, according to AASW, cross-cultural practice also refers to work acknowledging 'other diverse identities, such as sexual, political, professional and organisational' (AASW 2009, p. 66).

Conceptualising culture as differences opens up a range of questions about what constitutes cross-cultural social work practice and cultural competency. Park (2005, p. 13) has carried out a critical discourse analysis of the concepts of culture in a number of leading social work journals and articles and observes that culture 'has become a key signifier of difference', replacing the categories of race and ethnicity. This raises the questions, differences from what? How do we see differences? If differences are to be cherished, how do we do that? What if the differences we see are against our view of what is right and what is good? As Park (2005, p. 21) aptly cautioned, differences may be viewed against a Western framework; the 'white' mainstream is used as the point of comparison for difference and divergence, as she writes:

> Against the blank, white backdrop of the 'culture-free' mainstream, the 'cultured' Others are made visible in sharp relief, and this visibility—a sign of separateness and differentiations from the standard—are inscriptions of marginality. Embedded in the conceptualization of culture as difference, in other words, is that of difference conceptualized as deficiency (Park 2005, p. 22).

Culture as relational and dynamic

Green (1999) maintains that a relational rather than essentialist view of culture is the only useful way to think about cultural differences in a complex, heterogeneous society. Culture is then what becomes meaningful in a cross–cultural encounter.

A case study in a neighbourhood with residents from diverse ethnic backgrounds in the capital city of Kuching, Sarawak, one of the two Borneo states of Malaysia, illustrates how different culture impacts on human interaction and the interpretation of a situation (Langub 2012, pers. comm.).

CULTURE: A SITE OF DIFFERENCES

An eight-year-old boy of *Bidayuh* background, while playing outside his house, was bitten by the Chinese neighbour's dog, which was let out. As a gesture of apology, the owner of the dog offered to pay the medical fee involved. The boy's father, a lawyer by background, was considering taking a lawsuit against the neighbour for his negligence. The incident coincided with the visit of the boy's 70-year-old grandfather from his rural village, who upon knowing all that had occurred, advised his son not to proceed with any legal action against the neighbour, nor did he want the neighbour to pay the medical fee. To both his son and the neighbour's astonishment, he requested the neighbour give a 10-cent coin and a jar. The grandfather then performed a ritual together with the boy and everything was then 'back to normal'.

This case clearly showed that the participants' actions were guided by their cultural world view. The neighbour's offer to pay the medical fee was guided by a sense of responsibility. The boy's father saw a failure on the part of the neighbour to ensure that his dog did not pose a danger to the neighbourhood. How do we explain the action of the grandfather? To understand his action, we need to understand the world view of the traditional *Bidayuh* people of Sarawak, which is steeped in spirituality. The prime concern for the grandfather was the spiritual wellbeing of the boy. The dog bite to the child was not so much a bodily harm as a disruption of the boy's spirit. It (the spirit) may leave him (literally) weak and thwart his growth into a strong man. To return his spirit to its original state, something of metal is needed to restore the strength of the spirit and something is required to contain his spirit—hence the 10-cent coin (the metal) and the jar. An act of restitution was made by the neighbour providing the items and the grandfather performing a ritual.

CASE STUDY **2.1**

Understanding of culture in everyday life and in social work practice can be further illustrated by this case. First, culture can be thought of as a cognitive map we use to guide behaviour and interpret experience (Barth 1995). Culture could therefore be conceptualised as the organised system of knowledge and belief whereby a people structure their experience and perceptions, formulate acts and choose between alternatives (Keesing & Strathern 1998). Second, culture, as a system of knowledge, is dynamic and changing. As this case demonstrates, the world view and beliefs of the older man are no longer held by his son. He and a younger generation of *Bidayuh* and other Indigenous groups of Sarawak are no longer holding on to the spiritual beliefs of their ancestors or practising the rituals associated with these beliefs. Modernisation, urbanisation and their conversion to Christianity have contributed to the changing culture (for further understanding of *Bidayuh* traditional culture, refer to Jarraw 1994; Langub 1994).

A point to highlight in this case study is that each party involved was willing to go by a particular set of beliefs, perhaps partly demonstrating a respect accorded to an older person in a plural community. What needs further highlighting is that the older man had in fact demonstrated respect and acceptance of the neighbour's different culture by not asking him to join in the ritual, whereas in the village setting, or if the neighbour was from the same ethnic background, he would have been required to do so. A pertinent question to raise here is what if a case like this develops into a neighbourhood dispute and a social worker is referred?

In this situation, how then would our cultural background impact on the way we see the situation? Cultural knowledge will therefore be important to provide us background knowledge about the cultural beliefs of the diverse cultural groups we work with. Yet knowledge of the culture of the people we work with is not enough; we have to have an awareness of our own culture and how this may impact on the way we view situations like this—the *cultural awareness* approach. On the other hand, while cultural knowledge provides a frame of reference for working with a client from a culture different from our own, it should be stressed that the knowledge we have about a certain culture is always provisional and incomplete:

> ... there is a need to take into account the diversity and heterogeneity which exists within, as well as across cultures, and in terms of rural–urban divides and religious differences. Furthermore, a person can move between cultures and be multicultural; as a result such a person might hold divergent worldviews and contradictory perspectives and values. This may include individuals who synthesize different blends of traditional spirituality and formal religion; who are of mixed heritage; who converted from one religion to another; or who are influenced by different cultures within and/or outside Sarawak. The result of this 'pluralization' of the lifeworld means that it is unlikely that a particular culture exists as a neat and discrete category in a multicultural world (Ling 2008, p. 103).

Dean says it well:

> ... our knowledge is always partial and we are always operating from a position of incompletion or lack of competence. Our goal is not so much to achieve competence but to participate in the ongoing process of understanding and building relationship (2001, p. 628).

Culture as a site of power differentials

The above case clearly illuminates the points made by Rosaldo (1993) that culture is reflected in the mundane practices of everyday life. Culture is the way a person or community constructs meanings and beliefs about family, child rearing, religion, kinship, social roles, parenting, health and mental health, ageing and death (see chapters 11 and 13). Child-rearing practices and childcare are much contested areas of social work practice, an arena in which it is all too easy for social workers' cultural and professional assumptions to take precedence (Fulcher 2012).

Several cases in Australia highlight the tendency for social workers to base their assessment on a white, middle-class framework of what constitutes positive parenting. Malin, Campbell and Agius (1996) discuss the Nunga Aboriginal way of encouraging self-regulating and self-reliant behaviour. Children are given more autonomy in their daily functioning, feeding themselves only when wanted. The writers explore how this is viewed as inadequate supervision and non-compliance in the eyes of white, middle-class Australians. Yeo (2003) explored current assessment practices in relation to bonding and attachment of Indigenous Australian children and found that assessment practices are predicated on an ethnocentric view based on Anglo-Celtic values. For example, child rearing in the Aboriginal culture is literally a family and community concern, not solely confined to the parents of the child. The child may therefore have multiple caregivers and their sense of security is derived from a network of multiple caregivers and acceptance in their community. Determining the appropriateness of Western-oriented assessment practices of bonding and attachment, without taking into account the historical spiritual and cultural contexts of Aboriginal cultural values, has serious repercussions. These include concerns that Indigenous children may continue to be removed from their communities and be significantly over-represented in the substitute care population. In this context, a power analysis approach is of great relevance to social work practice across cultures.

This discussion highlights again that social work knowledge and practice methods are very much a product of a certain culture. We now turn to examining the idea of social work as a culture.

A way forward—seeing social work as a culture

Social work theory, knowledge and skills are socially constructed, influenced by the socio-cultural milieu in which social work occurs (Payne 1997). Green (1982, 1999) argues that social work itself can be seen as a culture, having a distinctive set of implicit and explicit values, a recognisable language, a body of knowledge and received traditions, its own set of institutions and activities of maintaining its own identity. Viewing social work as a culture redirects our thinking in the following ways.

First, when we bring social work across borders, we need to be mindful that the process does not lead to the displacement, marginalisation or domination of the world views of the people or community whose wellbeing social work purports to uplift. Second, social work, as one of the cultures of helping in relation to the other existing cultures of helping, needs to consider whether it might dominate or obliterate these other cultures. Third, social work, whether as a profession or as a culture, is 'what social workers do' (Payne 1996) in the same way that culture is lived and experienced by members of that culture. Social work knowledge, as culture, is constantly being interpreted and enacted by social workers according to contexts—societal and organisational—and mediated by individuals' culture, gender, age, life experience and social position.

On the other hand, some will resist the view of social work as *one* culture given the divergent and even opposing theoretical positions of social work. The wide array and ever-emerging theories of social work, which have varying perspectives about individuals and society and the purpose and nature of social work, make social work a very diverse culture, if it is to be considered as a culture. This again rings true for all cultures, whether it is for the Chinese living in China or Chinese in different parts of the world (Sin 2008) or the *Bidayuh* in Sarawak in the case study above. Further, the assumption of a monolithic body of Western social work knowledge is debatable (Sin 2008; Yan & Tsui 2007). Multicultural social work could be extended to refer to social work itself, in addition to social work that deals with cultural diversity. Social work, whether it is developed and practised in the West or in societies in which social work is yet to take root as a profession, needs to be conceptualised as a multicultural profession interacting with multi-cultures of helping practices and multi-cultures of people we work with (Ling 2008).

Promoting multicultural social work

The fluid position of multicultural social work offers a way that a plurality of approaches for cross-cultural social work can engage with one another. Given that much social and cultural interaction takes place within societies and among peoples of the world, not all Western social work theories and approaches are irrelevant to non-Western societies. Similarly, social work approaches developed from the authentisation position and Indigenous social work will be able to influence, and indeed has already influenced, Western social work (Harrison & Melville 2010).

In addition, a multicultural view of social work draws attention to the monocultural outlook of cultural knowledge and cultural awareness approaches. Both have tended to focus primarily on how Western social work relates to non-Western contexts, and do not consider other types of cross-cultural social work interaction. In a similar way, the authentisation position and Indigenous social work, concerned with developing social work that reflects the local culture, do not pay due consideration to the multicultural nature of most societies today, nor do they acknowledge the heterogeneous nature of any one cultural grouping. For example, a social worker may be a non-Western person working with clients of Western backgrounds, or both the social worker and client may be from different non-Western backgrounds, or they may share the same cultural heritage but from different geographical, national or class backgrounds. A multicultural perspective requires one to move away from the concern of 'West meeting East' to a consideration of all cross-cultural or multicultural relationships (Dungee-Anderson & Beckett 1995). As Shayne Walker and Anaru Eketone discuss in the context of Aotearoa New Zealand (see Chapter 5), cross-cultural practice refers to social workers of one cultural background working with clients of a different background and this should not exclude a Māori social worker working with a *Pākehā* (European Settlers and their descendents) client.

Social work practice as an intersection of different cultures

No-one is culture-free. Very often we are not aware of our own culture until we come across situations that are not within our frame of reference. It is possible for us to operate from our own assumptions and world views and become oblivious to other assumptions and world views. It is not an overstatement to say that every social work encounter is an intersection of different cultures. Social workers bring into their day-to-day practice their own culture and the social work (professional) culture, working under an organisational culture with clients who also bring their own culture. The crux of the matter is, in the interplay of all these cultures is the client's culture acknowledged and appreciated? Or do we, unknowingly, in doing what we think is good for our clients, impose our culture(s) on them? Does our organisational culture—our office settings and our care facilities—consider and make provisions for the diverse cultural backgrounds of our clients? Further, is cultural diversity taken into consideration in the formulation of services and programs?

Social work system and organisational culture

A recent study by Harrison and Turner (2010) of social workers in Queensland, Australia, found that organisational context was seen to be very influential in determining how well practitioners respond to the cultural needs of clients. Some of the impediments to culturally responsive practice were cited as administrative tasks, bureaucratic barriers and resource constraints (see also Chapter 3). An important point raised was the incongruence between the service model employed by the organisation, which is inclined towards individual work, and the need for family and group involvement. This highlights the point that service provision, including the method of service delivery, needs to take into consideration the central role of culture in help-giving and help-seeking practices in different communities. If social work services are offered as an alternative to existing helping systems, then the services should be provided in ways that tap community resources, thereby strengthening and empowering existing community helping systems (see Chapter 8).

In cases where residential care is the solution to a person's situation, we need to question whether cultural diversity is being taken into account. For example, when a child is admitted to a residential care facility we should consider whether it provides any sense of cultural safety. As elucidated by Fulcher (2002a), cultural safety is a state of being in which the child or young person's social and cultural frames of reference are acknowledged, even though not fully understood. Similarly, formulation of policies and programs needs to occur in consultation with various communities, taking into consideration community needs and aspirations, using community self-determination and empowerment as guiding principles.

Education and knowledge development

Conceptualising social work as multicultural has implications for social work education and knowledge development. How do we provide students and practitioners a framework of embracing diversity, yet be critical of the various approaches of culturally appropriate practice? How do we instil in students the importance of recognising culture as core to social work practice—having cultural knowledge and awareness, yet at the same time, having a critical perspective of the power analysis approach? Social work education curricula and the educational process are once again an intersection of different cultures. As Pedersen (1984) discusses, social work educators bring their own culture(s), work with students from diverse cultures and teach a third culture (social work) in the environment of a fourth culture (the educational institution). This intersection of cultures has meant for some a marginalising experience when their ways of knowing and being are incompatible with the individualised, competitive system of education, as studies with Indigenous students in Australia and New Zealand have shown (Foster 2000; Lynn et al. 1990; Tait-Rolleston et al. 1997; see Chapter 6 on social work education in India). The key issue is for the educational process to be an enriching experience for all.

Related to education is an area often overlooked in discourse on culturally appropriate social work practice: research to develop knowledge and theory. Research to generate social work knowledge and practice theory has been largely conducted using Western-centric research methodology that has ignored Indigenous ways of knowing and precluded the uncovering of local knowledge. Therefore, developing culturally appropriate practice needs to be accompanied by a process of decolonising methodologies (Smith 1999) and affirming the knowledge of clients and local practitioners (see Chapter 7).

Conclusion

The creation of an open cultural space

This chapter has explored major discourses on developing culturally appropriate practice theory and approaches. The authentisation, Indigenous social work, cultural knowledge and cultural awareness approaches guide us towards practice in which culture is given centre stage. The authentisation and Indigenous social work approaches remind us that cultural identity is a source of strength that steers a people towards community self-determination in developing their own ways of problem-solving and enhancement. The cultural knowledge approach encourages knowing about other cultures, while the cultural awareness approach extols awareness of self and an appreciation of cultural differences. The power analysis approach highlights the socio-political context that marginalises certain cultural groups and privileges others, and the inherent power differentials between social workers and their clients. Further examination of the concept of culture as used in social work approaches suggests the use of the concept of social work as a culture, thereby promoting the idea that, as different cultures are to be respected and embraced, different approaches to working with cultural diversity can also be mutually enriching.

In concluding this chapter, I call for the creation of a metaphorical intercultural space for open dialogue and mutual exchanges towards a greater understanding of developing culturally appropriate social work practice both locally and globally.

Internationally, much more learning can take place between Western and non-Western social work practitioners and educators in an open and equal partnership. When Midgley (2008) revisits the state of professional imperialism three decades on, he observes that some innovations originating from the developing world have been adopted in Western social work (see also Midgley 1990, 1992, 1994). Family group conferencing and micro-finance serving low-income communities are two examples of the West learning from developing countries. Likewise Gandhian philosophy, which has influenced social work in India, has inspired community development approaches in social work in Western contexts. More avenues need to be created through conferences and the use of technology to promote truly reciprocal exchanges.

Memoranda of understanding about various areas of exchanges, including knowledge-building, staff and students' exchanges and research, could be increased to facilitate two-way collaboration. A noteworthy example of collaboration is the student and academic exchange between RMIT, Australia, and Universiti Malaysia Sarawak, Malaysia, which has been ongoing for the past eight years. In particular, student exchanges, in which selected students conduct their studies in respective universities for one semester, have yielded much insight for the content and delivery of culturally relevant curriculum and the development of teaching and learning practices. These have greatly benefited students and staff from both institutions (Martin & Ling 2010).

The complementarity of the various approaches calls for a more dialogic understanding and mutual engagement so that cross-fertilisation of ideas will generate new insights for the personal and professional development of social work practitioners and educators. An intercultural open space in which the spirit of humility and curiosity prevails to engender greater understanding of cultural diversity and professional differences may well be the way forward.

REFLECTIVE QUESTIONS

1 Reflect on an experience of a cross-cultural encounter in your social work practice or other relevant situation. How do you think the approaches discussed in the chapter are relevant?
2 Reflect on an experience of working with a person of the same cultural and linguistic background as you. Did anything strike you as different? How did this experience influence the way you think about culture and cross-cultural practice?
3 What is your view of 'social work as a culture'?
4 Do you agree with the statement: 'All social work encounters are cross-cultural'? Explain your answer.
5 Is there a place for authentisation and Indigenous social work? What might be some of the issues and challenges in promoting these approaches?
6 'Socio-political and economic contexts impinge on cross-cultural social work practice.' Explain your understanding of this statement.

FURTHER READING

Dean, RG 2001, 'The myth of cross-cultural competence', *Families in Society: The Journal of Contemporary Social Services*, vol. 82, no. 6, pp. 623–30.
Walton, RG & Abo-El-Nasr, M 1988, 'Indigenization and authentization in terms of social work in Egypt', *International Social Work*, vol. 31, no. 1, pp. 135–44.
Weaver, HN 2008, 'Indigenous social work in the United States: reflections on Indian tacos, Trojan Horses and canoes filled with Indigenous revolutionaries', in M Gray, J Coates & M Yellow Bird (eds), *Indigenous Social Work Around the World: Towards Culturally Relevant Education and Practice*, Ashgate, Aldershot, pp. 71–81.

REFERENCES

Al-Krenawi, A & Graham, JR 1996, 'Social work practice and traditional healing rituals among the Bedouin of the Negev, Israel', *International Social Work*, vol. 39, no. 2, pp. 177–88.
Al-Krenawi, A & Graham, JR 1999, 'Gender and biomedical/traditional mental health utilization among the Bedouin-Arabs of the Negev', *Culture, Medicine and Psychiatry*, vol. 23, no. 2, pp. 219–43.

Australian Association of Social Workers 2009, *Statement of Specific Cross-cultural Curriculum Content for Social Work Qualifying Courses*, Australian Association of Social Workers, Canberra.

Bar-On, A 1999, 'Social work and the missionary zeal to whip the heathen along the path of righteousness', *British Journal of Social Work*, vol. 29, no. 1, pp. 5–26.

Barise, A 2005, 'Social work with Muslims: insights from the teaching of Islam', *Critical Social Work*, vol. 6, no. 2, pp. 114–32.

Barth, F 1995, 'Other knowledge and other ways of knowing', *Journal of Anthropological Research*, vol. 51, no. 1, pp. 65–8.

Bender, K, Negi, N & Fowler, DN 2010, 'Exploring the relationship between self-awareness and student commitment and understanding of culturally responsive social work practice', *Journal of Ethnic and Cultural Diversity in Social Work*, vol. 19, no. 1, pp. 34–53.

Bhatti-Sinclair, K 2011, *Anti-racist Practice in Social Work*, Palgrave Macmillan, Basingstoke.

Bose, AB 1992, 'Social work in India: developmental roles for a helping profession', in MC Hokenstad, SK Khinduka & J Midgley (eds), *Profiles in International Social Work*, National Association of Social Workers, New York.

Brislin, RW, Cusher, K, Cheerie, C & Yong, M 1986, *Intercultural Interaction: A Practical Guide*, Sage, Newbury Park, CA.

Canda, ER, Shin, SI & Canda, HJ 1993, 'Traditional philosophies of human services in Korea and contemporary social work implications', *Social Development Issues*, vol. 15, no. 3, pp. 84–104.

Chan, KL 2006, 'The Chinese concept of face and violence against women', *International Social Work*, vol. 49, no. 1, pp. 65–73.

Cheung, M & Liu, M 2004, 'The self-concept of Chinese women and the indigenization of social work in China', *International Social Work*, vol. 47, no. 1, pp. 109–27.

Chow, NWW 1987, 'Western and Chinese ideas of social welfare', *International Social Work*, vol. 30, no. 1, pp. 31–41.

Chow, N 1996, 'Social work education—east and west', *Asian Pacific Journal of Social Work and Development*, vol. 6, no. 2, pp. 5–15.

Coombe, V & Little, A 1992, *Race and Social Work: A Guide to Training*, Routledge, London.

Cox, DR 1989, *Welfare Practice in a Multicultural Society*, Prentice Hall, Sydney.

Cox, DR & Pawar, MS 2006, *International Social Work: Issues, Strategies and Programs*, 2nd edn, Sage, Thousand Oaks.

Crabtree, SA, Husain, F & Spalek, B 2008, *Islam and Social Work: Debating Values, Transforming Practice*, The Policy Press, University of Bristol.

Dean, RG 2001, 'The myth of cross-cultural competence', *Families in Society: The Journal of Contemporary Social Services*, vol. 82, no. 6, pp. 623–30.

Devore, W & Schlesinger, EG 1999, *Ethnic-Sensitive Social Work Practice*, 5th edn, Allyn & Bacon, Boston.

Dixon, J & Scheurell, RP 1995, *Social Welfare with Indigenous People*, Routledge, London.

Dominelli, L 1988, *Anti-Racist Social Work*, Macmillan, Basingstoke.

Dominelli, L 2002, *Anti-Oppressive Social Work Theory and Practice*, Palgrave Macmillan, New York.

Dungee-Anderson, D & Beckett, JO 1995, 'A process model for multicultural social work practice', *Families in Society: The Journal of Contemporary Human Services*, vol. 76, no. 8, pp. 459–68.

Ewalt, P 1999, *Multicultural Issues in Social Work: Practice and Research*, National Association of Social Workers, Washington DC.

Fong, R & Furuto, S 2001, *Culturally Competent Practice: Skills, Interventions and Evaluations*, Allyn & Bacon, Boston.

Fong, R & Mokuau, N 1994, 'Not simply Asian Americans: periodical literature review on Asian and Pacific Islanders', *Social Work*, vol. 39, no. 3, pp. 285–305.

Foster, S 2000, 'Addressing bi-culturalism in a teaching institution', *Social Work Review*, vol. 12, no. 1, pp. 3–6.

Fulcher, LC 2002a, 'Responsive child and youth care at home and away from home', *National Council of Voluntary Child Care Organisations Annual Journal*, no. 3, pp. 67–94.

Fulcher, LC 2002b, 'Cultural safety and the duty of care', *Child Welfare*, vol. 81, no. 5, pp. 689–708.

Fulcher, LC 2003a, 'The working definition of social work doesn't work very well in China and Malaysia', *Research on Social Work Practice*, vol. 13, no. 3, pp. 376–87.

Fulcher, LC 2003b, 'Rituals of encounter that guarantee cultural safety', *Journal of Relational Child and Youth Care Practice*, vol. 16, no. 3, pp. 20–7.

Fulcher, LC 2012, 'Culturally responsive work with indigenous children and families', *Reclaiming Children and Youth*, vol. 21, no. 3, pp. 53–7.

Goldstein, H 1986, 'Education for social work practice: a cognitive, cross-cultural approach', *International Social Work*, vol. 29, no. 2, pp. 149–64.

Graham, JR, Bradshaw, C & Trew, JL 2009, 'Adapting social work in working with Muslims clients', *Social Work Education: The International Journal*, vol. 28, no. 5, pp. 544–61.

Gray, M & Coates, M 2008, 'From "indigenization" to cultural relevance', in M Gray, J Coates and M Yellow Bird (eds), *Indigenous Social Work Around the World: Towards Culturally Relevant Education and Practice*, Ashgate, Aldershot, pp. 13–31.

Gray, M, Coates, J, Yellow Bird, M (eds) 2008, *Indigenous Social Work Around the World: Towards Culturally Relevant Education and Practice*, Ashgate, Aldershot.

Green, J 1999, *Cultural Awareness in the Human Services: A Multi-ethnic Approach*, 3rd edn, Allyn & Bacon, Boston.

Gross, ER 1995, 'Deconstructing politically correct practice literature: the American Indian case', *Social Work*, vol. 40, no. 2, pp. 206–13.

Harrison, G & Melville, R 2010, *Rethinking Social Work in a Global World*, Palgrave Macmillan, Basingstoke.

Harrison, G & Turner, R 2011, 'Being a "culturally competent" social worker: making sense of a murky concept in practice', *British Journal of Social Work*, vol. 41, no. 2, pp. 333–50.

Hart, MA 2002, *Seeking Mino-Pimatisiwin: An Aboriginal Approach to Helping*, Halifax, Fernwood.

Hart, MA 2006, 'An Aboriginal approach to social work practice', in T Heinonen & L Spearman (eds), *Social Work Practice: Problem-Solving and Beyond*, 2nd edn, Neilson, Toronto, pp. 235–60.

Hazlehurst, KM 1994, *A Healing Place: Indigenous Vision for Personal Empowerment and Community Recovery*, Central Queensland University, Rockhampton.

Henderson, G 1994, *Social Work Intervention: Helping People of Color*, Bergin & Garvey, London.

Herberg, DC 1993, *Frameworks for Cultural and Racial Diversity*, Canadian Scholars Press, Toronto.

Hollinsworth, D 2012, 'Forget cultural competence: Ask for an autobiography', *Social Work Education: The International Journal*, iFirst, pp. 1–13.

Huang, Y & Zhang, X 2008, 'A reflection on the indigenisation discourse in social work', *International Social Work*, vol. 51, no. 5, pp. 611–22.

Ife, J 1997, *Rethinking Social Work: Towards Critical Practice*, Longman, Melbourne.

Ife, J 2000, 'Local and global practice: relocating social work as a human rights profession in the new global order', paper presented at the Eileen Younghusband Memorial Lecture, IFSW/IASSW Biennial Conference, Montreal, 31 July.

Ife, J 2008, *Human Rights and Social Work: Towards Rights-based Practice*, Cambridge University Press, Cambridge.

International Federation of Social Workers 2012, Definition of social work, at <http://ifsw .org/policies/definition-of-social-work>.

Jamrozik, A, Boland, C & Urquhart, R 1995, *Social Change and Cultural Transformation in Australia*, Cambridge University Press, Cambridge.

Jarraw, B 1994, 'On the origin of shamanism and the concepts of sickness', *Sarawak Gazette*, vol. 121, no. 1527, pp. 15–18.

Jayasuriya, L 1990a, 'The problematic of culture and identity in cross-cultural theorising', in M Clare & L Jayasuriya (eds), *Issues in Cross Cultural Practice*, University of Western Australia, Nedlands.

Jayasuriya, L 1990b, 'Rethinking Australian multiculturalism: towards a new paradigm', *Australian Quarterly*, vol. 62, no. 1, pp. 50–63.

Jordan, B 1990, *Social Work in an Unjust Society*, Harvester Wheatsheaf, Hemel Hempstead.

Keesing, RM & Strathern, AJ 1998, *Cultural Anthropology: A Contemporary Perspective*, 3rd edn, Harcourt Brace, Philadelphia.

Koegel, P 1992, 'Through a different lens: an anthropological perspective on the homeless mentally ill culture', *Medicine and Psychiatry*, vol. 16, no. 1, pp. 1–22.

Langub, J 1994, 'Majlis Adat Istiadat and the preservation of the Adat of the natives of Sarawak', *Sarawak Museum Journal*, vol. 68, no. 1, pp. 7–16.

Ling, HK 2003, 'Drawing lessons from local designated helpers to develop culturally appropriate social work practice', *Asia Pacific Journal of Social Work and Development*, vol. 13, no. 2, pp. 26–45.

Ling, HK 2004, 'The search from within: research issues in relation to developing culturally appropriate social work practice', *International Social Work*, vol. 47, no. 3, pp. 336–45.

Ling, HK 2007, *Indigenising Social Work: Research and Practice in Sarawak*, Strategic Information and Research Development Centre, Selangor.

Ling, HK 2008, 'The development of culturally appropriate social work practice in Sarawak, Malaysia', in M Gray, J Coates & M Yellow Bird (eds), *Indigenous Social Work Around the World: Towards Culturally Relevant Education and Practice*, Ashgate, Aldershot, pp. 97–106.

Lum, D (ed.) 2003, *Culturally Competent Practice: A Framework for Understanding Diverse Groups and Justice Issues*, Brooks/Cole, Toronto.

Lynch, EW & Hanson, MJ 1992, *Developing Cross-Cultural Competence: A Guide for Working With Young Children and Their Families*, Paul H Brookes, Maryland.

Lynn, R, Pye, R, Atkinson, R & Peyton-Smith, J 1990, 'Antiracist welfare education: pie in the sky?', in J Petruchenia & R Thorpe (eds), *Social Change and Social Welfare Practice*, Hale & Iremonger, Sydney, pp. 83–5.

Malin, M, Campbell, K & Agius, L 1996, 'Raising children in the Nunga Aboriginal way', *Family Matters*, vol. 43, Autumn, pp. 43–7.

Martin, J & Ling, HK 2010, 'International education and student mobility: curriculum design and delivery', *Global Studies Journal*, vol. 3, no. 1, pp. 119–28.

Midgley, J 1981, *Professional Imperialism: Social Work In the Third World*, Heinemann. London.

Midgley, J 1990, 'International social work: learning from the Third World', *Social Work*, vol. 35, no. 4, pp. 295–301.

Midgley, J 1992, 'Is international social work a one-way transfer of idea and practice methods from the United States to other countries?—Yes', in E Gambrill & R Pruger (eds), *Controversial Issues in Social Work*, Allyn & Bacon, Boston.

Midgley, J 1994, 'Transnational strategies for social work: towards effective reciprocal exchanges', in RG Meinert, JT Pardeck & WP Sullivan (eds), *Issues in Social Work: A Critical Analysis*, Auburn House, Westport, CT, pp. 165–80.

Midgley, J 2008, 'Promoting reciprocal international social work exchanges: professional imperialism revisited', in M Gray, J Coates & M Yellow Bird (eds), *Indigenous Social Work Around the World: Towards Culturally Relevant Education and Practice*, Ashgate, Aldershot, pp. 31–48.

Mohanty, CT 1991, 'Under Western eyes: feminist scholarship and colonial discourses', in CT Mohanty, A Russ & L Torres (eds), *Third World Women and the Politics of Feminism*, Indiana University Press, Bloomington, pp. 51–80.

Morrissette, V, McKenzie, B & Morrissette, L 1993, 'Towards an Aboriginal model of social work practice: cultural knowledge and traditional practices', *Canadian Social Work Review*, vol. 10, no. 1, pp. 91–108.

Nakanishi, M & Rittner, B 1992, 'The inclusionary cultural model', *Journal of Social Work Education*, vol. 28, no. 1, pp. 27–35.

Ngan, R 1993, 'Cultural imperialism: Western social work theories for Chinese practice and the mission of social work in Hong Kong', *Hong Kong Journal of Social Work*, vol. 27, no. 2, pp. 47–55.

O'Collins, M 1997, 'Social work in the international context: strength from diversity', paper presented at the 25th AASW National Conference, November, Australia National University, Canberra.

Okun, BF, Fried, J & Okun, ML 1999, *Understanding Diversity: A Learning-as-practice Primer*, Brooks/Cole, Pacific Grove, California.

Osei-Hwedie, K 1993, 'The challenge of social work in Africa: starting the indigenization process', *Journal of Social Development in Africa*, vol. 8, no. 1, pp. 19–30.

Ow, R 1990a, 'Social behaviour in an Asian cultural setting', in M Clare & L Jayasuriya (eds), *Issues of Cross Cultural Practice*, University of Western Australia, Nedlands, pp. 100–14.

Ow, R 1990b, 'Asian perception of interventions', in M Clare & L Jayasuriya (eds), *Issues of Cross Cultural Practice*, University of Western Australia, Nedlands, pp. 83–99.

Ow, R 1990c, 'Working with Asian families', in M Clare & L Jayasuriya (eds), *Issues of Cross Cultural Practice*, University of Western Australia, Nedlands, pp. 69–82.

Park, Y 2005, 'Culture as deficit: a critical discourse analysis of the concept of culture in contemporary social work discourse', *Journal of Sociology and Social Welfare*, vol. 32, no. 3, pp. 11–33.

Payne, M 1996, *What is Professional Social Work?*, Venture Press, Birmingham.

Payne, M 1997, *Modern Social Work Theory: A Critical Introduction*, 2nd edn, Macmillan, London.

Pedersen, P 1984, 'Cultural assumptions of education and non-western alternatives', in D Sanders & P Pedersen (eds), *Education for International Social Welfare*, School of Social Work, University of Hawaii, Honolulu.

Prager, E 1985, 'American social work imperialism: consequence for professional education in Israel', *Journal of Jewish Communal Service*, vol. 62, no. 2, pp. 129–38.

Rao, M 1990, 'International social welfare: global perspectives', *Encyclopedia of Social Work*, 18th edn, National Association of Social Workers Press, Silver Springs, MD.

Ragab, IA 1990, 'How social work can take root in developing countries', *Social Development Issues*, vol. 12, no. 3, pp. 38–51.

Rogers, G 1995, 'Practice teaching guidelines for teaching ethnically sensitive, anti-discriminatory practice: a Canadian perspective', *British Journal of Social Work*, vol. 25, no. 4, pp. 441–57.

Rosaldo, R 1993, *Culture and Truth: The Remaking of Social Analysis*, Beacon Press, Boston.

Ruwhiu, LA, Baucke, H, Corrigan, R, Herewini, M, Davis, N & Ruwhiu, PTO 1999, 'Whaka-whanau-nga-tanga—a touch of class—we represent', paper presented at the Joint Conference of AASW, IFSW, APASWE and AASWWE, Brisbane, 26–29 September.

Silavwe, GW 1995, 'The need for a new social work perspective in an African setting: the case of social casework in Zambia', *British Journal of Social Work*, vol. 25, no. 1, pp. 71–84.

Sin, R 2008, 'Refiguring "Chineseness" in the international discourse on social work in China', in M Gray, J Coates & M Yellow Bird (eds), *Indigenous Social Work Around the World: Towards Culturally Relevant Education and Practice*, Ashgate, Aldershot.

Smith, L 1999, *Decolonising Research Methodologies*, Zed Books, London and New York.

Sue, DW 2005, *Multicultural Social Work Practice*, John Wiley & Sons, New York.

Tait-Rolleston, W, Cairns, T, Fulcher, L, Kereopa, H & Nia Nia, P 1997, 'He Koha Kii—Na Kui Ma, Na Koro Ma: a gift of words from our ancestors', *Social Work Review*, vol. 9, no. 4, pp. 30–6.

Thompson, N 2006, *Anti-discriminatory Practice: Equality, Diversity and Social Justice*, 4th edn, Palgrave Macmillan, Basingstoke.

Tsang, AKT & Yan, MC 2001, 'Chinese corpus, Western application: the Chinese strategy of engagement with Western social work discourses', *International Social Work*, vol. 44, no. 4, pp. 433–54.

Wakefield, JC 1995, 'When an irresistible epistemology meets an immovable ontology', *Social Work Research*, vol. 19, no. 1, pp. 9–23.

Walton, RG & Abo-El-Nasr, M 1988, 'Indigenization and authentization in terms of social work in Egypt', *International Social Work*, vol. 31, no. 1, pp. 135–44.

Watson, L 1988, 'An Aboriginal perspective: developing an indigenous social work, in E Chamberlain (ed.), *Change and Continuity in Australian Social Work*, Melbourne, Longman Cheshire.

Weaver, HN 1998, 'Indigenous people in a multicultural society: unique issues for human services', *Social Work*, vol. 43, no. 3, pp. 203–12.

Weaver, HN 1999, 'Indigenous people and the social work profession: defining culturally competent services', *Social Work*, vol. 44, no. 3, pp. 217–25.

Weaver, HN 2008, 'Indigenous social work in the United States: reflections on Indian tacos, Trojan Horses and canoes filled with Indigenous revolutionaries', in M Gray, J Coates & M Yellow Bird (eds), *Indigenous Social Work Around the World: Towards Culturally Relevant Education and Practice*, Ashgate, Aldershot, pp. 71–82.

Webber-Dreadon, E 1999, 'He Taonga Mo o Matou Tipuna A gift handed down by our ancestors', paper presented at the Joint Conference of AASW, IFSW, APASWE and AASWWE, Brisbane, 26–29 September.

Wikaira, B, Prasad, P, Davis, J & Halbert, M 1999, 'Inclusion of cultural social work perspectives within a monocultural system', paper presented at the Joint Conference of AASW, IFSW, APASWE and AASWWE, Brisbane, 26–29 September.

Yan, MC & Tsui, MS 2007, 'The quest for western social work knowledge: literature in the USA and practice in China', *International Social Work*, vol. 50, no. 5, pp. 641–53.

Yan, MC & Wong, YR 2005, 'Rethinking self-awareness in cultural competence: toward a dialogic self in cross-cultural social work', *Families in Society*, vol. 86, no. 2, pp. 181–8.

Yao, J 1995, 'The developing models of social work education in China', *International Social Work*, vol. 38, no. 1, pp. 27–38.

Yeo, SS 2003, 'Bonding and attachment of Australian Aboriginal children', *Child Abuse Review*, vol. 12, no. 5, pp. 292–304.

Yip, K 2001, 'Indigenization of social work in Hong Kong', *Hong Kong Journal of Social Work*, vol. 35, no. 1–2, pp. 51–78.

Yuen-Tsang, AWK & Wang, S 2002, 'Tension confronting the development of social work education in China: challenges and opportunities', *International Social Work*, vol. 45, no. 3, pp. 375–88.

3

Cultural competence: a critical analysis

Gai Harrison

Introduction

Cultural competence is a well-established construct in social work as well as a range of other professions spanning psychology, medicine, allied health and education. It is equally an influential discourse in government policy pertaining to health care, mental health and child and family welfare in countries such as Australia, Canada, New Zealand and the United States. Cultural competence has been embedded in professional codes of ethics, government department mission statements, organisational policies and human resources training. In fact, Gallegos, Tindall and Gallegos (2008, p. 51) claim that 'cultural competence has become ubiquitous in human services language and settings'.

It is important to state at the outset that cultural competence encompasses much more than working in cross-cultural contexts at the interpersonal level. One of the most commonly cited definitions of cultural competence was developed by Cross et al. (1989, p. iv), who define it as 'a set of congruent behaviours, attitudes and policies that come together in a system or agency or among professionals that enable effective interactions in a cross-cultural framework'. In other words, cultural competence goes beyond the level of the individual worker and recognises the need for an integrated approach that targets professional, organisational and structural factors. Accordingly, it is not just the attitudes and behaviours of workers that come under the spotlight, but also the policies, structures and practices of organisations. In this regard, cultural competence has much in common with social work's concern with the effects of broader systems on people's lives (Gallegos, Tindall & Gallegos 2008).

Culturally competent care is recognised as an important aspect of health-service provision. In response to concerns expressed about health disparities, it has become a prominent catchphrase in health care in many Western, multi-ethnic countries, subsequently being incorporated into government regulation. In these locations, culturally competent care is seen as the way to eliminate health inequalities and improve health outcomes for people from minority cultural and linguistic backgrounds (Horvat et al. 2011). For example, in Australia, the National Health and Medical Research Council (NHMRC 2006) has identified cultural competency as 'core business' at all levels of the health system, encompassing the individual, professional, organisational and systemic levels. Given that social workers comprise the largest group of allied health professionals in Australia (Australian Association of Social Workers 2011), this suggests that cultural competence is considered to be their 'core business' as well. It is therefore important to recognise that cultural competence is not only a professional discourse but is also written into many organisational policies that frame social work practice.

Despite its strong endorsement in the health and welfare sectors across a range of countries, cultural competence has been subjected to considerable debate in both the social work and broader literature. Johnson and Munch (2009) contend that although cultural competence is a well-entrenched discourse in social work, this should not exempt it from critical scrutiny. Instead, they argue that all taken-for-granted discourses in social work need to be subjected to ongoing evaluation to enable 'an attempt at reassessment or remedy' (Johnson & Munch 2009, p. 221). Thus, the primary aim of this chapter is to provide a critical analysis of cultural competence by identifying its underlying assumptions, surveying existing critiques and examining the evidence base for its effectiveness in practice. In doing so, I draw on some views of social workers elicited from an exploratory study conducted in Queensland, Australia, which investigated their perspectives on the utility of cultural competence for practice (Harrison & Turner 2011). The practitioners' comments are reproduced in boxes throughout the chapter to illustrate various points.

The first part of this chapter examines how cultural competence is conceptualised and understood in the literature. In recognition that cultural competence is more than a professional discourse and encompasses organisational policies, government regulations and interdisciplinary work, a broad literature base is canvassed. Next, the main critiques of cultural competence that exist in the literature are explored before examining what is known about its actual effectiveness in the real world. Consideration is then given to some of the broader political, system and organisational constraints to responding appropriately to the needs of people from diverse backgrounds. The chapter concludes with suggestions for how social work practitioners can make strategic use of cultural competence at the organisational level of practice, without losing sight of its limitations and ambiguities.

Making sense of cultural competence

There is an extensive body of literature on cultural competence as well as a plethora of policy documents relating to its implementation. There is no one universally accepted definition of cultural competence, although in principle it denotes the provision of culturally appropriate services to a diverse clientele in order to address disparities in health status and wellbeing (Cross et al. 1989). In the social work field, Boyle and Springer (2001, p. 55) claim that 'there are literally hundreds of conceptual definitions of cultural competence'. Other related terms that feature in the literature include cultural sensitivity, cultural awareness, cultural responsiveness and cultural safety. Some authors conceptualise these attributes as being part of cultural competence (Horvat et al. 2011; Lum 2011; Nayar & Tse 2006), while others clearly differentiate these terms from cultural competence (Brach & Fraser 2000; Kirmayer 2012a).

Abrams and Moio (2009) have charted the changing discourse of cultural competence in social work, highlighting how it has evolved from a primary focus on working with minority ethnic groups to include a range of groups at risk of exclusion on the basis of factors such as sexuality, ability, age and religion. The language of cultural competence also features in quite distinct ways with reference to specific populations and institutions. For example, Mancoske et al. (2012) outline a model of cultural competence for improving children's mental health outcomes while Charnley and Langley (2007) expand on a cultural competence framework for anti-heterosexist practice. Arguably, cultural competence only makes sense if it is contextualised with regard to how it is applied on a local level in a particular institutional context. Clearly no one size fits all. Moreover, along with being context-specific, what constitutes cultural competence is open to value judgments (Gallegos, Tindall & Gallegos 2008).

Confusion appears to reign in social work as to whether cultural competence is a theory or perspective (Gallegos, Tindall & Gallegos 2008), or more realistically reflects a movement (Lum 2011). However, despite these conceptual dilemmas, what most contemporary definitions of cultural competence do have in common is an understanding of the need to adopt a systemic approach to practice. For example, Lum offers a working definition of cultural competence for practice that

> involves the mutual consent of the worker and the client to become culturally proficient by participating together in the exploration and learning of cultural and ethnic history, values, and behavioural issues which are relevant to understanding particular problems in the helping relationship as part of the micro practice process and to work toward the development of meso and macro policies and programs which benefit clients who are culturally and ethnically diverse (2011, p. 20).

This definition demonstrates that cultural competence is a participatory approach to working with people that operates at the micro (individual), meso (institutional) and macro (community) levels. Moreover, it assumes that all levels of practice are interdependent. In this way, cultural competence is concerned with addressing system-wide barriers to responsive care that equally impact on a social worker's capacity to work effectively at the interpersonal level. In addition, it acknowledges that social work takes place in an organisational context, and that the organisation and its policies may be the target of change. The following two comments by social workers illustrate this broader systemic approach, which is integral to culturally competent practice.

> In fact, policies and attitudes and behaviour, particularly when they are put all together, will achieve the best results. I think that's cultural competence.
>
> Anna

> I think that it [cultural competence] comes down to the community capacity building side of social work, where you would look broader than the individual; it's agency but also community.
>
> Sarina

For example, at an organisational (meso) level, enacting cultural competence may entail increasing the numbers of Indigenous staff, including those in leadership roles, while at the individual (micro) level it may involve training staff to identify and challenge ethnocentric values and beliefs (Centre for Cultural Competence Australia 2010). At a broader community (macro) level, it may translate into consulting with target groups to identify and dismantle barriers they face in accessing culturally responsive services. In contrast to cultural awareness, which is seen as a passive approach to working with people, cultural competence is seen to have the potential to bring about behavioural and system change because it adopts an integrated approach that targets all levels of practice (Centre for Cultural Competence Australia 2010).

However, it is questionable whether such a coordinated approach actually occurs in practice, especially if adequate resources are not made available by funding bodies (Opper 2007). In these instances it is likely that cultural competency interventions are implemented in an ad hoc rather than a carefully planned and integrated fashion. Alternatively, the responsibility for the provision of culturally responsive services falls to individuals involved in front-line work. This dilemma is exemplified by Lily's comment below, in which she describes how she is charged with the responsibility of implementing a new program that is inadequately resourced.

> My role is with developing the suicide prevention strategy, and culturally diverse groups are a key priority, but over the five-year strategy there have been actually really low amounts of funding directed into that ... the application of organisational policy and priorities is what concerns me at times—how much of that actually filters down to your actual service delivery?
>
> Lily

What can be extrapolated from the preceding discussion is that cultural competence encompasses a systemic approach to practice, although policy may not always be adequately translated into practice if it is afforded low priority. At the same time, it is an evolving rather than a static concept and will take on different meanings in different situations. This lack of conceptual clarity, along with a number of other perceived flaws of cultural competence, is explored below.

What's the problem with cultural competence?

The idea of culturally competent practice has attracted its fair share of criticism in social work and allied disciplines. Part of the perceived 'problem' with cultural competence relates to the previous discussion, in which it was pointed out that the term defies a concrete and universally accepted definition. This makes it difficult to operationalise cultural competence for the purposes of evaluating its effectiveness in social work practice (Boyle & Springer 2001; Gallegos, Tindall and Gallegos 2008).

Culture is complex, contextualised and changeable

Several authors in social work argue that cultural competence is based on the faulty premise that acquiring cultural knowledge will result in competent social work practice (Dean 2001; Jani et al. 2011; Johnson & Munch 2009). A related criticism is that it fails to acknowledge that a person's relationship with culture is complex, contextualised and changeable. For example, Dreher and MacNaughton (2002, p. 182) observe that 'Some members of a culture may embrace its traditional norms, others may reject them, and still others may deploy cultural values situationally'. This complexity is illustrated by Harjeet's comment that while his cultural beliefs have changed over time through a cross-cultural marriage, he still identifies with his cultural group in India.

> For example, in my family—I am different—I'm the only person who has married cross-culturally; my life has changed so my cultural outlook and beliefs are definitely different to my other siblings and family group … Individuals will have their variances and different viewpoints [but] I'm still part of my cultural group and family in India.
>
> Harjeet

To be fair, some proponents of cultural competence have attempted to address this criticism by changing the focus from learning about discrete cultures—if indeed they ever existed—to recognising that cultures are constantly in flux and have blurred boundaries (Lum 2011). In more contemporary versions of cultural competence training, educators encourage practitioners to identify and critically appraise their own cultural beliefs as well as their professional culture. Nonetheless, there is still confusion in the literature in relation to this point. For example, Laird (2008, p. 39) urges social workers to 'learn about other cultures' while guarding against adopting essentialist understandings of people's cultural identities. However, Johnson and Munch (2009) question whether this approach is compatible with social work's value base, which requires workers to elicit each client's unique narrative rather than draw on a generalised knowledge of group characteristics and norms to inform their assessment.

This raises the vexed question of what it actually is that practitioners should learn in order to practise in a culturally competent manner, especially when they are urged to acquire knowledge about different cultures but to avoid seeing them as isolable, bounded entities. This ambiguous discourse is even more confusing when culture is conflated with ethnicity, race or nationality in the literature (Kleinman & Benson 2006). Below, Tim and Megumi point out that there is no standard guide for learning about different cultures and that, even within the same family, individuals may experience different cultural realities.

> You know, there's not a Lonely Planet guide for every culture. There's a Lonely Planet guide for countries, but there's no guide for every culture.
>
> Tim

> You can get four people from the same family and get four different views of that culture.
>
> Megumi

The directive for social workers to become culturally competent suggests that culture is meaningful to people. It would be hard to quibble with this view. Culture is something that most people intuitively identify with, although they may not be able to clearly state what it is or how it impacts on their way of life and identity. This is possibly because culture relates to the mundane and ordinary aspects of people's day-to-day lives (Kleinman & Benson 2006). In the case of mental health, for example, it may include the way a person expresses her symptoms, how she accounts for these symptoms, and the manner in which she seeks help for and manages her illness. If a practitioner is operating from a dominant cultural construction of mental illness, this will have ramifications for how this person's behaviour is interpreted and the options made available to her. For instance, the term 'flat affect' is used in Western classificatory systems of mental illness to signify how a person's mood deviates from what is considered the norm. However, such norms are 'culturally sanctioned' rather than universal (Qureshi et al. 2008, p. 552).

At the same time, variations in behaviour and meaning-making in relation to illness may be evident within the same social group. Factors such as age, religion, political affiliation, socioeconomic status and personality will equally influence a person's expression of illness (Kleinman & Benson 2006). This is illustrated by Sarah's comment below, in which she advocates a more holistic understanding of cultural identity that goes beyond ethnicity and race.

> I think a lot of people think of culture as ethnicity and race, but it goes to everything like age, gender, sexual orientation, history, values, family history, everything.
>
> Sarah

In recognition of the complex interplay of these factors in people's lives, some writers in social work have argued for the importance of incorporating the concept of *intersectionality* into a cultural competence framework (Jani et al. 2011; Lockhart & Mitchell 2010; Lum 2011). Intersectionality is premised on the understanding that a person's experiences will be shaped by the unique intersection of a range of social divisions such as employment status, (dis)ability, ethnicity and sexual affiliation at a particular point in time. Intersectionality is believed to address some of the limitations of cultural competence because it encourages workers to think beyond culture and recognise that people can have a multiplicity of social locations that interact in historically specific ways. It acknowledges that a person can be both privileged and disadvantaged, while taking account of the specific relational dynamics in operation at the time (Jani et al. 2011).

Cultural politics and culturalism

Although respect for culture is viewed as being part and parcel of 'good' social work practice, there are dangers in adopting an uncritical view of how it is applied in practice. Revering culture hosts its own dangers in social work, especially when certain acts that are carried out under its name victimise or oppress some individuals or groups. Strongly ingrained cultural beliefs have been implicated in maintaining gender inequalities and violating the rights of less powerful groups such as children. The literature on cultural competence, however, does not do justice to these 'cultural politics' or give direction as to how practitioners should negotiate these power dynamics (Jani et al. 2011). Below, Erica and Sophie describe the ethical dilemmas that can arise in practice when culturally condoned beliefs and behaviours are deemed to be harmful to another party, especially when children are involved.

> You aim to be sensitive to culture, but ... there are ethical dilemmas around childcare and the whole parenting thing.
>
> Erica

> What perhaps might be the norm in another country or within a family, in the Australian context could be quite harmful or inappropriate, or illegal.
>
> Sophie

Alternatively, it may be the case that too much importance is given to culture when other factors such as poverty are equally or more important in accounting for disparities in health and wellbeing (Kleinman & Benson 2006; Simon & Mosavel 2008). *Culturalism* refers to a tendency to relate all social problems back to culture, as well as locating the solutions to such problems within the same framework (Schierup & Ålund 2011, p. 48). However, Kleinman and Benson (2006, p. 1673) point out that 'cultural factors are not always central to a case, and might actually hinder a more practical understanding of an episode'. In other words, there are dangers attached to adopting a culturally determined view of people's lives. Kleinman and Benson (2006) therefore urge practitioners to adopt an ethnographic approach to understanding each person's 'local world' rather than employing a cultural framework to understand presenting issues.

Cultural competence has been critiqued in social work on the basis that it minimises power inequities and institutional discrimination, as well as historic injustices perpetuated on the basis of race, ethnicity, gender or location (Abrams & Moio 2009; Jani et al. 2011). Critics have equally lamented the lack of attention given by advocates of cultural competence to race relations, including a failure to acknowledge white privilege in those locations where whiteness operates as an unacknowledged normative ethnicity (Abrams & Moio 2009; Furlong & Wight 2011; Pon 2009). According to these writers, cultural competence represents a failure to decentre whiteness and remove white privilege.

For others, cultural competence represents an attempt to maintain the status quo. In health care, for example, Lee and Farrell (2006) argue that cultural competence is implicated in producing and reproducing patient 'compliance', where adhering to prescribed treatment regimens is unquestionably viewed as a good health outcome. Kirmayer (2012a) argues that once dominant cultural constructions of health become embedded in healthcare systems, they regulate what types of problems attract attention and the sorts of help made available to people.

Writers who adopt a postcolonial perspective suggest that cultural competence encourages practitioners to focus on the cultural 'other' rather than how the 'self' may be complicit in historical and ongoing colonisation (Downing & Kowal 2011). This preoccupation with the 'other' is particularly prominent in training and texts that aim to impart content on the cultures of different groups, which inadvertently risks reinforcing existing stereotypes (Johnson & Munch 2009).

> [Cultural competence training] all seems to be about 'them, them, them', and I think there's a bit of a problem in that.
>
> Carla

This criticism, however, assumes that practitioners themselves are part of a dominant group, which Sakamoto (2007) points out is not always the case. In addition, it fails to acknowledge that many people straddle a number of linguistic and cultural backgrounds that need to be understood within their particular spatial and historical dimensions. The 'self' of the social worker is a similarly complex entity in which, depending on the particular interactional context, some facets of the person's identity may be more prominent than others. Below, Nancy describes how she has been ascribed different identities at various times in her life that relate specifically to her nationality, ethnicity and religion.

> My current frame of thought is towards culture being both 'fixed' and dynamic and evolving. It relates very much to identity and time. What makes others see me as Chinese or a Catholic? What would identify me as Singaporean and not Australian? What would identify me as Singaporean Chinese and not mainland China Chinese?
>
> Nancy

In summary, what this survey of the literature suggests is that while there is clear evidence of a strong and active cultural competence movement, there is also a number of vocal critics of this framework for practice. The snapshot of social workers' perspectives presented in the preceding discussion also highlights their interest in this debate, especially since they are the ones charged with demonstrating cultural competence in their day-to-day practice. Perhaps, however, the more important issue is whether utilising a cultural competence framework in practice makes a difference to people's lives. The following section examines the research on cultural competence as well as what is known about how effective training programs are at promoting this form of competence in workers.

The evidence base for cultural competence

A fundamental problem in researching cultural competence in social work is its conceptual ambiguity, which in turn makes it difficult to operationalise for the purposes of evaluation (Gallegos, Tindall & Gallegos 2008). While there is an extensive literature on cultural competence in social work, much of this work is conceptual or theoretical rather than empirical. On a broader level, research that assesses the effects of culturally responsive care is in the early stages of development and no studies have systematically examined outcomes for service users (Bhui et al. 2007). Most of the existing research on cultural competence is focused on the health sector; this literature is explored below.

To date, there is limited evidence to support the assertion that cultural competence actually improves outcomes for the people who are on the receiving end of this form of service delivery (Bhui et al. 2007; Brach & Fraser 2000; Goode, Dunne & Bronheim 2006; Kleinman & Benson 2006; Lie et al. 2011; Oakes 2011). Moreover, of the studies that have been conducted, many demonstrate methodological shortcomings. For example, Brach and Fraser (2000) observe that much research on cultural competence fails to account for the role of confounding variables such as education and class in health disparities.

A systematic literature review conducted on the effectiveness of cultural competence strategies in managing or preventing chronic disease in culturally and linguistically diverse communities indicated that the use of bilingual community health workers may be linked with better health outcomes (Henderson, Kendall & See 2011). The authors of this review looked specifically at the use of bilingual health workers, the provision of cultural competence training for staff, the use of interpreter services, health promotion media and the establishment of community services for people with chronic disease. They concluded that bilingual workers played a pivotal role in encouraging people from these communities to make greater use of prevention measures such as health screening. In addition, these workers facilitated follow-up care and promoted better communication between health workers and clients. However, most of the studies reviewed were limited to the extent that it was not possible to ascertain any long-term health outcomes (Henderson, Kendall & See 2011).

Despite the lack of an evidence base for long-term health benefits, Dreher and MacNaughton (2002) suggest that cultural competence can be effectively employed in public health, especially when educators are trying to bring about behavioural change at the population rather than at the individual level. Information about group norms and behaviour, for example, can be used to inform educational programs aimed at improving a particular population's uptake of services or target groups that under-utilise health screening. Accordingly, culturally competent health promotion is seen to have the potential to improve health outcomes for marginalised populations

(NHMRC 2006). Similarly, there is evidence that a cultural competence framework can be effectively employed at the community level, particularly when members are involved in identifying both their needs and what services would meet these needs (Dreher & MacNaughton 2002).

Cultural competency interventions have also been evaluated to determine whether they improve rehabilitation outcomes for individuals with disabilities. Hasnain et al. (2011) conducted a systematic review of those studies that employed randomised controlled trials, which demonstrated that culturally adapted interventions do improve rehabilitation outcomes for individuals with disabilities, particularly in three areas: reducing disability-related symptoms, increasing client knowledge of their disability and improving psychosocial outcomes. However, the authors stated a caveat that their findings only applied to persons with disabilities who live in 'Western cultural contexts' (Hasnain et al. 2011, p. 9).

In mental health, Kirmayer (2012b) is critical of much research on the effectiveness of interventions that operate from a predetermined framework for what are considered to be desirable outcomes. In this regard, most research focuses on the abatement of symptoms and behavioural change, which may not necessarily coincide with 'culturally relevant outcomes' at the individual, family and community levels (Kirmayer 2012b, p. 249). This includes Indigenous ways of understanding mental health and healing, which have not received due attention in evaluation research. Accordingly, Kirmayer (2012b) concludes that evidence-based practice and cultural competence may actually be incompatible constructs and calls for a broader understanding of what constitutes evidence.

Notably, much of the existing research on cultural competence that has been subjected to review has emanated from English-speaking high-income countries (Horvat et al. 2011). Moreover, as indicated earlier, few studies have focused specifically on the outcomes of social work interventions. In terms of therapeutic work, Lee (2011) highlights some empirical research that suggests a link between cultural competence and increased client satisfaction and lower attrition rates. However, Oakes (2011) comments that the significance of the practitioner's receptivity to developing cultural competence is under-recognised in much of the literature. Similarly, a person's degree of open-mindedness towards difference has been identified as a factor that is likely to strongly influence receptivity to cross-cultural training (Fischer 2011). In other words, those individuals who are not open to understanding cultural differences are less likely to benefit from such training.

There is significant variation in the curricula that informs cultural competence training programs, and few studies have evaluated their impact in a rigorous manner. There is a lack of consensus concerning what cultural competence training should be aiming to achieve, what content should be covered and how it should be implemented

(Kirmayer 2012a; Littrell & Sallas 2005; Oakes 2011). In a review of the literature on training for cultural competence in the health sector, Oakes (2011, p. 47) concluded that 'cultural competency training has been policy driven' and lacks a clear evidence base or sound theoretical framework. Nonetheless, training on cultural competence is routinely employed in many workplaces.

A systematic review of the effects of cultural competency training for health professionals revealed limited evidence for a positive relationship between training and improved outcomes for service users (Lie et al. 2011). In an earlier review, Beach et al. (2005) concluded that cultural competence training does impact on the knowledge, attitudes and skills of health professionals and improves service–user satisfaction. However, it is difficult to substantiate a cause–effect relationship between training for cultural competency and cultural responsiveness in workers because of methodological weaknesses in most studies (Lie et al. 2011).

The above discussion suggests that the existing evidence on the impact of cultural competence is mixed. Notably, very little research has been conducted on what clients understand as culturally competent service delivery. In one study conducted by Davis (2007, cited in Johnson & Munch 2009, p. 224) that elicited community members' and practitioners' views on culturally competent practice, many of the community members' descriptions mirrored what would be considered to be 'good' social work practice with reference to values such as treating people with respect and valuing client input. Clearly, more research is needed to determine what service users actually expect in terms of culturally responsive services. Another dimension of cultural competence that has been subject to minimal investigation is the role of organisations in integrating and implementing this framework for practice. This aspect of culturally competent care is addressed in the following section.

The organisational base—a help or hindrance to culturally competent practice?

> I think certainly the organisation does play a big role in terms of the capacity to work flexibly and creatively when needed. That's often, though, dictated by funding and the way the funding is granted.
>
> Tina

> There's always never enough funding no matter—I don't think I've come across anybody saying, 'Are we done yet?'
>
> Sophie

Policy gets lost in translation in big organisations and government organisations.

Val

These comments made by social workers suggest that without an organisational commitment to cultural competence and adequate funding, it is difficult to practise in a way that is responsive to the different cultural realities of clients. As mentioned earlier, cultural competence is applied not only at the individual and professional levels, but also at the systemic and organisational levels. On an organisational level, the availability of interpreters and translated materials, the physical environment, the mechanisms for community consultation, dedicated training and the allocation of adequate funds to implement policy are just some of the factors that are thought to determine the cultural competence of an agency (Rice 2007). However, limited research has been conducted on the role of these organisational factors in the provision of culturally responsive service delivery (Goode, Dunne & Bronhiem 2006; Rice 2007; Whaley & Longoria 2008).

Arguably, unless an agency has the mindset, commitment, funds and time to incorporate a cultural competence framework in all its operations, policies and action plans are unlikely to achieve much in practice (Harrison & Turner 2011). Cultural competence is meaningless, for example, if people cannot access health or welfare services in the first place. Alternatively, if some groups are distrustful of mainstream services due to previous or ongoing experiences of discrimination, then it is unlikely that the cultural competence of practitioners alone will remedy this situation. Yet the literature tends to focus on the perceived cultural insensitivity of practitioners rather than the organisational constraints that these workers may be operating under (Charnley & Langley 2007; Harrison & Turner 2011). As a result, responsibility for outcomes is individualised, which in turn detracts attention from broader structural issues such as access to services and the distribution of resources.

Large caseloads, working to deadlines, competing priorities, policy getting lost in translation, funding constraints and rigid organisational practices have all been identified by social workers as factors that prevent them from providing responsive care to a diverse clientele (Allain 2007; Ayón & Aisenberg 2010; Harrison & Turner 2011). In a study that examined how practitioners negotiate clients' cultural expectations in child welfare practice in California, Ayón and Aisenberg (2010) observed that the workers' efforts were compromised by organisational constraints. Practitioners reported that they often had insufficient time to forge meaningful relationships with the families they worked with, which in turn adversely impacted on their ability to address their cultural needs (Ayón & Aisenberg 2010). In contrast, some practitioners from community-based agencies report that they are able to offer culturally responsive services because their organisations allow them adequate time to establish relationships with people and work in a flexible manner (Harrison & Turner 2011).

Clearly, more research is needed to determine the impact of organisational factors on culturally responsive service delivery. There may equally be a need to rethink the organisational dimensions of cultural competence given that they have been largely determined by expert opinion rather than reflecting community views (Whaley & Longoria 2008). More recently, a 'business case' for cultural competence has been identified by some writers whereby organisations such as hospitals are encouraged to pursue this form of competence for financial gain (Betancourt et al. 2002; Goode, Dunne & Bronheim 2006; Weech-Maldonado et al. 2012). This is a worrying development on one level because it may encourage managers to focus predominantly on the cost benefits of cultural competence rather than achieving good outcomes for people (Weech-Maldonado et al. 2012). Alternatively, organisations may become preoccupied with minimising liability rather than being genuinely committed to making their organisations accessible and responsive to a diverse clientele.

Conclusion

The above discussion has highlighted how cultural competence can evoke multiple meanings and, in its different articulations, needs to be understood in context. A social worker practising in a mental health setting will have a different understanding of culturally responsive care than a colleague working with survivors of violence. This fluidity in meaning is both a strength and a limitation of cultural competence: it is a strength in the sense that it can be adapted to different situations as needed, but it is also a limitation in that it is not easy to operationalise for the purposes of evaluation.

In assessing the utility of cultural competence for social work practice, it is important to locate this framework in the contemporary political and social context. Currently, there is evidence of a significant backlash against multiculturalism across Europe, North America and Australia. Some groups, including 'conservative religious groups, far-right movements … and increasingly a spoken-for "white majority" have even identified themselves as the victims of multiculturalism' (Lentin & Titley 2011, p. 181). Minority groups are now constructed as 'problems' to be solved because of their perceived failure to integrate, which in turn legitimises racism, albeit in a new form, based on the reification of cultural difference. In this way, culture becomes a signifier for race (Lentin & Titley 2011). Groups are slotted neatly into different cultures, allowing for a distinction between 'good diversity' and 'bad diversity', which in turn legitimises the state's role in evaluating, managing and controlling difference. Thus, overemphasising cultural difference can have adverse outcomes for those groups relegated to the 'bad diversity' category (Lentin & Titley 2011, p. 176).

Does this mean that cultural competence, via its privileging of culture, is a dangerous framework for practice? This depends on how it is employed in practice and whether it is deployed in an uncritical fashion. As Brach and Fraser (2000, p. 203) remark: 'Like anything else, cultural competency techniques can be sound or unsound, done well or not well'.

The cultural competence movement has alerted practitioners to the importance of recognising and advocating service users' rights, but not necessarily changing the systems that deny people social justice in the first place. Arguably, the issue of white privilege and associated power relations has not received adequate attention in the cultural competence literature, along with the constraints impacting on practitioners in terms of the organisational context of their practice. Nonetheless, cultural competence can be used strategically by social workers to improve organisational responses by identifying the organisation as an ally or target of change. The challenge for social workers is to think creatively about how they can work at the meso level to assist in transforming the organisational culture when it hinders the provision of culturally responsive services.

Social workers can, for example, appeal to organisational policies on equity and anti-discrimination and associated standards for cultural competence to advocate change. If government regulations stipulate that all service users have the right to an accredited interpreter, such regulations can be used strategically to argue for appropriate service provision. Although organisational standards for cultural competence may not assume a high priority in the workplace, they can be cited to remind managers of their responsibilities and facilitate compliance. Alternatively, social workers can appeal to external advocacy groups to bring such issues to the attention of the agency.

It is also important to think about the collective power of social workers, particularly in the health sector where they make up a significant proportion of the allied health workforce. Professional subcultures in organisations can be powerful drivers of change. Social workers in particular are less likely to accept the status quo if it works against the needs of service users. As Bloor and Dawson (1994, p. 285) found in their study on how professional groups influence organisational culture, out of all the allied health professions, social workers were more likely to 'advocate on behalf of clients, even in the face of medical authority dissension'. Promisingly, Bloor and Dawson (1994, p. 285) reported that the social workers in their study represented 'a dissenting professional subculture' who could potentially uproot the prevailing healthcare philosophy of the organisation.

Another potential role for social workers is to conduct research on the expectations of service users in relation to culturally responsive services. To date, limited research has been carried out in this area, but having empirical evidence to support the need for organisational change and presenting data in a timely manner can assist in increasing the awareness of staff and management. It is equally a requirement of agencies stipulated by cultural competence standards. Such evidence may then be used to inform service planning and implementation.

It would be easy to dismiss cultural competence out of hand as policy rhetoric, especially given the gulf between the rhetoric and reality on the ground. However, the other alternative is for practitioners to make strategic use of this rhetoric for the purposes of advancing the needs of service users and making a case for the development of culturally responsive services. Social workers do need to develop a critical awareness of the limitations and ambiguities of cultural competence. Equally, they should be familiar with the evidence base for its effectiveness in practice. Finally, it is important to remember that cultural competence is an evolving practice framework, which means that it is possible for practitioners to contribute to its ongoing development.

REFLECTIVE QUESTIONS

1   How does the construct of cultural competence fit with your own framework for social work practice?
2   Do you think cultural competence equates to 'good' social work practice? Why or why not?
3   *Culturalism* refers to a tendency to relate all social problems back to culture. What might be some examples of this?
4   What are the limitations of adopting a culturally determined view of people's identities in social work practice?
5   How can social workers use cultural competence standards and policies strategically to work towards making organisations more responsive to the needs of service users?

FURTHER READING

Johnson, Y & Munch, S 2009, 'Fundamental contradictions in cultural competence', *Social Work*, vol. 54, no. 3, pp. 220–31.
Kirmayer, L 2012, 'Cultural competence and evidence-based practice in mental health: epistemic communities and the politics of pluralism', *Social Science & Medicine*, vol. 75, no.2, pp. 249–56.
Kleinman, A & Benson, B 2006, 'Anthropology in the clinic: the problem of cultural competency and how to fix it', *PLoS Medicine*, vol. 3, no. 10, pp. 1673–6.
Sakimoto, I 2007, 'An anti-oppressive approach to cultural competence', *Canadian Social Work Review*, vol. 24, no. 1, pp. 105–14.

REFERENCES

Australian Association of Social Workers 2011, *AASW Health Reform Position Paper*, viewed 20 December 2012, <www.aasw.asn.au>.
Abrams, LS & Moio, JA 2009, 'Critical race theory and the cultural competence dilemma in social work education', *Journal of Social Work Education*, vol. 45, no. 2, pp. 245–61.

Allain, L 2007, 'An investigation of how a group of social workers respond to the cultural needs of black, minority ethnic looked after children', *Practice*, vol. 19, no. 2, pp. 127–41.

Ayón, C & Aisenberg, E 2010, 'Negotiating cultural values and expectations within the public child welfare system: a look at familismo and personalismo', *Child & Family Social Work*, vol. 15, no. 3, pp. 335–44.

Beach, M, Price, E, Gary, T, Robinson, K, Gozu, A, Palacio, A, Smarth, C, Jenckes, M, Feuerstein, C, Bass, E, Powe, N & Cooper, L 2005, 'Cultural competence: a systematic review of health care providers' educational interventions', *Medical Care*, vol. 43, no. 4, pp. 356–73.

Betancourt, J, Green, A & Carrillo, J 2002, *Cultural Competence in Health Care: Emerging Frameworks and Practical Approaches*, The Commonwealth Fund, New York.

Bhui, K, Warfa, N, Edonya, P, McKenzie, K & Bhugra, D 2007, 'Cultural competence in mental health care: a review of model evaluations', *BMC Health Services Research*, vol. 7, no. 15, p. 15.

Bloor, G & Dawson, P 1994, 'Understanding professional culture in organizational context', *Organization Studies*, vol. 15, no. 2, pp. 275–95.

Boyle, D & Springer, A 2001, 'Toward a cultural competence measure for social work with specific populations', *Journal of Ethnic and Cultural Diversity in Social Work*, vol. 9, no. 3–4, pp. 53–71.

Brach, C & Fraser, I 2000, 'Can cultural competency reduce racial and ethnic health disparities? A review and conceptual model', *Medical Care Research and Review*, vol. 57, no. 1, pp. 181–217.

Centre for Cultural Competence Australia 2010, *About CCCA*, viewed 23 July 2012, <http://ccca.com.au>.

Charnley, H & Langley, J 2007, 'Developing cultural competence as a framework for anti-heterosexist social work practice: reflections from the UK', *Journal of Social Work*, vol. 7, no. 3, pp. 307–21.

Cross, T, Bazron, B, Dennis, K & Isaacs, M 1989, *Towards a Culturally Competent System of Care: A Monograph on Effective Services for Minority Children Who are Severely Emotionally Disturbed*, vol. 1, University Child Development Center, Washington DC.

Dean, R 2001, 'The myth of cross-cultural competence', *Families in Society: The Journal of Contemporary Human Services*, vol. 82, no. 6, pp. 623–30.

Downing, R & Kowal, E 2011, 'A postcolonial analysis of Indigenous cultural awareness training for health workers', *Health Sociology Review*, vol. 20, no. 1, pp. 5–15.

Dreher, M & MacNaughton, N 2002, 'Cultural competence in nursing: foundation or fallacy?', *Nursing Outlook*, vol. 50, no. 5, pp. 181–6.

Fischer, R 2011, 'Cross-cultural training effects on cultural essentialism beliefs and cultural intelligence', *International Journal of Intercultural Relations*, vol. 35, no. 6, pp. 767–75.

Furlong, M & Wight, J 2011, 'Promoting "critical awareness" and critiquing "cultural competence": towards disrupting received professional knowledges', *Australian Social Work*, vol. 64, no. 1, pp. 38–54.

Gallegos, J, Tindall, C & Gallegos, S 2008, 'The need for advancement in the conceptualization of cultural competence', *Advances in Social Work*, vol. 9, no. 1, pp. 51–62.

Goode, T, Dunne, M & Bronheim, S 2006, *The Evidence Base for Cultural and Linguistic Competency in Health Care*, National Center for Cultural Competence, Center for Child and Human Development, Georgetown University, Washington DC.

Harrison, G & Turner, R 2011, 'Being a "culturally competent" social worker: making sense of a murky concept in practice', *British Journal of Social Work*, vol. 41, no. 2, pp. 333–50.

Hasnain, R, Kondratowicz, D, Borokhovski, E, Nye, C, Balcazar, F, Portillo, N, Hanz, K, Johnson, T & Gould, R 2011, 'Do cultural competency interventions work? A systematic review on improving rehabilitation outcomes for ethnically and linguistically diverse individuals with disabilities', *FOCUS Technical Brief*, 31, SEDL, National Center for the Dissemination of Disability Research, Austin, TX.

Henderson, S, Kendall, E & See, L 2011, 'The effectiveness of culturally appropriate interventions to manage or prevent chronic disease in culturally and linguistically diverse communities: a systematic literature review', *Health and Social Care in the Community*, vol. 19, no. 3, pp. 225–49.

Horvat, L, Horey, D, Romios, P & Kis-Rigo, J 2011, 'Cultural competence education for health professionals', *Cochrane Database of Systematic Reviews 2011*, Issue 10. Art. No. CD009405. DOI: 10.1002/14651858.CD009405.

Jani, J, Ortiz, L, Pierce, D & Sowbel, L 2011, 'Access to intersectionality, content to competence: deconstructing social work education diversity standards', *Journal of Social Work Education*, vol. 47, no. 2, pp. 283–301.

Johnson, Y & Munch, S 2009, 'Fundamental contradictions in cultural competence', *Social Work Special Issue on Racial and Ethnic Minorities)*, vol. 54, no. 3, pp. 220–31.

Kirmayer, L 2012a, 'Rethinking cultural competence', *Transcultural Psychiatry*, vol. 49, no. 2, pp. 149–64.

Kirmayer, L 2012b, 'Cultural competence and evidence-based practice in mental health: epistemic communities and the politics of pluralism', *Social Science & Medicine*, vol. 75, no. 2, pp. 249–56.

Kleinman, A & Benson, P 2006, 'Anthropology in the clinic: the problem of cultural competency and how to fix it', *PLoS Medicine*, vol. 3, no. 10, pp. 1673–6.

Laird, S 2008, *Anti-Oppressive Social Work: A Guide for Developing Cultural Competence*, Sage, London.

Lee, E 2011, 'Clinical significance of cross-cultural competencies (CCC) in social work practice', *Journal of Social Work Practice: Psychotherapeutic Approaches in Health, Welfare and the Community*, vol. 25, no. 2, pp. 185–203.

Lee, S & Farrell, M 2006, 'Is cultural competency a backdoor to racism?', *Anthropology News*, vol. 47, no. 3, 9–10.

Lentin, A & Titley, G 2011, *The Crises of Multiculturalism: Racism in a Neoliberal Age*, Zed Books, London.

Lie, D, Lee-Rey, E, Gomez, A, Bereknyei, S & Braddock, C 2011, 'Does cultural competency training of health professionals improve patient outcomes? A systematic review and proposed algorithm for future research', *Journal of General Internal Medicine*, vol. 26, no. 3, pp. 317–25.

Littrell, L & Sallas, E 2005, 'A review of cross-cultural training: best practices, guidelines, and research needs', *Human Resource Development Review*, vol. 4, no. 3, pp. 305–34.

Lockhart, L & Mitchell, J 2010, 'Cultural competence and intersectionality: emerging frameworks and practical approaches', in L Lockhart and F Danis (eds), *Domestic Violence, Intersectionality and Culturally Competent Practice*, Columbia University Press, New York, pp. 1–28.

Lum, D 2011, *Culturally Competent Practice: A Framework for Understanding Diverse Groups and Justice Issues*, 4th edn, Brooks/Cole, Belmont, CA.

Mancoske, R, Lewis, M, Bowers-Stephens, C & Ford, A 2012, 'Cultural competence and children's mental health service outcomes', *Journal of Ethnic and Cultural Diversity in Social Work*, vol. 21, no. 3, pp. 195–211.

National Health and Medical Research Council 2006, *Cultural Competency in Health: A Guide for Policy, Partnerships and Participation*, Commonwealth of Australia, Canberra.

Nayar, S & Tse, D 2006, 'Cultural competence and models in mental health: working with Asian service users', *International Journal of Psychosocial Rehabilitation*, vol. 10, no. 2, pp. 79–87.

Oakes, K 2011, 'Health care disparities and training in culturally competent mental health counseling: a review of the literature and implications for research', *International Journal of Humanities and Social Science*, vol. 1, no. 17, pp. 46–57.

Opper, I 2007, *Multicultural Action Plans: A Map for Change in Queensland? Report 2, An Independent Review of Multicultural Action Plans 2006/2007*, Ethnic Communities Council of Queensland, Brisbane, viewed 3 August 2009, <www.eccq.com.au>.

Pon, G 2009, 'Cultural competency as new racism: an ontology of forgetting', *Journal of Progressive Human Services*, vol. 20, no. 1, pp. 59–71.

Qureshi, A, Collazos, F, Ramos, M & Casas, M 2008, 'Cultural competency training in psychiatry', *European Psychiatry*, vol. 23, no. 1, pp. 49–58.

Rice, M 2007, 'A post-modern cultural competency framework for public administration and public service delivery', *International Journal of Public Sector Management*, vol. 20, no. 7, pp. 622–37.

Sakamoto, I 2007, 'A critical examination of immigrant acculturation: toward an anti-oppressive social work model with immigrant adults in a pluralistic society', *British Journal of Social Work*, vol. 37, no. 3, pp. 515–35.

Schierup, C & Ålund, A 2011, 'The end of Swedish exceptionalism? Citizenship, neoliberalism and the politics of exclusion', *Race & Class*, vol. 53, no. 1, pp. 45–64.

Simon, C & Mosavel, M 2008, 'Key conceptual issues in the forging of "culturally competent" community health initiatives: a South African example', *Cambridge Quarterly of Healthcare Ethics*, vol. 17, no. 2, pp. 195–205.

Weech-Maldonado, R, Elliott, M, Pradhan, R, Schiller, C, Dreachslin, J & Hays, R 2012, 'Moving towards culturally competent health systems: organizational and market factors', *Social Science & Medicine*, vol. 75, no. 5, pp. 815–22.

Whaley, A & Longoria, R 2008, 'Assessing cultural competence readiness in community mental health centers: a multidimensional scaling analysis', *Psychological Services*, vol. 5, no. 2, pp. 169–83.

4

Incorporating *whiteness* into the teaching and learning of anti-racist social work

Ann Joselynn Baltra-Ulloa

Introduction

I begin this chapter the way I begin my teaching—by introducing myself, revealing where my thinking, my practices and my way of being in the world come from. This introduction locates me within a particular context, invested in particular relationships, all of which inevitably shape my work. It is also a way of showing respect to and earning the respect of the reader. I became a social worker so that in my work I could stay connected to land, to each other, to spirit, to freedom and to our need for peace. I am Mapuche, so as an Indigenous South American to me 'to be born Indigenous is to be born political' (Tovey, cited in Briskman 2008, p. 91). I grew up being taught that we were all people of the land—interdependent and interconnected by our human need to survive, to care for each other and be cared for by others. I came to Australia as a refugee. My refugee and resettlement experiences reinforced my belief in our interconnectedness and interdependency; however, these experiences also exposed me to the reality that there are socio–cultural conditions that shape this world unequally 'along relational divisions of class, race, gender, sexuality and other social divisions' (Pease 2010, p. 3). I bring this personal context and journey to everything I am and do in life.

In this chapter, I critically reflect on my personal experiences of introducing and teaching *whiteness* theory in Australian anti-racist social work, as a Western-trained social worker of non-Western cultural background to a largely Euro-Australian student cohort in an all-European-Australian educational context. My rationale for using the terms 'Western' and 'Euro-Australian' mirrors the explanations given by Walter, Taylor and Habibis (2012, p. 232) for their 'labelling' of the majority of white Australians as 'Euro-Australians'. I take a similar political and critical stance by describing the majority white Australian population as 'raced' given that 'non-white [Australians] are always described by race, such as Indigenous Australians, but Euro-Australians tend to be either termed "Australian" without an attached qualifying racial descriptor, or described in terms of not being raced [for example] "non-Indigenous Australians"' (Walter, Taylor & Habibis 2012, p. 232).

I share my critical observations and reflections of how I consider anti-racist social work education to be caught between two places. On the one hand, the teaching of anti-racist social work in Australia is focused on teaching critical reflexivity and racial cognisance, while conversely it supports the crossing of cultures via cultural competence as a fixed recipe for achieving anti-racist social work practice. This situation results from and preserves whiteness, creating a divide between knowing, being and doing (Martin 2003, p. 1) in social work. Introducing whiteness theory to the teaching of anti-racist social work was a way of posing the question 'why?'.

This chapter discusses the many issues faced in the teaching of whiteness that alerted me to the problems described above. Issues faced during the experience included instructor legitimacy in teaching, the effects of political correctness and racial privilege, and assessing students' engagement with whiteness. The pedagogical merits of dialogue and mutuality are also explored. These became methods and tools for teaching that facilitated relationships with students. In these relationships, the incongruence of teaching whiteness in social work from within an educational and professional context that preserves whiteness became visible. However, seeing this incongruence marked not the end of the experience but the beginning of a journey many others can add to. There is no 'one size fits all' recipe for teaching and learning whiteness theory in anti-racist social work. Highlighted for the reader are several questions as thinking points. The aim is to add to debate, to open the door to dialogue and to continue hearing multiple stories as we make sense of not just what we *do* in social work but also what we *know* and how we *are* in social work.

What is whiteness theory?

The concept of whiteness is most commonly understood in the Australian literature as 'the invisible norm against which "other" races are judged in the construction of identity, representation, subjectivity, nationalism and the law' (Moreton-Robinson, cited in Walter et al. 2011, p. 7). The common descriptor of whiteness as 'the invisible norm' derives from critical race theory's understanding that socio-cultural conditions have allowed, accepted and perpetuated white people's voices to be representative of all people's voices (Pease 2010), while people who are not white can often only speak on behalf of their own race and no one else's (Dyer 2002, cited in Pease 2010, p. 113). Whiteness's original conceptualisation lay in critical race scholarship, predominantly driven by African–American scholars motivated by and responding to the civil rights movement in the United States (Abrams & Moio 2009; Jeyasingham 2012).

Whiteness is an elusive ideology; beyond skin colour it is an identity (Ware & Black 2002), 'a structure, location/space and discourse' (Haggis 2004, p. 58) that denies that race has anything to do with the way people experience and have access to life opportunities. It is embedded in the way the West takes for granted its power, its sense of superiority and its privileged position in seeking homogeneity across the globe. In the case of Australia, 'Whiteness is a foundational claim to identity, belonging and ownership that at no point connects with Indigenous ways of being in the land' (Haggis 2004, p. 56). The concept of whiteness, however, does not in itself theorise how we undo white power and privilege. Its relevancy and usefulness to social work and social work education lies in its capacity to provide a platform for examining and explaining why power and privilege are discursive, invisible and raced (Young 2004). Such examinations and explanations help social work unsettle some of its own taken-for-granted understandings of how social justice is achieved cross-racially (Walter, Taylor & Habibis 2012, p. 237). Theorising a future practice beyond one embedded in the context of whiteness lays in our capacity as social workers and as a profession to think, feel and act from a fundamental belief that we fight racism, oppression, colonisation and injustice for all our sakes and not just for the sake of the 'other' (Yamato, cited in Young 2004, p. 117).

Following Frankenberg (1993), Walter, Taylor and Habibis (2012) argue that whiteness 'needs to be conceived across three dimensions: [as] a location of structural advantage or privilege; a set of cultural practices that are unmarked and unnamed; and, as standpoint, the place from where those who are white look at themselves and others' (Walter, Taylor & Habibis 2012, p. 232). Whiteness theory's usefulness to social work is fundamentally about extending the scope of critical, anti-oppressive and anti-racist theories that have promoted the use of a critically reflexive stance in social work. This stance calls for practitioners to self-examine and self-identify aspects of their cultural self that affect practice while also engaging critically in structural change aimed at redressing issues of social inequality. This contention falls short on two fronts. First, as Foley (1998) and Yan and Wong (2005) have identified, critical self-reflexivity relies on the worker being the 'all knower', capable of identifying and rectifying the impact of cultural bias on practice. This 'one-way process' (Yan & Wong 2005, p. 184) privileges individuality, a Western prerogative offering limited chances for self to be confronted with its own sources of power and privilege in relation to and by the 'other' (Young 2004). Second, critical, anti-oppressive and anti-racist theories fail to problematise the issue of race, often diluting it from arguments about oppression (Young 2004). This prevents critical questions from being asked, such as *'[why are] negative life chances disproportionally affecting non-white people'* [emphasis added] (Young 2004, p. 115). Studying whiteness in anti-racist social work does not involve ignoring the role that issues such as class, gender, sexuality, age and able-bodiedness play in creating and propelling oppression. The study of whiteness in anti-racist social work allows us to consider the racialised nature of life chances. Frankenberg states:

> Whiteness as a site of privilege is not absolute but rather is cross-cut by a range of other axes of relative advantage and subordination: these do not erase or render irrelevant race privilege, but rather inflect or modify it (2001, p. 76).

While Pease concludes:

> The starting point for any form of anti-racism by white people must be an acknowledgment that they are white ... white people have privileges accruing to their whiteness ... they are personally implicated in the reproduction of the ideologies and structures of white dominance. White people must come to understand that what we do in the world reproduces our privileges ... whiteness is useful as part of the critique of white supremacy because it is important to challenge the invisibility of whiteness as normative (2010, p. 127).

The dichotomy between the thinking and the practice of anti-racist social work

The Australian Association of Social Workers (AASW) has decided to progress the profession's journey in responding to issues of cultural diversity and Aboriginal disadvantage by introducing cross-cultural (AASW 2009) and Aboriginal and Torres Strait Islander curriculum content (AASW 2011) to social work qualifying courses. Universities across Australia have integrated this content into their teaching in various forms: some have introduced specific standalone courses dedicated to multicultural practice, cross-cultural practice and anti-racist practice, while others have ensured that every course offered in the social work program covers diversity-focused content. In the case of my university, a standalone course has been introduced, while all other units in the social work program are expected to offer diversity-focused content.

Social work practice is evolving alongside these educational contexts. Australia favours cross-cultural competency approaches to social work practice with culturally diverse groups (Walter, Taylor & Habibis 2012). The current privileging in Australian social work practice of this approach, juxtaposed with anti-racist curricula, leaves little room for considering social work knowledge and practice as products of a particular culture and race. The word 'culture', for example—one of the most confusing, ambiguous and contested terms—continues to be forced into fixed meanings by Western social work (Dean 2001; Gray, Coates & Yellow Bird 2008; Park 2005). Culture continues to be associated in social work literature with racial difference (Park 2005, p. 13), which is still mostly attributed to 'non–white people' (Pease 2010, p. 111). The racially different are spoken of as minorities and seen as marginal in Western societies, and this marginal status leads to these 'minorities' being socially disadvantaged (Baltra-Ulloa 2013). A focus on 'culturally competent and sensitive practice' is born of this context. What this context does not facilitate is an examination of how race plays a central role in who actually gets to define:

- who has the power to determine what culture is and what it is not
- who has the power to decide what aspects of culture are worthy of knowing or not knowing
- who has the power to determine the skills that are necessary to deem someone to be 'culturally competent' outside their own culture.

These observations have led me to take a critical stance on the pedagogical merits of culturally competent social work practice for anti-racist social work education.

The cultural competency approach to practice presents many challenges for anti-racist social work education. First, the curriculum standards set by AASW promote a 'critical appraisal of knowledge in ... cultural and race theories; culturally safe and sensitive practice; specific historical and contemporary cross-cultural issues in Australia [and] international cross-cultural issues' (AASW 2009, p. 68), while also supporting 'teaching environments [that] are culturally safe places for all ... [where] the Aboriginal lens of Ways of Knowing, Being and Doing (Martin 2003) is used' (AASW 2009, p. 3). The curriculum content relies fundamentally on social workers learning to question their own values, attitudes, knowledge and skills base in the face of a genuine desire to learn from the 'cultural other' about what works and what does not during a social work encounter (AASW 2009, 2011). Further, the values, attitudes, knowledge and skill base that the curricula support are framed on being able to engage in relationships with people. In relationships with people social workers are said to learn of clients' ever-changing and evolving contexts, their histories and stories (AASW 2009, 2011). Yet the cultural competency approach preferred by the Australian social work field relies heavily on the social worker mastering the culture of the client, learning sets of knowledge, skills and practices that facilitate a crossing of cultural contexts. This is problematic on several fronts.

There is mounting evidence that social workers can no longer speak of crossing cultures competently with any assurance (Abrams & Moio 2009; Dean 2001; Park 2005; Yan 2008). Generally, cross-culturally competent approaches to social work practice have been designed, developed and evaluated by Western social workers in the belief they are effective helpers across multiple cultural contexts, although they know very little about whether the recipients of their help would actually agree (Baltra-Ulloa 2013). Further, in Australia, AASW describes 'culturally competent safe and sensitive practice' (2010, p. 43) as a model that builds from social work's general principles and ethical standards. The underlying assumptions made by AASW in its *Code of Ethics* (2010) and, similarly, by Laird (2008), Lum (2007), O'Hagan (2001), National Association of Social Workers (NASW) (2001) and Patni (2006), are multiple: anti-racist social work is associated with the social worker who implicitly knows their own culture and is unreservedly thought of as able to identify how culture affects practice, and is able to juggle knowing their culture with learning about the culture of the client all the while remaining 'sensitive to difference'.

Lastly, there is no need for the social worker to ask 'why' at any stage of this process. The culturally sensitive and competent practitioner needs to know how to do culturally sensitive and competent practice to be an anti-racist social worker, but this practitioner remains immune to having to ask why the need exists (Baltra-Ulloa 2013). Cultural competency in this context 'depoliticises race and promotes "othering"' (Pon 2009, cited in Harrison & Turner 2011, p. 336) while also assuming the superiority of the dominant culture—mainly the culture of the worker (Sakamoto 2007, cited in Harrison & Turner 2011, p. 336).

In essence, the teaching of cross-cultural and Aboriginal and Torres Strait Islander social work in Australia is unfolding in a context whereby praxis is problematic because this context promotes social work as 'synonymous with diversity management and the development of competencies' (Jeffery 2005, p. 409). The teaching paradigm centres on delivering valuable curricula aimed at learning cross-cultural practice. However, the epistemological foundations of such a teaching paradigm, practice and curricula remain largely uncontested in the face of issues of race, white power and privilege and their nuanced connections to the maintenance and perpetuation of oppression and inequality (Abrams & Gibson 2007, p. 150).

Introducing the study of whiteness to a largely Euro-Australian student cohort represented my teaching attempt at examining and contesting the epistemological foundations of anti-racist social work knowledge and practice. My aim was to turn the gaze back to social work, to relearn our professional history, examine it as a Western construction shaped by the Western cultural tradition of privileging Western ways of knowing, being and doing (Martin 2003) above all others—a form of continuing colonisation.

Teaching whiteness theory in social work: challenges and critical reflections

The teaching of the unit incorporating whiteness theory involved delivering content specifically related to social work practice with Aboriginal and Torres Strait Islander peoples and culturally and linguistically diverse communities. Table 4.1 summarises the content of the unit's modules.

All lecture material, films, vignettes, interviews and debates were pre-recorded and made available online across three regional campuses. Guest speakers attended tutorials and were organised regionally to assist students in linking with local people.

Table 4.1   Unit's content schedule

Week/ module	Lecture and tutorial topic
Week 1 Module 1	■ Introducing the unit coordinator and tutors (personal and professional contexts, teaching and practice styles, values and ideologies) ■ Introduction to the unit: what is anti-racist practice, postcolonialism, whiteness, dialogue and mutuality ■ Teaching and learning expectations ■ How to participate in feedback and evaluation of the unit and teaching
Week 2 Module 1	■ Historical contexts: colonisation, oppression, human rights and multiculturalism ■ Self-stocktake: Who am I? What is my historical context? How am I situated within the global historical context?
Week 3 Module 1	■ The story of invasion, resistance and social action—Aboriginal and Torres Strait Islander peoples and the intergenerational impact of colonisation ■ Interview with Nick—growing up Aboriginal in Tasmania ■ Self-stocktake continues: How much do I know about Indigenous Australians? Why do I know what I know?
Week 4 Module 1	■ Performance and cast interview by African youth theatre group—Culture to Culture: 'From home to camp to the space in between' (refugee and resettlement experience) ■ Reflecting on what we know about refugees and asylum seekers. Why do we know what we know?
Week 5 Module 2	■ Power, privilege and whiteness in the context of anti-racism ■ Film: debate on whiteness by social work professionals ■ What's in my backpack of privilege?
Week 6 Module 3	■ Understanding culture and identity ■ Film: *Go back to where you came from*
Week 7 Module 3	■ Opening Pandora 's box: how *white* is Australian social work? ■ Where there is oppression there is always resistance—learning from Aboriginal and civil rights activism
Week 8 Module 2	■ Stocktake: What are we understanding about the relevance of whiteness for anti-racist social work? ■ Week of reflection
Week 9 Module 2	■ 'How many rooms are there in the tower of Babel?' Intercultural dialogue and mutuality for anti-racist social work practice ■ Learning to sit comfortably and ethically with the constant discomfort of not knowing
Week 10 Module 3	■ Film: *Yudum* ■ Learning from Aboriginal and Torres Strait Islander peoples' ways of knowing, being and doing ■ Learning to yarn with big ears and small mouths
Week 11 Module 3	■ Decolonised ways of knowing, being and doing with migrants, refugees and asylum seekers ■ Community guest speakers share their thoughts on social work with people of refugee background

(continued)

Table 4.1   Unit's content schedule *(continued)*

Week/ module	Lecture and tutorial topic
Week 12 Module 3	▪ Decolonised ways of knowing, being and doing with and via interpreters and bicultural workers (filmed vignettes) ▪ A new kind of multidisciplinary work, mutual cultural decoding and valuing the bicultural professional
Week 13 Module 3	▪ Preparing for the real world—becoming a decolonised ally and learning when to step aside

The face-to-face component occurred via weekly two-hour regional tutorials. Weekly topics and discussions were supported by relevant readings and a blog site on which students shared their learning experiences with each other, with me and the tutors, and where questions were answered and resources shared. As unit coordinator, I also visited the three regions to connect with students beyond the virtual world. Students provided feedback on course content and the teaching and learning experience via two anonymous evaluations, one mid-semester and another at the end of the course.

The teaching experience took into consideration that whiteness theory within Australian social work is not yet widely recognised. As such, much of the body of pedagogical theory critically examining methods and tools for teaching whiteness has come from the experiences of North American and British contexts (Walter, Taylor & Habibis 2012). This more widely available body of work has emerged from the influences of critical race theory, postmodern, postcolonial and feminist thought and the Freirean liberatory educational movement (Miller, Hyde & Ruth 2004). These traditions have shaped the values and principles that underpin the teaching of whiteness as part of a multicultural and/or cross-cultural teaching agenda. According to Miller, Hyde and Ruth (2004, p. 411) these values and principles include:

▪ The understanding of oppression as multifaceted, multidimensional and ever-changing. Oppression is rooted in the way we think, the way we are in the world and the way we act in the world. It is also in the social structures we have created to support our ways of knowing, being and doing in the world (Martin 2003).
▪ No person, space or system is neutral—when we teach and learn about oppression, power, privilege, whiteness, race and, indeed, social justice, everything and everyone is implicated.
▪ The classroom, therefore, and the experiences had in it are also never neutral.
▪ Learning about whiteness must be also about learning how to take action against dominance and the concentration of power and privilege. Beyond learning to become self-aware, teaching and learning about whiteness must include strategies to move beyond intellectual understanding and towards active tangible change and transformation.

The challenges associated with teaching whiteness under such a framework are documented across disciplines. In the field of education, Cochran-Smith (1991, 1995a, 1995b, 1999 & 2000), hooks (1994), Frankenberg (1997), Giroux (1997), Howard (1999) and Levine-Rasky (2000) all record the resistance of students in the face of being taught material that argues that whiteness exists and that it exists unbeknown to most white people. Gillespie, Ashbaugh and Defiore (2002) document the literature in sociology that argues that the teaching of whiteness as part of multicultural cross-cultural education attracts student and institutional resistance because it racialises power and privilege, making being white about belonging to a particular culture, race and tradition that values thinking of itself as the norm.

In social work literature the arguments are similar. Whiteness is spoken of as an unacknowledged, unexamined and invisible element of race that operates secretly through social, political and cultural systems (Jeyasingham 2012, p. 671). Teaching involves presenting these systems as racialised systems that claim, on the surface, to have no reference to race but inevitably support and propel the privileged position of white people over others (Pease 2010). Students of social work also tend to resist learning about whiteness, similarly because it threatens their sense of 'normal' self and shifts perceptions of social work as a culture-less, race-less, benevolent and neutral caring profession (Baltra-Ulloa 2013). Teaching whiteness in social work has ensued from efforts to find pedagogical ways to prepare graduates for culturally competent and sensitive social work practice (Gollan & O'Leary 2009). However, the literature documents that there are problems with how these efforts incorporate whiteness because they remain largely epistemologically underpinned by professional values, theories and practices that still favour Eurocentric ways of being, knowing and doing (Walter, Taylor & Habibis 2012).

Jeffery (2005) makes a powerful case for how educators often fall into a paradox when teaching whiteness. She argues that in teaching anti-racist social work, we teach students to be racially cognisant via a self-reflexive consideration of how whiteness is present and enacted, and this inevitably means we become critical of social work (p. 410). Students, as '[prototypically] free modern liberal subjects' (Jeffery 2005, p. 410) struggle to reconcile why social work would benefit from turning the gaze inwards and challenging itself. Writers such as Fellows and Razack (1998), Razack (2002) and Roman (1993) elaborate by stating that the free moral Western subject sees the self as rational and capable of learning cross-cultural competencies that lead to mastery and autonomy, so when called to challenge social work and examine how social work is a site of whiteness there is this redemptive retreat to social work practice. Social work practice is where the *doing* of social work becomes the means by which the *being* of whiteness is perceived to be conquered. Jeffery's (2005, p. 410) paradox is thus described as 'if you have to "give up" whiteness, how can you be a good social worker?'. This is the challenge of teaching and learning whiteness in social work as we hold on to cultural competency as the preferred approach to practice.

Ultimately, the literature highlights many aspects that characterise the teaching and learning of whiteness in social work and the issues that result from the teaching and learning experience. Whiteness does not just exist and therefore exposing it becomes the pedagogical aim. Whiteness is performed in context and comes into being through the relationships in the classroom. So, teaching in a manner that facilitated students remaining implicated in critiquing whiteness in self, and in social work theory and practice, proved crucial to the experience I reflect on here. The contextuality of whiteness as a performance made me aware that perhaps the most valuable teaching tool I could take with me to the teaching of whiteness was to learn to sit comfortably and ethically with constant discomfort.

This highly contextual, localised, emotional and labour–intensive teaching and learning experience was filled with challenges and learnings. An explanation of how the content was taught is beyond the scope of this chapter; however, the discussion below grapples with how whiteness theory impacted on the teaching and learning experience. In an effort to succinctly articulate what might be most relevant to others attempting similar journeys I have adopted Miller, Hyde and Ruth's (2004) pedagogical challenges for the teaching of whiteness with a particular focus on *instructor legitimacy* and *racial privilege*.

Instructor legitimacy

It is documented that the teaching of whiteness is often perceived as best delivered by coloured people (Walter, Taylor & Habibis 2012) and, as Miller, Hyde and Ruth (2004) highlight, this perception derives from the underlying belief that white bourgeois subjectivity is raceless and cultureless; therefore, the coloured 'other' is seen as the legitimate speaker of race and culture. As the 'non–Euro–Australian other', I encountered this perception in my students, many of whom felt that my position as non–Euro–Australian teacher afforded me less 'white guilt' and 'pressure' to transform whiteness. My attempts at modelling the process of identifying whiteness and owning the privileges it afforded me during the teaching (even as a non–Euro–Australian teacher) seemed to counter some of these perceptions. Further, posing critically reflective questions to students assisted in deepening their understanding of how whiteness functions to privilege the experience of white people over others. However, what was most useful was realising that discussions about feeling white guilt and pressure were products of whiteness acting to position students and teacher outside systems of power, privilege, race and oppression (Jeyasingham 2012, p. 676).

Shifting conversations from the personal to the political became the pedagogical tool for engaging students in unpacking how social, cultural, economic and political systems influence and define white guilt and pressure as negative by–products of conversations about race and racism. This unpacking also highlighted how issues of race and racism are often able to be avoided by the white population, while non-white people, particularly Aboriginal and Torres Strait Islander peoples, are regularly confronted with their race and made responsible for addressing racism as the product of their 'difference' (Moreton-Robinson 2004).

Legitimacy for the non-Euro-Australian teacher teaching whiteness in this context was about being able to lead these kinds of conversations. Leading them delicately meant balancing the interconnectedness between the personal and the political without buying into 'political correctness', which, as an agent of whiteness, often defines sensitive conversation as taboo. Legitimacy in this context was about taking risks, transformative dialogue, mutuality, releasing some control and not divorcing the personal from the political for the sake of being the 'nice teacher'. For example, I was told by students that my brown skin did not bother them as they saw me simply as their lecturer. Messages of support and encouragement from students for my work followed as though being the brown teacher somehow meant I needed to be reassured my race was of no consequence to my teaching ability. This resulted in classroom conversations about colour blindness, racism and the perverseness of whiteness in encouraging people to believe that, in the West, we can 'see past colour' to the person they are. Pease (2010) talks about these instances as 'unconscious racism' (p. 111), instances of colour-blindness that result from the power and privilege of being white and living in a Western system that allows people to ignore how racialised social structures and life experiences are. Ignoring race and ethnicity might be something Euro-Australians can take for granted, but for many non-white and Aboriginal and Torres Strait Islander peoples, race is ever-present and also a source of identity, empowerment and great pride (Pease 2010).

What proved most powerful in exploring instances of 'unconscious racism' was being able to hear from non-Euro-Australian students about their experiences of race and their sense of pride over their skin colour, their connection to their people, their identity and their sense of belonging in being 'different'. For them, transcending their race and ethnicity was not an option, and that made many Euro-Australian students reflect on how much they were able to transcend being white. I allowed these conversations to unfold, monitoring conversations both in class and on blogs and participating when asked. It was then that I described the joy I felt at seeing students interact and take risks in their public conversations. I also apologised to the non-Euro-Australian students in the course for any offence the comments directed at me as being a person devoid of my race and ethnicity might have caused them and I shared my personal feelings of being patronised by those comments. I asked students 'have you posted messages of support and encouragement to the other lecturers, letting them know it doesn't matter that they're white Euro-Australians because they're doing a great job and they're just lecturers to you?' It was not easy asking such questions. It proved to me that white people can observe these experiences like cultural voyeurs, not burdened by having to acknowledge how whiteness ensures that responsibility continues to fall to the non-white 'other' to unveil and make a case against it.

Racial privilege

Miller, Hyde and Ruth (2004), Nylund (2006), Abrams and Gibson (2007) and Jeyasingham (2012) warn that the process of unveiling whiteness, owning the privileges it bestows and decoding its influences on what is considered normal requires 'introspection, re-education and a willingness to practice new interactional skills, all of which can be personally threatening ... destabilizing ... and profoundly unsettling' (Miller, Hyde & Ruth 2004, p. 413). My experience of teaching whiteness certainly gave credence to this warning. I was deeply humbled by the willingness students showed in engaging with all that this course offered and how they continued to attend class even when there was tension, emotion and fatigue, and the material at times seemed so 'against the grain'. However, in making these statements, I'm not seeking to gloss over instances in which there was racism and discrimination and a need to act against them, such as the times students felt aggrieved at acknowledging Aboriginal land rights and asylum seekers as legally entitled to travel in boats to seek asylum in Australia. Similarly, I'm not seeking to continue to uncritically support the idea that only 'raced others' should teach the 'race bits' in social work programs (Walter, Taylor & Habibis 2012) but rather that there are considerations for all involved in teaching and learning whiteness that need to be acknowledged as they influence what takes place in the classroom and what will eventually take place in the field.

First, understanding and confronting whiteness is a lifelong journey and must start with the self—every self, no matter what racial background. Once a social work program contains the teaching of whiteness, whether as a standalone subject and/ or as integrated material across units, it is inevitable that students will make links to other areas of their learning experience and question their relevancy. These links extend to the social work field, as students become social work graduates, taking their learning to their practice, their colleagues, their organisations and, more importantly, their clients. This has multiple implications; for example:

- How will the non-Euro-Australian teacher be perceived and therefore supported?
- How will students be supported to engage with curriculum that essentially questions the legitimacy of what they are learning in social work?
- How will the rest of a social work program be designed to integrate material on whiteness?
- How will field educators be briefed and supported to welcome students who learn about whiteness in social work?
- How will organisations respond to social work graduates who seek to challenge Whiteness?
- How will clients respond to a social worker who challenges whiteness?

Second, whiteness acts on the anti-racist social work classroom to reward certain behaviours, such as political correctness, and the reflexive subject who is willing to acknowledge their implication in systems of oppression. For example, as a non-Euro-Australian teacher, I was able to push the boundaries more in my teaching because political correctness made it difficult for the majority Euro-Australian students in an all Euro-Australian educational system to challenge me as a 'raced other'. I will not deny that I was challenged and confronted by racism and that, as a social work educator, I welcomed being respectfully challenged because it confirmed that a space for dialogue, mutual learning and safe exploration of differences existed. However, add to this dynamic other issues of power and privilege, such as class, gender, age and the teacher–student role, and the product is far from a straightforward teacher–student relationship but rather a multidimensional and complex association needing to be constantly negotiated. Ahmed (2004, cited in Jeyasingham 2012, p. 676) points out that while the study of whiteness may enable people to identify their participation in systems of oppression and inequality, it also celebrates and supports those who claim reflexive transformative understandings of their own power and privilege.

Critical and anti-racist theory may have also theorised how political correctness and the rewarding of the reflexive subject occur as products of socio-cultural contexts that are dominated by Euro-American values (Boulet 2009). What whiteness theory adds to these critiques, however, is a consideration of how much political correctness and the rewarding of the reflexive subject may occur to protect the discomfort white people feel when issues of race are discussed or debated (Young 2004). On reflection, this is what occurred in assessing students.

Assessing students' engagement with whiteness

Assessments in this unit involved a learning experience journal; an essay relating students' personal framework for the practice of anti-racist social work integrating understandings of whiteness, power and privilege; and a major piece developing a mock intervention plan that integrated their personal framework for anti-racist practice. Students who were able to recognise their own sources of power and privilege and position these within larger systems that support inequality and then connect these realisations to social work and its practice generally performed well as they mirrored an anti-racist stance in their work. Those unable to make these realisations and connections were deemed to struggle with anti-racist and reflexive social work and performed less successfully.

The implications were that, as teacher, although I could satisfy structural requirements around criteria-based assessments, defining an anti-racist social work student as a 'critically reflexive, culturally sensitive communicator who avoids stereotypes', I could not assess the validity of the opposite stance as anti-racist social work. How could students who held a strong opposition to political correctness or who valued collective rather than individual reflexivity or other forms of non-Western retrospection be part of what was considered anti-racist social work learning? My teaching context provided no room to examine these deeper manifestations of whiteness. Perhaps Jeyasingham (2012) best summarises my thoughts on this issue:

> ... reflexive work ... does not, in itself, challenge racism; it only changes the position that the speaker takes up in relation to racism. Such statements are therefore a way of claiming that we are good, anti-racist people that, ironically, are only possible to make for certain people who are privileged through Whiteness (p. 676).

The question beckons: is reflexively acknowledging whiteness enough for the teaching and learning of whiteness in social work? I think not. As social workers are we not invested in action that leads to change? So, the journey is far from over. Much work is yet to be done to influence the unveiling of whiteness within academe and the systems that shape the teaching and learning of anti-racist social work. The challenge remains for social work to find decolonised alternatives, allow for what is comfortable to be replaced by what is uncomfortable—ways of knowing, being and doing (Martin 2003, p. 1) that allow for difference to become the norm.

Conclusion

The teaching and learning of whiteness in anti-racist social work is everybody's business; it should not become the sole responsibility of the non-Euro-Australian 'other', teaching content that inevitably challenges the foundations of much of what is taught and thought of as anti-racist social work. This work represents an opportunity to examine the fundamental epistemological and ontological foundations of social work. As such, there is an opportunity to gaze inwards and towards unveiling and staying implicated in implicit elements of social work's ways of knowing, being and doing (Martin 2003, p. 1). We have for too long focused on the 'hows' at the expense of examining the 'whys'.

In Australia, we have a statement of specific Aboriginal and Torres Strait Islander curriculum content for social work qualifying courses that promotes the Aboriginal lens of ways of knowing, being and doing (Martin 2003, cited in AASW 2011, p. 3). This document calls on social workers to not separate their mind from their heart—thinking, being and doing as one interconnected process. Conversely, we have AASW's statement of specific cross-cultural curriculum content for these courses, promoting the crossing of cultures via a set of knowledge, skills, attitudes and values. The expectation is that these documents are relevant only to social work that involves Aboriginal and Torres Strait Islander peoples or people of culturally and linguistically diverse backgrounds. I think this is where whiteness hijacks effort, and much could be gained in all aspects of social work teaching, learning and practice from understanding what these documents essentially promote: '... Ways of Doing [social work] are a synthesis and an articulation of [our] Ways of Knowing and [our] Ways of Being' (Martin 2003, p. 11).

The way forward is therefore messy, risky, uncomfortable and painful but also incredibly transformational as we are talking about opening up to change, not only for the sake of others, but for the sake of our own relevancy and survival as a profession in an increasingly interconnected and interdependent world.

REFLECTIVE QUESTIONS

1   Why do we do what we do in social work?

2   Is there a social work culture?

3   How do our reasons for doing what we do in social work interface with our clients' lived experience of our practices?

4   How do you think non-white or Aboriginal and Torres Strait Islander peoples would feel about being told by white people that they make them feel guilty and pressured for being white?

FURTHER READING

Bennett, B, Green, S, Gilbert, S & Bessarab, D (eds) 2012, *Our Voices: Aboriginal and Torres Strait Islander Social Work*, Palgrave Macmillan, South Yarra, Victoria.

Gray, M, Coates, J, Yellow Bird, M & Hetherington, T (eds) 2012, *Decolonizing Social Work*, Ashgate, Aldershot.

Pease, B 2010, *Undoing Privilege in a Divided World*, Zed Books, London.

REFERENCES

Australian Association of Social Workers 2009, *Statement of Specific Cross-Cultural Curriculum Content for Social Work Qualifying Courses*, Australian Association of Social Workers, Canberra.

Australian Association of Social Workers 2010, *Code of Ethics*, Australian Association of Social Workers, Canberra.

Australian Association of Social Workers 2011, *Australian Social Work Education and Accreditation Standards: Statement of Specific Aboriginal and Torres Strait Islander Curriculum Content For Social Work Qualifying Courses*, Australian Association of Social Workers, Canberra.

Abrams, LS & Gibson, P 2007, 'Teaching notes: Reframing multicultural education: teaching white privilege in the social work curriculum', *Journal of Social Work Education*, vol. 43, no. 1, pp. 147–60.

Abrams, L & Moio, J 2009, 'Critical race theory and the cultural competence dilemma in social work education', *Journal of Social Work Education*, vol. 45, no. 2, pp. 245–61.

Baltra-Ulloa, AJ 2013, 'Why decolonized social work is more than crossculturalism?', in M Gray, J Coates, M Yellow Bird & T Hetherington (eds), *Decolonizing Social Work*, Ashgate, Aldershot, pp. 87–104.

Boulet, J 2009, 'For a solidarity based practice in the globalising context', in J Allan, L Briskman & B Pease 2009, *Critical Social Work*, Allen & Unwin, Crows Nest, NSW, pp. 281–94.

Briskman, L 2008, 'Decolonizing social work in Australia: prospect or illusion', in M Gray, J Coates & M Yellow Bird (eds), *Indigenous Social Work Around the World: Towards Culturally Relevant Education and Practice*, Ashgate, Aldershot, pp. 82–93.

Cochran-Smith, M 1991, 'Learning to teach against the grain', *Harvard Educational Review*, vol. 61, no. 3, pp. 279–310.

Cochran-Smith, M 1995a, 'Color blindness and basket making are not the answers: confronting the dilemmas of race, culture, and language diversity in teacher education', *American Educational Research Journal*, vol. 32, no. 3, pp. 493–522.

Cochran-Smith, M 1995b, 'Uncertain allies: understanding the boundaries of race and teaching', *Harvard Educational Review*, vol. 65, no. 4, pp. 541–70.

Cochran-Smith, M 1999, 'Learning to teach for social justice', in G Griffin (ed.), *98th Yearbook of NSSE: Teacher Education for a New Century: Emerging Perspectives, Promising Practices and Future Possibilities*, University of Chicago Press, Chicago, IL, pp. 114–44.

Cochran-Smith, M 2000, 'Blind vision: unlearning racism in teacher education', *Harvard Educational Review*, vol. 70, pp. 157–90.

Dean, RG 2001, 'The myth of cross-cultural competence', *Families in Society: The Journal of Contemporary Social Services*, vol. 82, no. 6, pp. 623–30.

Fellows, ML & Razack, S 1998, 'The race to innocence: confronting hierarchical relations among women', *Journal of Gender, Race and Justice*, vol. 1, no. 2, pp. 335–52.

Foley, D 1998, 'On writing reflexive realist narratives', in G Schacklock & J Smyth (eds), *Being Reflexive in Critical Education and Social Research*, Falmer Press, London, pp. 110–29.

Frankenberg, R 1993, *White Women, Race Matters: The social conctruction of whiteness*, Routledge, London.

Frankenberg, R (ed.) 1997, *Displacing Whiteness: Essays in Social and Cultural Criticism*, Duke University Press, Durham, NC.

Frankenberg, R 2001, 'The mirage of an unmarked whiteness', in B Rasmussen, E Klineberg, I Nexia & M Wray (eds), *The Making and Unmaking of Whiteness*, Duke University Press, Durham, NC.

Gillespie, D, Ashbaufgh, L & Defiore, J 2002, 'White women teaching about white privilege, race cognizance and social action: toward pedagogical pragmatics', *Race, Ethnicity and Education*, vol. 5, no. 3, pp. 237–53.

Giroux, H 1997, 'Rewriting the discourse of racial identity: Towards a pedagogy and politics of whiteness', *Harvard Educational Review*, vol. 67, no. 2, pp. 285–320.

Gray, M, Coates, J & Yellow Bird, M (eds) 2008, *Indigenous Social Work Around the World: Towards Culturally Relevant Education and Practice*, Ashgate, Aldershot.

Gollan, S & O'Leary, PJ 2009, 'Teaching culturally competent social work practice through black and white pedagogical partnerships', *Social Work Education*, vol. 28, no. 7, pp. 707–21.

Haggis, J 2004, 'Thoughts on a politics of whiteness in a (never quite post) colonial country: abolitionism, essentialism and incommensurability', in A Moreton-Robinson (ed.) 2004, *Whitening Race*, Aboriginal Studies Press, Canberra, pp. 48–58.

Harrison, R & Turner, R 2011, 'Being a "culturally competent" social worker: making sense of a murky concept in practice', *British Journal of Social Work*, vol. 41, no. 2, pp. 333–50.

hooks, B 1994, *Teaching to Transgress: Education as the Practice of Freedom*, Routledge, New York.

Howard, GR 1999, *We Can't Teach What We Don't Know: White Teachers, Multiracial Schools*, Teachers College Press, New York.

Jeffery, D 2005, 'What good is anti-racist social work if you can't master it? Exploring a paradox in anti-racist social work education', *Race, Ethnicity and Education*, vol. 8, no. 4, pp. 409–25.

Jeyasingham, D 2012, 'White noise: a critical evaluation of social work education's engagement with whiteness studies', *British Journal of Social Work*, vol. 42, no. 4, pp. 669–86.

Laird, J 1998, 'Theorizing culture: narrative ideas and practice principles', in M McGoldrick (ed.), *Re-visioning Family Therapy*', Guildford, New York, pp. 20–36.

Levine-Rasky, C 2000, 'Framing whiteness: working through the tensions in introducing whiteness to educators', *Race, Ethnicity, and Education*, vol. 3, no. 3, pp. 272–92.

Lum, D 2007, *Culturally Competent Practice: A Framework for Understanding Diverse Groups and Justice Issues*, Thomson Higher Education, Belmont.

Martin, K 2003, 'Ways of knowing, being and doing: a theoretical framework and methods for Indigenous and Indigenist re-search', *Journal of Australian Studies: Voicing Dissent*, vol. 27, no. 76, pp. 203–14.

Miller, J, Hyde, C & Ruth, BJ 2004, 'Teaching about race and racism in social work: challenges for white educators', *Smith College Studies in Social Work*, vol. 74, no. 2, pp. 409–26.

Moreton-Robinson, A 2004, *Whiteness, Epistemology and Indigenous Representation: Whitening Race*, Aboriginal Studies Press, Canberra, pp. 75–88.

National Association of Social Workers 2001, *Standard of Cultural Competence Practice*, NASW, Washington DC.

Nylund, D 2006, 'Critical multiculturalism, whiteness and social work: towards a more radical view of cultural competence', *Journal of Progressive Human Services*, vol. 17, no. 2, pp. 27–42.

O'Hagan, K 2001, *Cultural Competence in the Caring Professions*, Jessica Kingsley, London.

Park, Y 2005, 'Culture as deficit: a critical discourse analysis of the concept of culture in contemporary social work discourse', *Journal of Sociology and Social Welfare*, vol. 32, no. 3, pp. 11–33.

Patni, R 2006, 'Race-specific vs culturally competent social workers: the debates and dilemmas around pursuing essentialist or multicultural social work practice', *Journal of Social Work Practice*, vol. 20, no. 2, pp. 163–74.

Pease, B 2010, *Undoing Privilege: Unearned Advantage in a Divided World*, Zed Books, London.

Razack, N 2002, 'A critical examination of international student exchanges', *International Social Work*, vol. 45, no. 2, pp. 251–65.

Roman, L 1993, 'White is a color! White defensiveness, postmodernism and anti-racist pedagogy', in C McCarthy & W Crichlow (eds), *Race, Identity and Representation in Education*, Routledge, New York.

Walter, M, Taylor, S & Habibis, D 2011, 'How white is Australian social work', *Australian Social Work*, vol. 64, no. 1, pp. 6–19.

Walter, M, Taylor, S & Habibis, D 2012, 'Australian social work is white', in B Bennett, S Green, S Gilbert & D Bessarab (eds), *Our Voices: Indigenous and Torres Strait Islander Social Work*, Palgrave Macmillan, South Yarra, Victoria.

Ware, V & Black, L 2002, *Out of Whiteness: Color, Politics and Culture*, University of Chicago Press, Chicago.

Yan, MC 2008, 'Exploring the meaning of crossing and culture: an empirical understanding from practitioners' everyday experience', *Families in Society*, vol. 89, no. 2, pp. 282–92.

Yan, MC & Wong, YR 2005, 'Rethinking self-awareness in cultural competence: toward a dialogic self in cross-cultural social work', *Families in Society*, vol. 86, no. 2, pp. 181–8.

Young, S 2004, 'Social work theory and practice: the invisibility of whiteness', in A Moreton-Robinson (ed.), *Whitening Race*, Aboriginal Studies Press, Canberra, pp. 104–18.

5

Biculturalism as an approach to social work

Shayne Walker and Anaru Eketone

Introduction

As a profession, social work in New Zealand has shown leadership among the 'people professions' by requiring its practitioners to be competent at working across cultures; in particular, with Māori, the nation's Indigenous people. Māori make up 15.4 per cent of the population, with 682 200 people identifying as Māori out of the total New Zealand population of 4 433 000 (Statistics New Zealand 2012). The high number of Māori who come to the notice of the authorities has meant that aspiring social workers are required to have a basic knowledge of Māori cultural constructs (*tikanga*), have undertaken an introductory course into the Māori language (*te reo*), and be aware of how to uphold and apply the Treaty of Waitangi, the nation's founding agreement signed between Māori and the British Crown in 1840.

This chapter looks at how and why social work students are trained to work biculturally in the first instance and from there develop a multicultural approach. The focus is on a local southern New Zealand approach developed at the University of Otago and includes a critical analysis of the wider New Zealand context and the New Zealand Social Workers Registration Board's requirement to demonstrate cross-cultural competency. We argue that biculturalism, based on the relationship established by the Treaty of Waitangi, is still the favoured approach to social work in Aotearoa New Zealand; however, within biculturalism is the capacity to include multiculturalism in regards to social work education, theory and practice.

A further objective of this chapter is to examine dilemmas present in teaching in a bicultural context as shown by research, and to suggest strategies from our own teaching experiences. These may have relevance for other contexts in which social work educators and practitioners are confronted with practice with minority cultural groups.

Historical and political context

In New Zealand, the social work profession has been at the forefront of the movement to require the various practitioners in the health and welfare sectors to be competent to work across cultures. This came about as New Zealand went through a process to examine its colonial past and set processes in place to restore the place and value of its Indigenous peoples, the Māori. The Treaty of Waitangi, signed between 512 tribal leaders and the British Crown in 1840, gave permission for the British to set up a colonial government; however, unwittingly from a Māori perspective, allowed a massive influx of British immigrants that soon dominated a Māori population that was shrinking due to introduced diseases (Walker 2004). While there is still dispute about the translation of the document (which was originally signed in the Māori language), essentially, in return for allowing British governmental rule (Article 1), the Treaty of Waitangi guaranteed the protection of Māori property rights such as for lands, fisheries and forests, and the continuation of tribal authority over local affairs (Article 2), while granting Māori the rights of British citizenship (Article 3) (Walker 2004).

The influx of settlers and the movement of control from the British colonial office to a settler-run government in 1854 placed power in the hands of a population who gradually undermined the agreement of the Treaty until, in 1877, the Chief Justice could declare the Treaty 'a simple nullity' because Māori were barbarians and savages and therefore incapable of understanding such an agreement (Morris 2004). The settlers sought to justify and validate the massive land grabs that ensued, while at the same time allowing Māori a lesser type of political and societal rights (Fleras & Spoonley 1999). While the latter part of the 19th century was a low point for Māori society, the latter part of the 20th century was highlighted by a reinvigoration of the Māori population.

Government policies towards Māori of assimilation and then integration had not created the equal society that Article 3 of the Treaty had promised (Tauri 1999). Many Māori *whānau* (extended families) struggled to maintain their language and culture and so this cultural reinvigoration was supported by political activism that also sought to have the promises made in the Treaty of Waitangi honoured. It can be argued that the Māori loss of sovereignty and its associated marginalisation by successive settler governments meant that three main issues had to find some form of resolution. The first related to Article 2 of the Treaty and the loss of 95 per cent of Māori-owned land, resources and influence over local affairs. Some of these losses were the result of military action, land confiscation, coercion, acts of parliament and shonky land deals, but all were part of an orchestrated government policy to gain lands for incoming British settlers (Walker 2004). The second issue related to Article 3 and the lack of real equality: Māori were prevented from taking the opportunities that their resources would have allowed, and the associated social and political marginalisation led to massive inequalities in health, education, welfare, housing and justice (Durie 1998). The third issue was the lack of recognition of the Māori people as a distinct, vital and valued Indigenous culture (Fleras & Spoonley 1999).

The reinvigoration and associated political and social action sought to bring change yet much of the advancement of Māori as a society in the last 60 years has been incremental. Two documents and one piece of legislation stand out as having particular relevance to social work: *Puao-Te-Ata-Tu: The Report of the Ministerial Advisory Committee on a Māori Perspective for the Department of Social Welfare* (Ministerial Advisory Committee 1986); the report by the Royal Commission on Social Policy (1988); and the *Children, Young Persons, and Their Families Act 1989* (CYP&F Act 1989).

Puao-Te-Ata-Tu was a ministerial review of New Zealand's Department of Social Welfare, which outlined, from a Māori perspective, what the department needed to do to improve outcomes for Māori. This extensive consultation exercise was conducted in Māori spaces such as *marae* (traditional Māori meeting places), using Māori protocols and language, and was chaired by leading Ngai Tūhoe elder John Rangihau. The report was heavily critical of the department's monocultural approach to both services and processes and set out 13 recommendations to reform the department. *Puao-Te-Ata-Tu* was scathing in its criticism of the Department of Social Welfare, describing it, from an organisational perspective, as being insensitive to the needs of Māori, institutionally racist and inflexible (Ministerial Advisory Committee 1986, p. 25).

The recommendations of the report were all-encompassing and gave a clear message to the department. Among other recommendations, the department was to

> attack all forms of racism in New Zealand that result in the lifestyle of the dominant group being regarded as superior to those of other groups, especially Māori by … incorporating the values; cultures and beliefs of the Māori people in all policies developed for the future of New Zealand (Ministerial Advisory Committee 1986, p. 9).

They were also:

> To attack and eliminate deprivation and alienation by:
>
> **(a)** Allocating an equitable share of resources.
> **(b)** Sharing power and authority over the use of resources.
> **(c)** Ensuring legislation which recognises social, cultural, and economic values of all cultural groups and especially Māori people.
> **(d)** Developing strategies and initiatives which harness the potential of all its people, and especially Māori people to advance (Ministerial Advisory Committee 1986, p. 9).

There were also specific recommendations relating to social work education and training:

(a) the Department take urgent steps to improve its training performance in all aspects of its work;

(b) the State Services Commission undertake an analysis of the training needs of all departments which deliver social services;

(c) the State Services Commission assess the extent to which tertiary social work courses are meeting cultural needs for those public servants seconded as students to the courses;

(d) the Department in consultation with the Department of Māori Affairs identify suitable people to institute training programmes to provide a Māori perspective for training courses more directly related to the needs of the Māori people;

(e) **(i)** additional training positions be established for training in Māoritanga at a district level;

   (ii) provision be made for the employment of staff to provide temporary relief while other staff attend training;

   (iii) assistance be provided to local Māori groups offering Māoritanga programmes (Ministerial Advisory Committee 1986, p. 40).

In the late 1980s, the Royal Commission on Social Policy consulted on a wide range of issues as part of a major government review of social policy and issued a report (1988) that, among other things, came up with a framework for how the Treaty of Waitangi could be applied to social issues by government departments. In particular, it proposed a set of principles that the commission believed were inherent in the Treaty that could be applied to the social policy areas of health, education, welfare, justice, housing, and so on. The three principles were partnership, participation and protection. Government departments were now expected to show how they implemented these principles in their dealings with Māori (Durie 1998).

These two reports, and the appalling statistics in regards to the care and protection needs of Māori children, led to changes in government legislation for social welfare provision.

Recommendation 4 of *Puao-Te-Ata-Tu* resulted in a review of the *Children and Young Persons Act 1974* and the establishment of the family group conference (FGC) process as part of the CYP&F Act 1989. FGCs have been exported throughout the world and New Zealand is considered to be the birthplace of and leader in practice (McKenzie & Walker 2007). The CYP&F Act 1989 is acknowledged worldwide as an example of how to empower families and deal effectively with care and protection and youth justice issues (Connolly & Cashmore 2009). The CYP&F Act has deepened the awareness of cultural sensitivity and encompasses traditional Māori social structures of *whānau* (extended family), *hapū* (village/sub-tribe) and *iwi* (tribe), and other Māori values and beliefs.

The *Puao-Te-Ata-Tu* report, the Royal Commission on Social Policy and the CYP&F Act all contributed to the then Labour Government's momentum to honour the agreements made in the Treaty of Waitangi (Barrett & Connolly-Stone 1998; Durie 1998). The government had already passed legislation that a permanent commission of inquiry, the Waitangi Tribunal, could look at all breaches of the agreement of the Treaty. In 1986 they had instituted a requirement that all policy referred to Cabinet had to 'draw attention to any implications for recognition of the principles of the Treaty of Waitangi and that departments should consult with appropriate Māori people on all significant matters affecting the application of the Treaty' (Durie 1998, p. 101).

Around that time, the government began to adopt a policy of biculturalism to uphold and acknowledge the value of Māori culture and thus force government departments, and organisations receiving government contracts, to remove the barriers of monoculturalism and so allow Māori culture, values and expectations to influence service provision (Durie 1998).

What is biculturalism?

Biculturalism, as a concept, has different meanings in different societies. It may refer to official policies of bilingualism or the recognition of two dominant cultures within a society. To Māori, its usual meaning is to be able to understand and live in two cultural worlds (Fleras & Spoonley 1999), but from a New Zealand government position, it was a policy that acknowledged that government departments operated from a Eurocentric view of the world whereby their values had become 'the norm and the marked standard by which others were judged and criticised' (Fleras & Spoonley 1999, p. 236). The answer to this Eurocentric monoculturalism in which *Pākehā* (European settlers and their descendants) dominated was advocacy for a type of biculturalism that recognised 'the co-existence of two distinct cultures, Māori and *Pākehā* within New Zealand society with the values and traditions of both cultures reflected in society's laws, practices, and institutional arrangements' (Durie 1998, p. 102).

Fleras and Spoonley (1999) observe that biculturalism became de facto government policy in 1986, with the passing of the State-Owned Enterprises Act, which began the trend for all government departments to report on their responsiveness to Māori and to the Treaty of Waitangi (Fleras & Spoonley 1999). There was, at times, vocal opposition to this course of events, particularly from those who considered Māori cultural practices and language as being irrelevant in the modern world (Barnes et al. 2012). However, many others had been uncomfortable that the country had not kept its promises and commitments to Māori and saw these policies as an opportunity to restore 'honour' to the country (Graham 2001).

One sector that was very supportive of the move towards biculturalism was the social work profession. Many of its clients, the most marginalised and disadvantaged in the community, were Māori. The extensive consultation process undertaken to produce *Puao-Te-Ata-Tu* fuelled a drive towards a bicultural perspective in the professional education and training of social workers, as mentioned previously (Ministerial Advisory Committee 1986). Social workers advocated strongly for biculturalism and chose to lead by example, giving greater acknowledgment to Indigenous social work policies and practices. As a result of this wider policy perspective, a Bicultural Code of Practice (NZASW 1993) was implemented, and the association changed its name from the New Zealand Association of Social Workers to the Aotearoa New Zealand Association of Social Workers (ANZASW) (Aotearoa being an Indigenous name for New Zealand). In the years before the New Zealand Social Workers Registration Board was set up in 2003, to be accepted as a competent social worker you had to be a member of the ANZASW and pass a competency assessment that included the Bicultural Code of Practice. The code included a statement that a bicultural society in Aotearoa New Zealand is 'one in which Māori and *Pākehā* contribute equally to policy, decision-making and have equal access to resources at all levels of society' and committed itself to achieving this (NZASW 1993, p. 21).

The Bicultural Code of Practice defined bicultural standards of ethical conduct, which recognised such things as traditional familial and social groupings, and the responsibility to empower the same. It recognised that Māori clients had the right to have a Māori social worker; that social work agencies should have policies, procedures and practices that are informed by the Treaty of Waitangi; and that 'Monocultural control over power and resources need to be relinquished so that Māori can achieve liberation' (NZASW 1993, p. 18). This included actively respecting cultural differences and consulting with Māori to ensure agencies and organisations 'avoid imposing monocultural values and concepts on Māori' (NZASW 1993, p. 18). Social workers were to commit themselves to learning about and understanding Māori perspectives, language, social structures and practice models.

As a document it was radical, progressive and sought to address the imbalance that had occurred in New Zealand society. It lasted for 14 years before it was superseded by the current ANZASW Code of Ethics (2008), which is more aligned to international codes of practice. Although the document claims that the Bicultural Code of Practice was incorporated into the Code of Ethics, it was in a diluted form. It was in the drafting of the new code that impetus came for Māori to establish a new independent, Indigenous Tangata Whenua Social Work Association. It was set up in part because of a belief that the Māori voice was diminishing and in part through a desire to be independent as an expression of greater *tino rangatiratanga* (self-determination). We are concerned that removing a large portion of Māori from the ANZASW may water down the profession's commitment to biculturalism even further, and lead to a greater focus on multicultural approaches.

Biculturalism and social work education

Where knowledge is gathered, wisdom should follow.

The commitment of the social work profession to biculturalism meant that social work trainers and educators had to lead the way both in what they taught and how they responded personally to the challenges put before them. We (the authors) both came into social work training in the 1990s as mature students in our thirties and were taught by social work educators that were committed to this bicultural ideal.

Knowledge of New Zealand history, the Treaty of Waitangi, colonisation, Māori language and culture is mandatory for social work students, as social statistics show Māori to be over-represented in most of the negative indicators (Ministry of Social Development 2006). Just as importantly, appropriate responses to working with and for Māori in a partnership authorised by the provisions of the Treaty are necessary to counter the wider hegemonic and discriminatory attitudes towards Māori. Accordingly, our social work courses are described as 'Treaty-based' (that is, they are underpinned by the inherent promises and principles of the Treaty of Waitangi). These approaches are taught within a broader social work theory and practice base of social justice, human rights, resiliency and strengths-based approaches, to name but a few. If people are going to work with Māori appropriately, they will have to learn how, and then practise these skills. Using the Treaty as 'moral blackmail' to develop bicultural practice is not the solution, as this can produce educated racists who use this knowledge to disempower Māori (Jackson 1994). Students often ask us to teach them Māori practice models designed by Māori practitioners for use in dealing with Māori clients; however, we are sometimes hesitant as the models can be devoid of contextual knowledge in a university setting.

In 2003 we were presented with an opportunity for a senior academic from another country to examine the efficacy of our program in Treaty-based, bicultural and cross-cultural education. Dr Susan Young's work is a useful case study for this chapter. Her research challenged us to develop new approaches to teaching students so that theory and knowledge related to cross-cultural work were more translatable into practice, providing improved outcomes for client families. While we have not done further research since making these changes, our anecdotal evidence is that we have had far fewer 'grumblings' from our Māori communities about the practice of our graduates.

Bicultural and cross-cultural education

Along with the ANZASW, the Social Workers Registration Board (SWRB) has also shown a commitment to biculturalism. The first two standards for SWRB registration and competency relate to practice with Māori and cultural 'others' (SWRB 2012).

AN OUTSIDER'S VIEW OF TREATY-BASED, BICULTURAL AND CROSS-CULTURAL EDUCATION

With the value of an outsider's perspective, Dr Susan Young, a visiting scholar from the University of Western Australia, came to the Department of Community and Family Studies at the University of Otago to undertake research with 24 recent social work gradu-ates of the social work program. She was interested in understanding how they translated what they had learnt about working biculturally and cross-culturally into daily social work practice. She wanted to know what helped, what hindered and what they would like to learn further (Walker, Walker & Eketone 2006; Young 2003, p. 3).

Considering the application of learning to practice, Young (2003) found that practi-tioners recognised a number of forms of learning as being important for their practice. There was the formal (prescribed) learning provided through the courses and readings undertaken at university. These readings covered knowledge of Māori language, culture and history; the nature and values connected to critical self-reflection; the holistic approach of social work; an understanding of cultural diversity and how this relates to self; and the plethora of generic skills that are necessary to provide social work services in a broad vari-ety of organisational settings.

Informal (less prescribed, but just as important) learning was linked to the secondary learning from peers and beyond the classroom, 'while experiential learning related to that gained through a range of experiences from childhood, other work and significantly those experiences in the classroom which may or may not have been specifically designed by lecturers to result in learning. Cultural workers and supervision in the workplace also con-tributed to learning' (Young 2003, pp. 3–4).

Young discovered evidence of a disjuncture between the 'knowing about' (head) (that is, being 'culturally literate') and 'being able to do' (hand) aspects of working with people from a different culture. The students interviewed (now practitioners) 'reflect the almost uniform view among these practitioners that they believed themselves to be unprepared for bicultural and cross-cultural ... social work practice' (Young 2003, p. 42) and made a number of important suggestions about linkages to Māori social services, continuing professional development, spirituality, child protection work and self-reflection (Walker, Walker & Eketone 2006).

To integrate this knowledge about 'others', students needed to take what really was 'head and heart' (intellectual and relational) learning and translate it into 'hand' (skills and methods) work (Kelly & Sewell 1988). This is a complex process, and Young concluded that 'it is the task of educators to capitalise on the opportunistic and design strategies to ensure all learners have the opportunity to learn using different strategies. What is signifi-cant here is the preparedness or the propensity for learning shown by some people's past experiences. How we as educators use these diverse situations and opportunities to assist students learn especially in the area of bicultural and cross-cultural practice is a challenge' (Young 2003, pp. 3–4).

Young's (2003) provision of a 'reflection in the mirror' and feedback from students inspired the University of Otago Social Work program to become more committed than ever to improving the theoretical and practice outcomes for students. When they leave the program, graduates must find their own place of praxis and be confident operating within it. Although their starting point is as a 'not knower', or humble expert that learns in relationship with others, they must not be overcome by the complexities of working with different cultural or ethnic groups. It would be useful to undertake further research to examine the efficacy of changes made as a result of Young's visit.

The expectation is that, while we have Treaty specialists in our teaching group, it is the responsibility of all educators to teach about the Treaty implications for their specialist courses. This is cognisant of the requirement that all social work educators be currently registered with current practice certificates; otherwise, the program is not accredited by the SWRB.

However, the Treaty of Waitangi is basically a structural (macro) document between two sovereign parties and sometimes does not equate to better bicultural practice among students (Walker, Walker & Eketone 2006; Young 2003). What we have done is include some cross-cultural approaches in our bicultural approaches. Again our pathway into this comes out of human rights, social justice and strengths-based approaches that emphasise the need for theoretical and experiential knowledge in specific cultures. For that reason we now utilise the approach outlined by Skutnabb-Kangas (1988) as the context for 'Treaty' teaching.

In discussing cultural competency, Perry and Tate-Manning (2006) translated the work of Finnish author Tove Skutnabb-Kangas (1988), which outlines cultural competency in a practice framework as having three major elements:

- cognitive knowledge
- affective competency
- behavioural competency.

Cognitive knowledge is regarded as knowledge about other cultures gleaned through secondary sources (books, movies and so on) and usually does not cause conflict with the values of one's own cultural view. Affective competency results in understanding the other culture from within and the ability to identify with some aspects of the culture, whereby it is viewed as a 'whole culture'. Comparison between cultures may take place, but it does not require an in-depth understanding of the culture; instead, it requires an acceptance that the difference has value. Behavioural competency is the ability to behave in an appropriate manner in a variety of cultural settings.

This requires an internalisation of some values of the other culture, which results in changes in behaviour (that is, learning new skills). Conflict may arise, and often does, if competing norms confront the person at the same time. This in a sense is the goal or endpoint, but good work can only be achieved if the first two competencies are addressed (Walker, Walker & Eketone 2006).

A graduate of any social work program in Aotearoa New Zealand should be able to, in the Māori language, *mihimihi* (greet others formally, stating who they are and their familial origins), *waiata* (sing appropriate songs or chants that support the occasion), *karakia* (provide prayers that bless food, and open and close meetings) and occasionally, if male, *whaikōrero* (give a ritual formal speech acknowledging a formal speech of welcome at a *marae*). More importantly, they should know something of the knowledge base that underpins these skills and processes. These are the basic practical skills to respect Māori culture—a bare minimum, in fact, but more than 'taking your shoes off at the door' or 'rubbing noses' (the *hongi* is the traditional Māori greeting whereby two individuals will greet each other by pressing their noses together). The authors assert that if a practitioner does not have these wider skills available as part of their practice repertoire, then how could they be declared competent to practice in Aotearoa New Zealand (Walker, Walker & Eketone 2006).

Young's (2003) results about the University of Otago social work program recognised achievement of cognitive competency. Students had a good understanding of the Treaty of Waitangi; some knowledge of history and the injustices perpetuated upon Māori, with the consequent impacts in terms of highly negative statistics; had attained a basic knowledge of Māori language (pronunciation, greeting, and so on); and had some understanding of important Māori cultural values. However, even with this knowledge base, what happened when they started practice? According to Young (2003), there was an illustrated lack of praxis in terms of affective and behavioural competency. We contend that social workers need to be exposed to clients from other cultures early in their careers, so that life is 'breathed' into all that they have learned in their university training, and so they can build on this and learn new skills because the context demands it. This, accompanied by good supervision, is good for new practitioners' growth. Training students to work cross-culturally can be threatening and intimidating for them; our task is to give them confidence while encouraging humility. The anecdotal evidence from students on placement in Māori contexts is that the urgency for skills and models development only happened in those contexts. The context itself speaks (Walker, Walker & Eketone 2006).

We have also used the 'Bennett Scale' (Bennett 1986, 1993), also called the 'Developmental Model of Inter-cultural Sensitivity' (DMIS), in training. The framework describes the ways in which people can react to cultural differences and what they can do to improve their skills. This is a process, or 'how to get there', approach that provides a safe place for students to reflect on their own attitudes. (Interestingly, this model was not found in social work literature but instead was found on the internet as part of cross-cultural literature for the business and finance sectors for people who were planning to conduct business in foreign cultures). In the social work field, people are often compelled to work with a social worker but, in business, customers may have a wide choice of people to do business with and so the impetus and motivation to communicate well cross-culturally may be stronger.

Bennett's approach explains how people construe cultural difference and encourages self-rating. The underlying assumption is that as one's experience of cultural difference becomes more complex, one's potential competence in intercultural relations increases (Walker, Walker & Eketone 2006). The Bennett Scale is a continuum with two endpoints: 'ethno-centric' and 'ethno-relative'. Ethno-centricism refers to using one's own standards and customs to judge all people, often unconsciously. Ethno-relativism is the opposite of ethno-centrism and refers to a person who is comfortable with many standards and customs, and who can be effective interpersonally by adapting their behaviour and judgments in many cultural settings. Each state has three orientations: denial; defence/reversal and minimalisation; and acceptance, integration and adaptation (Bennett 1993). People move through these states and orientations as they acquire intercultural competence. The approach allows the possibility for students to safely understand their own position and 'isms' (Walker, Walker & Eketone 2006). However, the inference from Young's work is that, for many students, this was still an abstraction that was, in the main, an intellectual exercise.

The Otago response

In using the ideas explored above in the Aotearoa New Zealand context, we believe that they must be applied first of all to the situational context of biculturalism and after that to the multicultural context. In applying both Skutnabb-Kangas's cognitive competence and Bennett's ethno-centric stage of development, a double step is required: first, recognising the place of Māori as *tangata whenua* (Indigenous people of the land) in the implementation of a bicultural structural relationship based on the Treaty of Waitangi and, second, working through the same process with respect to other cultures. Therefore, while we shall be primarily talking about Treaty-based education and social work practice in such a setting, we also imply the necessity for understanding the culturally specific elements of each culture to fulfil the requirements of multiculturalism. In seeking to respond, we are attempting to develop our teaching along lines of promoting further intellectual (cognitive) learning as well as modelling expected behaviours, experiential learning and practicum experience. It might seem paradoxical to begin with cognitive learning when Young's research acknowledged this as being successfully achieved, but what the cross-cultural material indicates is that while graduates may have worked through Bennett's stage of 'ethno-centrism', it is far less certain that they will have achieved full ethno-relativism.

As we have noted above, for students their journey is initially an intellectual one, which is more important than just learning about another culture. So how do you create theoretical pathways for students to have a safe place to debate 'inter' and 'intra' issues? Our approach is to provide an intellectual space for students to move away from binary thinking (Sands & Nuccio 1992) and deconstruct their own discourses about the cultural or ethnic 'other', hopefully decentring the oppositional hierarchies that value or privilege one group over another. This is more than useful in terms of cross-cultural or bicultural thinking. The discovery of multiple discourses, one's own subjectivity in constructing reality, and meaning and subsequent identity(s), can lead a student to realise that these things are contextually influenced and therefore changing, sometimes contradictory and often multifaceted. This is often not discovered until they are in practice (Young 2003). This form of intellectual 'unsettling' can be challenging or just 'mind games' for some but it sets the scene for an analysis of power in regards to the production of knowledge about the cultural or ethnic other (Said 1978). This can also be a point of conscientisation and emancipation (Friere 1972) as the unsettling can be transformative, with felt responses that provide opportunities to translate into practice.

We (educators, practitioners and students) may all have our own particular 'isms', but do we ask ourselves the right questions? For practitioners that work with those groups that have been ascribed minority status, this academic viewing may move them on from the 'put on a smile' approach that can result in paternalistic bicultural and cross-cultural practice. The continued professional development expectations of ANZASW and SWRB require ongoing learning where, epistemologically, we must always be asking ourselves 'How are we thinking about our thinking?' (Sewpaul 2012). This is a question of pro-social modelling if we are to produce students who ask themselves the same question.

It is important for students and practitioners to be exposed to the culturally and ethnic 'different' and, where possible, develop strong relationships because this is often where the best learning takes place. The ideal is to learn competencies of a culture from within that particular cultural setting. Some students clearly enjoyed experiential learning, but things like language, culture and history were only relevant if they were associated with the right processes, settings and people (Walker, Walker & Eketone 2006).

One of the things we try to do is immerse students in unfamiliar settings. *Noho marae* is an event where we formally enter a *marae* and all sleep on mattresses on the floor in the *wharenui* (ancestral long house). The subsequent use of *pōwhiri* (ritual speeches of welcome and engagement to remove the potential corruption of the outside world) brings the students into this process and often touches their hearts and their *wairua* (spirit). They practice their own *mihimihi* (extended formal greeting in the Māori language explaining their familial position) for the occasion—which is often fraught with fear and nervousness—and are examined and awarded marks for their greeting, yet no one has ever complained once they have done it. Staying on the *marae* is an experience in itself as they share the *wharenui* with up to 60 others. They often get tired and irritable and we get to see the best and worst of attitudes and actions. All of these things 'breathe some life' into the university classroom learning and make it come alive for some students.

However, it is a somewhat artificial version; although we use the community's facilities, processes and values, often the community itself is not there as we do not want to impose on their lives so we use their facilities when they are free. Despite this, it is still for many the beginning of a long-term relationship with the culturally different. The objective is to get students to relate these processes at the *marae* to how they will work with Māori in their everyday working life. One of the regular pieces of feedback is that the students absolutely enjoy getting to know the staff outside of a university classroom and seeing whether staff 'walk the talk' and do their *mihimihi* and *waiata*. Relationship-building that is constructive and engages with Māori requires practice in Māori settings to develop knowledge and skills. *Noho marae* are a good start, as the combination of theory and experience is a way of getting emotional (heart) and intellectual (head) buy-in from students. The *noho marae* are organised through our department, but due to the costs involved, only occur one or two nights a year and, while many students cherish the experience (Young 2003), for some this may just be cultural voyeurism and not become part of ongoing relationship development and accountability.

Modelling—towards behavioural competence and ethno-relativity

Another strategy that we use is to co-teach courses in which Māori social work knowledge is delivered (in 2012, this was through compulsory courses at second and third year and an optional course at fourth year). Team teaching provides a number of advantages for the students; they are exposed to multi-tribal and sometimes conflicting approaches to issues and different knowledge. We highlight the differences we have over traditional and contemporary expressions of Māori culture. One teacher belongs to the local tribe and the other is from a tribe 1000 kilometres away. Our different perspectives on ethnicity and identity, and our different beliefs about the primacy of local, tribal and national Māori groups, can create a healthy debate that exposes students to the idea that Māori are a diverse community and are not all the same. It guards against an essentialism whereby students think that if they just learn a certain grouping of knowledge they can just use a 'tickbox' to assess Māori clients or to move in and out of Māori environments. Our skill bases complement each other to provide a more consistent and deeper approach both in terms of practice and theory. Anaru has always worked in and with Māori organisations, Shayne to a lesser degree, and our varied and sometimes oppositional professional backgrounds provide students with great ways to illustrate theory and practice. We both endeavour to maintain strong links with the local Māori communities and pro-socially model the necessity for good, strong, ongoing and hopefully accountable relationships. We 'spark' off each other and the students 'spark' off us. The feedback from students about this is very good.

Change in New Zealand society has been slow and, even after 20 years, the development of bicultural practice is still at such an emergent phase that the opportunities for all but a few students on practicum placements to fully grapple with and 'try out' their bicultural skills are limited, although the program does try to share learning through intensive small-group weekly fieldwork tutorials. This, however, is an area we hope to develop further, as the knowledge and practice itself develops in the 'real world'.

Bicultural and cross-cultural competency and the Social Workers Registration Board

While we have sought to implement and adapt our philosophies, we have had to do so in a context in which the SWRB has had a growing influence and impact on the profession. One of the interesting aspects of the SWRB's competency process is that it seems to assume that social workers are white. Social workers have to prove ten competencies, including two culture-based competencies:

1 competence to practise social work with Māori
2 competence to practise with different ethnic and cultural groups in Aotearoa New Zealand (SWRB 2012).

Critiquing these competencies from a Māori perspective, as social workers are expected to be able to work with Māori and with different ethnic groups, the assumption is that social workers are white. This became clear when we were part of a group inquiring with a board member about how we as educators (not currently practising social workers) could demonstrate the necessary competencies when we went through the registration process. When the second competency was discussed, one of the authors innocently said 'Well, that's good, I can work with *Pākehā*'. There was a mixture of laughter from other staff and shock and some shortness by the board member, showing to all in attendance that white New Zealanders were not to be considered one of the 'different' ('other') cultures that the competency process was meant to refer to. We do not believe that the intention of the question is to ask Māori about their ability to work with *Pākehā* clients, but to question their competency to work with non-*Pākehā* clients.

Despite this, we believe that biculturalism is itself a stepping stone to other approaches such as multiculturalism, although it is viewed with suspicion by some Māori. It is not that Māori disagree with other cultures being dealt with appropriately, but instead that multiculturalism often seems to be an argument for maintaining the domination of Eurocentric approaches. We have been in numerous forums where biculturalism was objected to, the argument being that, despite Māori being at the bottom of most social indices, social workers can't be expected to learn about every culture, therefore Māori should not be privileged by forcing social workers to learn about them. The logic of their argument is that it is more appropriate that already disadvantaged groups adjust themselves to be worked with in a way that *Pākehā* social workers find appropriate. It should be untenable for a social worker to expect that it is the client who must change their cultural world view and take on the values, beliefs and customs of the dominant culture, particularly if this dominant culture has also been responsible for their marginalisation and even oppression. This is where ethno-relativism has its strength. Young's (2003) research showed that knowing about Māori history, culture and language, and using this knowledge to the benefit of all parties concerned, is what bicultural education should be aiming for.

One of the changes in social work education at Otago is that there are greater numbers of Māori joining the course. In the past, they were often mature 'second-chance' students but now more Māori are coming through the traditional university pathways. Is this better for clients? Certainly, having more trained Māori social workers is desirable, but there is still much to be done. Being Māori does not make you a 'genetically pre-packaged' bicultural social worker, and Māori practitioners also have added expectations placed on them by their communities. Biculturalism then has been a pathway to creating greater social change and equality both for Māori extended families and Māori social workers.

The future for bicultural education

What then for the future? In this increasingly multicultural context, how do we maintain the rights of Indigenous peoples? Fleras and Spoonley (1999) argue that biculturalism and multiculturalism clash, that there is little space for them to sit comfortably together, as the dominant settler culture can play off one minority against another. It means that they can deny Māori rights of cultural understanding because, to some, under multiculturalism, you can't learn about everyone so therefore you learn about no-one. Fleras and Spoonley's (1999) answer was a form of bi-nationalism in which Māori as *tangata whenua* are on 'one chair' and *Pākehā* (including all other immigrants to Aotearoa) are in 'another chair', facing each other and sharing power—multiculturalism within a bicultural framework.

In terms of the accreditation of social work programs in New Zealand, particularly through the SWRB and the New Zealand Qualifications Authority, programs must show a clear mapping of their taxonomy of learning outcomes in regards to knowledge and practice necessary for working with Māori in a well-considered bicultural manner. Points of integration must be layered into the curriculum year after year to ensure prospective social workers are prepared to work with Māori biculturally and other groups multiculturally. Integration with other social work theory—that is, human rights, social justice and strengths-based approaches—is critical, and is a logical outcome of Young's (2003) research in regard to curriculum development.

We foresee students needing to spend more time in bicultural situations during their training; for example, by running a university social work course that is completely based in the traditional Māori environment of the *marae*. Students generally desire to be good at cross-cultural and bicultural social work but as Young (2003) found, they must be put in positions to make them use the associated skills and knowledge.

Durie (2012) discusses three phases of intervention for practice with Māori that can be applied here: *whakpiri* (engagement), *whakamārama* (enlightenment) and *whakamana* (empowerment). The 'domains of enlightenment' (Durie 2012, p. 26) are followed by responses to the social work process. Students (future social workers) must think broadly and creatively and think differently about their responses to questions about such things as *ngākau, puku, wairua, mātauranga* and *whānau* (Durie 2012):

- What is your *puku* (stomach) saying to you? (physical response)
- What is your *ngākau* (heart) saying to you? How have you connected with the people you are working with and what they are saying and doing? (felt response)
- What is your *wairua* (spirit) saying to you? (sensed response)
- What does *te ao Māori/Pākehā mātauranga* (mind) theory say to you? (thought response)
- What are the *whanaungatanga* (family making) issues that resonate here? (relational response)
- What kind of fabric is being woven? (the distinctiveness that comes from a number of variants in this cultural context) (integration response) (Durie 2012).

Each of these questions is followed by a response by the client and the worker. This encourages ownership of the process by both. The questions are part of the essence of working biculturally with Māori as they are informed by the meaning-making frameworks of many Māori, including us. The aim of bicultural practice is surely *mana*-enhancing practice (Ruwhiu 2009) that leads to better outcomes for Māori from the social work process. Our intention is not to end this chapter arrogantly but, if this interests you, find out what *mana* is and how you can enhance it in others.

Conclusion

In many ways, the New Zealand situation is unique. Not only do we have an Indigenous population that has reinvigorated and is reinvigorating itself, but we also have a large portion of the descendants of the colonial settler population acknowledging the errors of the past and seeking a way forward that not only supports this reinvigoration but also embraces the change in society that has encouraged it. The acceptance of biculturalism may not have lived up to political expectation but it has created an environment and opportunity for organisations like ANZASW to embrace bicultural approaches to social work and see it as a way forward both for Māori and the country. As Indigenous social work educators at the University of Otago we have been privileged to participate in this journey.

While much of the knowledge we try to impart is underpinned by a Māori world view, we have adopted international theoretical frameworks that help our students understand not only the context in which they work, but also encourage them to be self-reflective in a way that we hope motivates them to learn as much about themselves as about others.

Our approach is not intended to be idealistic; the focus on cognitive knowledge, affective competency and behavioural competency highlights a broad approach to practice through which, theoretically, anyone can work with anyone. However, each cultural group needs culturally specific skill and knowledge 'packages'. These can only be taught in a general manner in an undergraduate program as generic multicultural approaches within a bicultural relational framework. Our worst fear is that we create, through our social work education programs, educated racists who use their power and knowledge to silence the voice and actions of their cultural other. We, as educators and practitioners, have a responsibility to uphold 'the right of Indigenous people to make sense of their time and place in this world' (Russell 2000, p. 10) in our teaching, learning and practice.

In this chapter we have endeavoured to explain the New Zealand bicultural approach to social work, exploring the rationale and processes behind it. We have even highlighted some of the tensions as we seek to improve outcomes for social work clients and create a more just society, all the while acknowledging and valuing the Indigenous culture. However, in the end it comes down to what we do and how we use the resources and knowledge that we have acquired.

Where knowledge is gathered, wisdom should follow.

REFLECTIVE QUESTIONS

1   What do you enjoy about other cultures?
2   When you consider the cultural diversity of your country, how would you rate your cognitive, affective and behavioural competencies to work with those groups that are ascribed minority status? Be honest and list evidence under each competency.

3   After doing this exercise, where would you be on the 'Bennett scale'? Be mindful that each of the two states (ethno-centric or ethno-relative) has three orientations: denial; defence/reversal and minimalisation; and acceptance, integration and adaptation.

4   It may vary between cultures, but how do you construe the culturally different other?

5   What 'isms' are blind spots for you (for example, racism or sexism) and are there any groups you regularly stereotype?

6   Who are the first nation, or Indigenous, people from your country, area and place of work? What are the specific knowledge, attitudes and behaviours necessary to work with this group in a confident and effective manner?

7   How do you celebrate cultural diversity in your daily life?

FURTHER READING

Bennett, MJ 1993, 'Towards ethno relativism: a developmental model of intercultural sensitivity', in RM Paige (ed.), *Education for the Intercultural Experience*, Intercultural Press, Yarmouth, ME, pp. 21–7.

Fleras, A & Spoonley, P 1999, *Recalling Aotearoa: Indigenous Politics and Ethnic Relations in New Zealand*, Oxford University Press, Auckland.

Mead, HM 2003, *Tikanga Māori: Living by Māori Values*, Te Whare Wānanga O Awanuiarangi, Huia, Wellington.

Perry, C & Tate-Manning, L 2006, 'Unravelling cultural constructions in social work education: journeying toward cultural competence', *Social Work Education*, vol. 25, no. 7, pp. 735–48.

Ruwhiu, L 2009, 'Indigenous issues in Aotearoa New Zealand', in M Connolly & L Harms (eds), *Social Work Contexts and Practice*, 2nd edn, Oxford University Press, Australia & New Zealand, pp. 107–20.

REFERENCES

ANZASW 2008, *Code of Ethics*, 2nd revision, Aotearoa New Zealand Association of Social Workers, Christchurch.

Barnes, AM, Borell, B, Taiapa, K, Rankine, J, Nairn, R & McCreanor, T 2012, 'Anti-Māori themes in New Zealand journalism—toward alternative practice', *Pacific Journalism Review*, vol. 18, no. 1, pp. 195–216.

Barrett, M & Connolly-Stone, K 1998, 'The Treaty of Waitangi and social policy', *Social Policy Journal of New Zealand*, no. 11, pp. 29–47.

Bennett, MJ 1986, 'A developmental approach to training for intercultural sensitivity', *International Journal of Intercultural Relations*, vol. 10, no. 2, pp. 179–96.

Bennett, MJ 1993, 'Towards ethno relativism: a developmental model of intercultural sensitivity', in RM Paige (ed.), *Education for the Intercultural Experience*, Intercultural Press, Yarmouth, ME, pp. 21–7.

Connolly, M & Cashmore, J 2009, 'Child welfare practice', in M Connolly & L Harms (eds), *Social Work Contexts and Practice*, 2nd edn, Oxford University Press, Australia & New Zealand, pp. 275–90.

CYP&F Act 1989, *Children Young Persons, and Their Families Act 1989*, Government Printer, Wellington.

Durie, M 1998, *Whaiora Māori Health Development*, 2nd edn, Oxford University Press, Auckland.

Durie, M 2012, 'Māori concepts of wellbeing: Intervening with Māori children, young people and families', Compass seminar, Invercargill, 20 July.

Fleras, A & Spoonley, P 1999, *Recalling Aotearoa: Indigenous Politics and Ethnic Relations in New Zealand*, Oxford University Press, Auckland.

Friere, P 1972, *The Pedagogy of the Oppressed*, Penguin, Middlesex.

Graham, D 2001, *The Legal Reality of Customary Rights for Māori*, Treaty of Waitangi Research Unit, Stout Research Centre, Victoria University, Wellington, New Zealand.

Jackson, M 1994, 'Seminar to Community and Family Studies Department', University of Otago, Dunedin.

Kelly, A & Sewell, A 1988, *With Head, Heart and Hand: Dimensions of Community Building*, Boolarong Publications, Brisbane.

McKenzie, M & Walker, S 2007, 'Experiences and challenges of FGC in New Zealand: a view from New Zealand', in L Schjelderup & C Omre (eds), 2007, *Veivisere for Et Fremtidig Barnevern*, Taper Akademisk Forlag, Trondheim, pp. 37–56.

Ministerial Advisory Committee 1986, *Puao-Te-Ata-Tu: The Report of the Ministerial Advisory Committee on a Māori Perspective for the Department of Social Welfare*, Government Printer, Wellington.

Ministry of Social Development 2006, *The Social Report 2006: Indicators of Social Wellbeing in New Zealand*, Ministry of Social Development, Wellington.

Morris, G 2004, 'James Prendergast and the Treaty of Waitangi: judicial attitudes to the treaty during the latter half of the nineteenth century', *VUWLR*, 35, pp. 117–44.

New Zealand Association of Social Workers 1993, *Code of Ethics and Bicultural Code of Practice*, NZASW, Dunedin.

Perry, C & Tate-Manning, L 2006, 'Unravelling cultural constructions in social work education: journeying toward cultural competence', *Social Work Education*, vol. 25, no. 7, pp. 735–48.

Royal Commission on Social Policy 1988, *The April Report*, Volumes I to IV, Royal Commission on Social Policy, Wellington.

Russell, KJ 2000, 'Landscape: perceptions of Kai Tahu', PhD thesis, University of Otago, Dunedin.

Ruwhiu, L 2009, 'Indigenous issues in Aotearoa New Zealand', in M Connolly & L Harms (eds), *Social Work Contexts and Practice*, 2nd edn, Oxford University Press, Australia & New Zealand, pp. 107–20.

Said, E 1978, *Orientalism*, Vintage Books, New York.

Sands, R & Nuccio, K 1992, 'Postmodern feminism and social work', *Social Work*, vol. 37, no. 6, pp. 489–94.

Sewpaul, V 2012, 'Inscribed in our blood: confronting the ideology of sexism and racism as possible seeds of liberation and radical change', Proceedings of the Joint World Conference on Social Work and Social Development: Action and Impact, Stockholm, 8–12 July.

Skutnabb-Kangas, T 1988, *Vahemmisto, Kieli ja Rasismi*, Painokaari Oy, Helsinki.

Statistics New Zealand Tatauranga Aotearoa 2012, 15 November, *Māori population grows more and lives longer*, media release, viewed 17 April 2013, <www.stats.govt.nz/tools_and_services/services/media-centre/additional-releases/māori-population-estimates-15-nov-2012.aspx>.

Social Workers Registration Board 2012, *Core Competence Standards*, viewed 17 April 2013, <www.swrb.govt.nz/competence-assessment/core-competence-standards>.

Tauri, J 1999, 'Explaining recent innovations in New Zealand's criminal justice system: empowering Māori or biculturalising the state', *Australian and New Zealand Journal of Criminology*, vol. 32, no. 2, pp. 153–67.

Walker, R 2004, *Ka Whawhai Tonu Mātou: Struggle Without End*, 2nd edn, Penguin, Auckland.

Walker, S, Walker, P & Eketone, A 2006, 'We can be equal as long as you'll be like me. Theory into practice: biculturalism and social work practice in a multicultural context', paper presented to the 33rd World Congress of the International Association of Schools of Social Work.

Young, S 2003, *Opening New Worlds: Stories from Fields of Bicultural and Cross-cultural Practice*, Department of Community and Family Studies, University of Otago, Dunedin.

6

Social work practice in India: the challenge of working with diversity

Supriya Pattanayak[1]

What is considered theory in the dominant academic community is not necessarily what counts as theory for women of colour. Theory produces effects that change people and the way they perceive the world. Thus we need *teorías* [theories] that will enable us to interpret what happens in the world, that will explain how and why we relate to certain people in specific ways, that will reflect what goes on between inner, outer and peripheral 'I's within a person and between the personal I's and the collective 'we' of our ethnic communities.

Theory then, is a set of knowledges. Some of these knowledges have been kept from us—entry into some professions and academia denied us. Because we are not allowed to enter discourse, because we are often disqualified and excluded from it, because what passes for theory these days is forbidden territory for us, it is vital that we occupy theorising space, that we not allow white men and women solely to occupy it. By bringing in our own approaches and methodologies, we transform that theorising space.

Gloria Anzaldúa (1990, p. xxv)

Introduction

India is a multilingual, multi-ethnic and multicultural country where diversity is the norm rather than an exception. There are approximately 3000 mother tongues, 4000 castes and communities, 4000 faiths and beliefs; the diversities that exist in India build up a single language and culture area. This cultural area is based on relationships, which, in the absence of a structured social protection system, have

---

1 The opinions expressed by the author are her own and not those of the organisation she represents, Department for International Development India.

been the bedrock of a community support and security system. This gets eroded by the values of individuality and profit, promoted by a capitalist monoculture and advocated by neo-liberal globalisation. Further, it is well documented that colonialism, modernisation and neo-liberal globalisation have played a part in repressing Indigenous peoples' ways of knowing and discouraging people from making use of their traditional knowledge in everyday life (Mosha 2000; Smith 1999; Venkataraman 1996).

Social work theory and practice in India is an import, often imposed, and does not take into account the extensive diversity in the Indian context. There is an urgent need, as Said (1993) indicates, to assess how knowledge production and theories of the past and present have been and continue to be shaped by the ideas and power relations of imperialism, colonialism and globalisation. India has a longstanding tradition of philosophical values and religious practices, embracing Hinduism, Islam, Buddhism, Christianity and a host of others, which all speak of 'respect for the other'. Gandhian principles of *satyagraha* (zeal for truth), non-cooperation, non-violence, self-reliance and self-governance also influence everyday lives of people and communities. Social work practice in India today does not embed these principles. Instead, the attempt is to integrate 'western knowledge, Indigenous knowledge and authentization knowledge into the mainstream social work education and practice' (Channaveer 2012, p. 118).

This chapter demonstrates the disjunct between social work theory and practice in India through a series of examples, while proposing the integration of Indigenous theory and practice principles.

Linguistic imperialism and the Indian education system

Linguistic imperialism, or the dominance of certain languages internationally and attempts to account for such dominance in an explicit theoretically founded way (Phillipson 2009), has shaped education policy and program formulation in India. In India, while maintaining diversity, both social and cultural, is espoused, it is in rhetoric only. Skutnabb-Kangas (2000) shows how state policies and actual practices in respect of languages leads to loss of linguistic diversity by denial of linguistic human rights in education and various forms of neglect of minority mother tongues. It has also been demonstrated (Fishman 1991; Skutnabb-Kangas 2000) that the survival and development of languages is enhanced by the use of languages in education. It has been the contention of most social work practitioners in India that there is a disjunct between theory and practice, language being a key component in this.

The lack of recognition of the diversity of cultures and languages in the Indian education system has led to a layered alienation of, at one level, the people from their relationships and, at another level, from the production of knowledge and valuing of the same. Colonial powers in India, recognising the value of the Sanskrit language, systematically ensured that Sanskrit did not become the language of mainstream education for the local population. Indian languages were not considered as languages of knowledge (science) or languages of development by the colonial powers or the rest of the world. In this manner, English came to be the dominant language and was imposed on a very diverse populace.

The imposition of the English language certainly helped to further the agenda of globalisation and a global system of marginalisation and exploitation. The state policy of 'education for all' thus by definition became 'education for few': for those who could access quality formal schooling and English language. Further, for young Indians today, the acquired competence in English remains the major benchmark for education. Mohanty (2010, p. 165) notes that 'multilingual societies are generally characterised by hierarchical power relationships among languages and their speakers. Some languages empower their speakers giving them privileged access to resources whereas others contribute to marginalisation and disadvantage for the community of the resources'. As language is a vehicle of cultural transmission, culture is also lost because of the loss of language. A set of theories, Western in origin and thought, alien to the lives of people, was also imposed. As a consequence, those who were meant to benefit from this education, either as consumers or clients, did so, if at all, by half measures.

History of social work in India

Historically, social work practice in India was firmly based within a welfarist perspective, evolving into a practice that:

> enhances social functioning of the individual, group or community within the prevailing social structure, and without any effort in uprooting the contemporary values of social life ... recognises equality, the worth and dignity of the individual ... human rights and social justice serve as the motivation and justification for social work. Social work intervenes at the point where people interact with each other in their environment (Sreerama Murty 2012, p. 87).

The Gandhian philosopher Dayal (1986) emphasised that social work in India was about adjustment, adaptation, reconciliation and the link between the individual and the social environment rather than bringing about fundamental changes in the social structure. Structural transformation was not the focus of social work in India; rather it was focused on the individual and their adjustment, adopting the Western ideology of individualism, although in India community was the basis of all life. Gandhi reiterated time and again that India lived in its 700,000 villages.

Sreerama Murty (2012) has systematically recorded a history of social work in India, a brief summary of which is presented below. In India, glimpses of the spirit of doing good to one's fellow beings, and initiating or taking part in activities for the welfare and common good of all are obtained through folk tales and legends, treatises on polity (Chanakya's *Arthashastra*, 350–283 BC), on sacred Hindu customary laws derived from the Vedas (the *Smritis*) and on the ancient laws that formed the basis for social and religious codes of conduct (the *Dharmashastras*). Undertaking public works (for example, roads, rest houses, hospitals, water supply) and ensuring sanitation and cleanliness, and care of the elderly, poor, disabled, deserted and orphans, are clearly spelt out in the *Arthashastra*, which also specifies responsibilities and penalties. Collective charity or alms-giving in times of famine are also recorded in the *Jatakas* (tales about Buddha). Helping the cause of education (*Vidyadana*) and making endowments or donations in the form of land (*Bhoomidana*) for the recurring expenses incurred by educational and other public institutions was considered highly meritorious. The subsequent Hindu and Muslim rulers also had the same spirit of social service.

The British came to India for the primary purpose of trade, and therefore had little interest in the welfare of the Indian people. The introduction of Western education and the Charter Act of 1813, which encouraged the provision of education, had a far-reaching impact on the local populace. English, as the medium of education, was introduced. Although initially the presence of Christian missionaries in India was for evangelical work, they soon became involved in social reforms, with the support of Indian leaders. The reforms included opposing child marriage, polygamy and female infanticide; upliftment of the lower castes; allowing widow remarriage; and abolishing *sati* (the Hindu practice in which widows would immolate themselves on their husbands' funeral pyres). Thus a large number of people changed their outlook and a different and new sense of values was introduced. This period was one of individual action and protest as well as the emergence of new movements (in the form of Bramho Samaj, Arya Samaj, Ramakrishna Mission and Theosophical Society) that were religious in nature but had an interest in social reforms. The greater communication and exchange between India and England resulted in the establishment of welfare organisations along the British model.

Following Indian independence in 1947 and the advent of industrialisation, the very foundation of Indian society, the villages (and its constituents the joint family system and the caste system) were shaken. New conditions called for new forms of intervention and organisation. There was increased government intervention on many fronts: regulating factories, controlling working conditions and protecting women and child workers. Increasingly, social reforms transformed from being embedded within religious change to a liberal and humanitarian perspective.

Professional social work in India was founded with the establishment of the social work course by Dr Clifford Manshardt, an American missionary, under the aegis of the Sir Dorabji Tata Trust. The Sir Dorabji Tata School of Social Work was established in 1936 to meet the emerging need for a trained workforce and was renamed the

Tata Institute of Social Sciences in 1944. Despite various universities and institutions initiating several social work programs, social work in India, however, could never establish itself as an independent profession (Singh & Singh 2011). Social work was embedded within industry when the labour laws were first enacted in India and slowly was transformed to human resource development. The establishment of the Tata Institute of Social Sciences meant that the conception of the role of government moved away from mere tax collection to establishing a society within the bounds of law to incorporate welfare measures and schemes of rural development with the engagement of rural communities. This led to the emergence of an organised voluntary effort, but the limitation as always was the availability of resources to manage these programs.

Access to education in India, especially higher education, has been restricted. Those who have access, complete a bachelor program and/or masters program in science or arts. Professional courses such as medicine or engineering are available to only a few. A whole range of other practice-oriented professional courses were available to still fewer. However, over the past two decades, a host of private providers have moved into higher education and a range of poor-quality courses have come into being. Social work courses abound. International aid and development agencies have played a significant role in determining the course of social work. While they determine policies, programs and strategies to address various structural disadvantages in society, they have failed to address their applicability to different cultures and have therefore been severely and quite justifiably criticised.

Epistemic violence and social work education in India

The term 'epistemic violence' was used by Spivak (1998) as a way of marking the silencing of marginalised groups. 'General non-specialists', 'the illiterate peasantry', 'the tribals' and 'the lowest strata of urban subproletariat' (pp. 282–3) are populations that are routinely silenced or subjected to epistemic violence. An epistemically violent side of colonialism is the devastating effect of the 'disappearing' or 'devaluing' of knowledge, whereby local or provincial knowledge is dismissed due to privileging alternative, often Western, epistemic practices. Spivak highlights that one way of executing epistemic violence is to damage a given group's ability to speak and be heard.

Nearly three decades ago Midgley (1981) first discussed the issue of professional imperialism to indicate how social work as a profession was a legacy of colonialism and had been imposed on the third world. The long history of philanthropy and attempts at self-reliance has been outlined above. Gandhi's program of alternating political activity with periods of 'constructive work' gave large segments of the population their first introduction to organised social activity. However, with the passage of time, a disjunct between theory and the reality it aimed to address has developed, so much so that Singh and Singh (2011, p. 103) advocate that 'government should take steps to weed out such unnecessary disciplines from our education system or consider modifying these to suit our conditions'.

For example, the impact of various development policies on women and other marginalised groups who are the users (or non-users) of services is often seen to operate passively within established (or implicit) rules of their communities. The established rules of the communities are seldom challenged by any of the development policies. The assumption that 'development' is the key to socioeconomic advancement (and subsequently the improvement of women's social status) in India has not provided insight into what it *actually* means to women as 'users' of the associated 'services' or as participants in the programs. What has assisted women to maintain their efforts in preserving their subsistence—or what Shiva (1989) has called their 'life base'—is different from the representations they have been ascribed in mainstream Western social science and feminist literature. In my experience, the Western representation is reinforced in Indian social work curricula and, however reluctantly, I am forced to adhere to the dominant discourse within social work and its hegemonic practices.

This view is associated with the nature of knowledge and truth and what knowledge is valued. The beliefs, nature and value of 'social good' are imported into the premises of academic programs. It can be argued that postcolonial theory can be used as a strategy for Western theorists to perpetuate control over knowledge related to colonised 'others', while at the same time ignoring their concerns and ways of knowing (Grande 2000; Smith 2000). Grande (2000) argues that postcolonial theory is a version of critical theory born out of a Western tradition that emphasises individuality, secularisation and mind–body duality. Therefore, concepts such as family, spirituality, humility and sovereignty have not found a place in a number of theoretical discourses. A middle ground has to be found for the dominant and the excluded to learn from each other.

The neo-liberal society demonstrates an overt domination that specifies who can know, who can create knowledge and which knowledge is of value. The term *academic imperialism* signifies this position well and refers to 'the unjustified and ultimately counterproductive tendency in intellectual and scholarly circles to denigrate, dismiss, and attempt to quash alternative theories, perspectives or methodologies' (Chilisa 2012, p 55). Ife (1997) has discussed extensively the inherent contradictions in the dual concerns of social work: social control and social change and transformation. It is important to unpack what social control and social change and transformation mean in different contexts. In the West, the structures of authority and control are well defined and operate within a fairly conservative environment. In India, control rests mainly within the family, although increasingly control of the social is veering to the conservative state. For example, in rural Odisha, several relational boundaries (for example, the social boundaries that disallowed a woman facing her husband's older brother, and the presence of the joint extended family) limited the possibility of domestic violence. Recently a Domestic Violence Act has been enacted that, while being protective of women, has fallen short of viewing society through a gendered lens. In a relationship-based society, there has been an erosion of relationships and establishment of contracts.

Several authors (see, for example, Ferguson & Woodward 2009; Ife 1997; Lavalette 2011) lament that social change and transformation in the West is limited to opposing spending cuts to the social sector and does not represent (as it should) the structural analysis and perceived need for fundamental social change. Proponents of neo-liberal globalisation are discussing new ideas, from debating the contours of a 'new consumer' to developing sustainable models for 'new consumptions'—all the dialogues seem to be circling around finding new definitions for old problems and new solutions to emerging paradigms. Social transformation in the Indian context also means change following a structural analysis but in the context of the local knowledge and long cultural history integrated with new knowledge (Dasgupta 2012). For example, the *Scheduled Tribes and Other Traditional Forest Dwellers (Recognition of Forest Rights) Act 2006* (called the Forest Rights Act) enacted by the government of India is aimed at redressing the historical injustice to the forest dwellers and conferring rights to forest lands on the dwellers. While the Act itself is progressive, the rules fall short and seem to perpetuate the historical injustice (AITPN 2012).

It has been reiterated time and again (Cox 1995; Lok 1993; World Bank 1990) that globalisation has led to greater marginalisation of vulnerable sections of society such as the unorganised or informal labour force, scheduled castes and scheduled tribes peoples, women, persons with disabilities, and so on. Yet, as part of present social work discourse in India, Roy (2011, p. 9) notes that 'globalisation also creates the preconditions for increased social justice and democracy'. While there are inherent contradictions in these positions, it is important to recognise that the Gandhian concept of *Gram Swaraj*, or the village republic, led to three-tiered decentralised governance in India, the *Panchayati Raj* system, extending to the village level. This has meant that there has been a grassroot engagement in governance since the 1960s. However, as mainstream governments did not truly believe in these people's institutions, they remain weak structures and leave scope for the empowerment of the grassroots to this day.

The question of what and whose knowledge is of value has confounded researchers and practitioners for a long time. The place of languages in the production of social work knowledge has been addressed in a limited manner in discourse (Hall, Slembrouck & Sarangi 2006; Hawkins, Fook & Ryan 2001), in approaches that incorporate bilingual perspectives (Harrison 2006), and as language in social work as a communication endeavour (Gregory & Holloway 2005). Languages have developed alongside cultural and knowledge systems. Elsewhere, I have discussed the significance of names and the naming process in India (Pattanayak 2011). I would like to highlight the nature of relationship terms and their significance, using an example from my mother tongue, Odia. Relationship terms are three-dimensional; for example, *mamu-jhia-bhauni* is a term that means this is my maternal uncle's (*mamu*) daughter and my sister (as in Odia, there is no word for 'cousin'). Likewise, *pisi-pua-bhai* is my paternal aunt's (*pisi*) son and my brother. These terms not only indicate the direction of the relationship, but also the depth of relationship and the relational boundaries within a culture. In English they get subsumed within a single term 'cousin'. Likewise *mamu, dada, kaka, chacha, badabapa, dadei* and *pisa* (male relational terms) all get subsumed within the English relationship term 'uncle' and *main, mousi, khudi* and *pisi* (female relational terms) all get subsumed in the term 'aunt'.

Chilisa (2012) notes that language expresses the patterns and structures of cultures and consequently influences human thinking, manners, values and judgment. Culture is lived, and language, through all its manifestations, projects that life, giving it form and texture. Proverbs highlight the obvious truth, familiar experience or values, as indicated by the examples below:

- *sakala sutrare ganita kasiba, aapana sutra na chadiba* (use the universal principles of maths, but do not do away with your own principles)
- *chali najani agaana ra doso* (not knowing how to walk, blame the floor)
- *chhata dekhile gori sundara, nithei dekhile kaali sundar* (look quickly and the fair one is beautiful, look closely and the dark is beautiful).

While many social work programs have begun to reflect a strong orientation towards social change, epitomised by embracing the concept of 'diversity', in reality the tools that enable students to respond to this diversity are lacking, ensuring that so-called intellectual neutrality prevails. Chilisa (2012) offers an Indigenous research paradigm, the principles of which can apply to social work theorising and practice, which I have in turn adopted for the Indian context. Theory and practice should be informed by Indigenous knowledge systems, critical theory, postcolonial discourses, feminist theories, critical race-specific (caste and class) theories and neo-Marxist theories. They should be based on socially constructed multiple realities shaped by the set of multiple connections that human beings have with the environment, the cosmos, the living and the non-living. Knowledge is relational as all Indigenous knowledge systems are built on relations. Practice should be guided by a relational accountability that promotes respectful representation, reciprocity and the rights of people. It should also be participatory, liberatory and transformative, and should rely on Indigenous knowledge systems and be culturally responsive. Skills should involve the use of language frameworks (proverbs, metaphors), Indigenous knowledge systems and stories.

Implications for social work theory and practice in India

Individualistic approaches are a product of their time and context in the Western world. Social work theory and practice based on the individualistic approaches are an import and imposed on the majority world; Western social work methods and practice principles are prescribed in the social work curriculum in India as well. In fact, Chaugule (2012, p. 215) notes that the 'American (and British) model(s) of social work education has been directly transplanted without any changes or modifications'. Although critiques of direct approaches in social work are alluded to in the majority world, there is little systematic effort to provide evidence as to why these are not or should not always be the appropriate methods of choice in the majority world. It has been argued by Molankal (2012) that some methods are more relevant than others to work with people in the Indian context. Community development and social action may be two such methods. Although these two approaches are not the exclusive domain of social work, practitioners must make greater attempts to relate themselves to larger democratic struggles and people's movements in the country.

However, there have been attempts to move away from Western approaches and bring about integration between methods that address the individual and the structural. Connolly (2001, p. 29) points out that 'not only is social work concerned with helping people, it is also concerned with changing systems that contribute to oppression and disadvantage'. She further points out that community action and social justice have created practice interventions that emphasise empowerment and build individual, family and community strengths; that skills can be transferred and that theoretical frameworks and critical reflection can be applied across the continuum of practice contexts (Connolly 2004).

Channaveer (2012), despite a host of literature (cited above) that critiques the hegemony of Western knowledge, proposes different ways of accepting and adapting imported knowledge systems to Indigenous situations. He proposes five steps:

> … first the imported knowledge system can be accepted as a model; secondly, the model can be made relevant to the local and native conditions; thirdly, the native literature and local cultural traditions need to be explored to comprehend the compatibility with the western knowledge; fourthly, there can be critical and reflective discourses for effective amalgamation of western and native knowledge systems; and lastly, both the knowledge systems need to undergo experimentation process for employing in the local conditions to bring desirable change and development (Channaveer 2012, p. 118).

Molankal (2012) too states that:

> ... the academic and field endeavours are of urgent need to re-conceptualise and re-contextualise social work education (in India), in order to make it more specific to local context and address the larger issues of people rather than the individual specific issues (p. 208).

Likewise, field education should also extend beyond institutional settings to communities and more unstructured settings around problem areas, campaigns and movements to allow students to strategise appropriately, taking into account the present social realities.

Channaveer (2012) highlights that integrated perspectives should take into account a global context, ecological context, human rights context and sustainable context. Molankal (2012) further points out that the lack of in-depth Indigenous study material based upon Indian culture and society has complicated the applicability of professional social work, as taught in the existing schools of social work. He claims that just as teachers find it difficult to derive various social work concepts in regional languages, students are also unable to understand these concepts in English, and he therefore calls for Indigenous foundations to social work education that incorporate dominant cultural philosophies.

Towards an integrated approach to theory and practice

Gandhian thought is inimical to Western values and is more relevant to India today than ever before. Gandhi understood the pulse of India and emphasised social justice and wellbeing of all (*sarvodaya*) and giving priority to the poorest and the disadvantaged sections of society (*antyodaya*). Some of the other key concepts he promoted were truthfulness (*satyagraha*), non-violence (*ahimsa*), and self-sufficiency and village independence (*swadeshi* is localism and self-sufficiency but at the same time interdependence and, in Gandhi's time, finally led to independence (*swaraj*)). Gandhi (1999, pp. 320–1) notes 'Swadeshi is an eternal principle whose neglect has brought untold grief to mankind'. Gandhi considered it a constructive program that involved production and distribution of articles manufactured in one's own country.

Gandhian thought concerned the reconstruction of society based on truth and non-violence and welfare of all, especially the poorest of the poor. Gandhi was transformational in his thinking and considered that it was necessary to bring about fundamental changes in the institutional framework and values of the society. He believed in social action as collective effort toward combating social problems. He proposed an 18-item constructive program for communal unity, removal of untouchability, prohibition of alcohol, *khadi* (homespun cotton, the symbol used for the boycott of foreign goods that was central to the Indian independence movement), village industries, village sanitation, new or basic education, adult education, women, education in health and hygiene, provisional languages, national language, economic equality, *kisans* (peasants), labour, *adivasis* (Indigenous population), lepers, and students. Central to his constructive program were core spiritual values such as truth, non-violence, non-discrimination, social justice and self-reliance. Gandhi's aim was to create a society that was free from conflict, poverty, discrimination, inequality, exploitation and disparities of income, wealth and opportunities. Gandhi specifically focused on the spiritual in his personal life and in the attainment of his reconstruction program. Others (see, for example, Canada 1988; Karnik & Suri 1995; Nash & Stewart 2005; Sermabeikian 1994) have since tried to elaborate on the use of spirituality in social work practice.

Conclusion

It is not in trying to find the compatibility of social work values with Gandhian values (Yasas, as quoted in Gangrade 2004) but also recognising the relevance of Gandhian thought to the social reality of India that ensures an integrated approach to social work in India. It is in the differences in Gandhian thought and in the recognition of the diversity that is India, rather than in its compatibility to Western social work theory and practice, that an integrated Indigenous approach relevant to Indian society can be found. Further, as indicated above, central to an integrated Indigenous approach is the recognition of the diversity in languages and cultures and the need for a critical theory approach to gain a clearer contextual and conceptual base and an understanding of the complex interplay between the global and the local. Central to this approach for a practitioner has to be the integration of Indigenous knowledge competence, values competence, cultural competence and related skills competence.

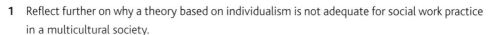

REFLECTIVE QUESTIONS

1   Reflect further on why a theory based on individualism is not adequate for social work practice in a multicultural society.
2   Do you agree with the concept of 'intellectual neutrality'? How do you think this manifests in social work theory?
3   Reflect further on how epistemic violence manifests in a multicultural society. Could a 'middle ground' be found where the dominant and excluded learn from each other?
4   Do you believe that integrated inclusive social work can help mitigate the effects of globalisation and perhaps even prevent them?
5   Gandhi's approach to social work and social service welded tradition, adaptation and invention. Do you think social work presently can do the same? (In other words, where do we go from here?)

FURTHER READING

Canda, ER & Furman, LD 2010, *Spiritual Diversity in Social Work Practice: The Heart of Helping*, 2nd edn, Oxford University Press, New York.

Dotson, K 2011, 'Tracking epistemic violence, tracking practices of silencing', *Hypatia*, vol. 26, no. 2, pp. 236–57.

Verkuyten, M & Martinovic, B 2006, 'Understanding multicultural attitudes: the role of group status, identification, friendships, and justifying ideologies', *Journal of Intercultural Relations*, vol. 30, no. 1, pp. 1–18.

Walz, T & Ritchie, H 2000, 'Gandhian principles in social work practice: ethics revisited', *Social Work*, vol. 45, no. 3, pp. 213–22.

REFERENCES

Anzaldúa, G (ed.) 1990, *Making Face, Making Soul: Creative and Critical Perspectives by Women of Color*, from *Borderlands/La Frontera: The New Mestiza*, copyright © 1987, 1999, 2007, 2012 by Gloria Anzaldúa. Reprinted by permission of Aunt Lute Books, San Francisco <www.auntlute.com>.

Asian Indigenous and Tribal Peoples Network 2012, *The State of the Forest Rights Act: Undoing of Historical Injustice Withered*, AITPN, New Delhi.

Canada, ER 1988, 'Conceptualizing spirituality for social work: insights from diverse perspectives', *Social Thought*, vol. 14, no. 1, pp. 30–46.

Channaveer, RM 2012, 'Contexts and approaches of social work education and practice: Indian perspective', in BS Gunjal & GM Molanklal (eds), *Social Work Education in India*, IBH Prakashana, Bangalore, pp. 117–30.

Chaugule, M 2012, 'Expanding horizons of higher education in social work and recognising its challenges', in BS Gunjal & GM Molanklal (eds), *Social Work Education in India*, IBH Prakashan, Bangalore, pp. 213–21.

Chilisa, B 2012, *Indigenous Research Methodologies*, Sage, Thousand Oaks, CA.

Connolly, M 2001, 'The art and science of social work', in M Connolly (ed.), *New Zealand Social Work: Contexts and Practice*, Oxford University Press, Auckland.

Connolly, M 2004, 'Practice approaches', in J Maidment & R Egan (eds), *Practice Skills in Social Work and Welfare*, Allen & Unwin, Australia.

Cox D 1995, Asia and the Pacific, in D Elliott, T Watts and NS Mayadas (eds), *International Handbook of Social Work Education*, Greenwood, Westport.

Dasgupta, S 2012, *Social Transformation in India*, Pearson Education, New Delhi.

Dayal, P 1986, *Gandhian Philosophy of Social Work*, Gujarat Vidyapeeth, Ahmedabad.

Ferguson, I & Woodward, R 2009, *Radical Social Work in Practice: Making a Difference*, Policy Press, Bristol.

Fishman, JA 1991, *Reversing Language Shift: Theoretical and Empirical Foundations of Assistance to Threatened Languages*, Multilingual Matters, Clevedon, UK.

Gandhi, MK 1999, *The Collected Works of Mahatma Gandhi*, electronic book, vol. 19, New Delhi Publications Division, Ministry of Information and Broadcasting, Government of India, New Delhi.

Gangrade, KD 2004, *Moral Lessons from Gandhi's Autobiography and Other Essays*, Concept, New Delhi.

Grande, S 2000, 'American Indian identity and intellectualism: the quest for a new red pedagogy', *Qualitative Studies in Education*, vol. 13, no. 4, pp. 343–59.

Gregory, M & Holloway M 2005, 'Language and the shaping of social work', *British Journal of Social Work*, vol. 35, no. 1, pp. 37–53.

Hall, C, Slembrouck S & Sarangi S 2006, *Language Practices in Social Work: Categorisation and Accountability in Child Welfare*, Routledge, New York.

Harrison, G 2006, 'Broadening the conceptual lens on language in social work: difference, diversity and English as a global language', *British Journal of Social Work*, vol. 36, no. 3, pp. 401–18.

Hawkins, L, Fook J & Ryan M 2001, 'Social workers use of the language of social justice', *British Journal of Social Work*, vol. 31, no. 1, pp. 1–13.

Ife, J 1997, *Rethinking Social Work: Towards Critical Practice*, Longman, Melbourne.

Karnik, SJ & Suri, KB 1995, 'The law of karma and social work considerations', *International Social Work*, vol. 38, no. 4, pp. 365–77.

Lavalette, M (ed.) 2011, *Radical Social Work Today: Social Work at the Crossroads*, Policy Press, Bristol.

Lok, HP 1993, 'Labour in the garment industry: an employer's perspective', in C Manning & J Hardiono (eds), *Indonesia Assessment*, Australian National University, Canberra, pp. 155–72.

Midgley, J 1981, *Professional Imperialism: Social Work in the Third World*, Heinemann, London.

Mohanty, AK 2010, 'Language policy and practice in education: negotiating the double divide in multilingual societies', in K Heugh & T Skutnabb-Kangas (eds), *Multilingual Education Works: From the Periphery to the Centre*, Orient Blackswan, Hyderabad, pp. 164–75.

Molankal, GM 2012, 'Social work education in India: areas of concern', in BS Gunjal & GM Molanklal (eds), *Social Work Education in India*, IBH Prakashan, Bangalore, pp. 199–212.

Mosha, RS 2000, *The Heartbeat of Indigenous Africa: A Study of the Chagga Educational System*, Garland, New York & London.

Nash, M & Stewart, B 2005, 'Spirituality and hope in social work for social justice', *Currents: New Scholarship in the Human Services*, vol. 4, no. 1, pp. 1–10.

Pattanayak, S 2011, 'Names: an address without a postcode', in M Kumar, S Pattanayak & R Johnson (eds), *Framing my Name: Extending Educational Boundaries*, Common Ground, Altona, Victoria, pp. 129–40.

Phillipson, R 2009, *Linguistic Imperialism Continued*, Routledge, New York and London.

Roy, S 2011, *Introduction to Social Work and Practice in India*, Akansha, New Delhi.

Said, EW 1993, *Culture and Imperialism*, Vintage, London.

Sermabeikian, P 1994, 'Our clients, ourselves: the spiritual perspective and social work practice', *Social Work*, vol. 39, no. 2, pp. 178–83.

Shiva, V 1989, *Staying Alive: Women, Ecology and Development*, Zed Books, London.

Singh, KK & Singh RS 2011, *An Introduction to Social Work*, ABD, New Delhi.

Skutnabb-Kangas, T 2000, *Linguistic Genocide in Education—or Worldwide Diversity and Human Rights*, Lawrence Erlbaum, Mahwah, NJ.

Smith, GH 2000, 'Protecting and respecting indigenous knowledge', in M Batiste (ed.), *Reclaiming Indigenous Voice and Vision*, University of British Columbia Press, Vancouver, Canada, pp. 207–24.

Smith, LT 1999, *Decolonizing Methodologies, Research and Indigenous Peoples*, Zed Books, London.

Spivak, GC 1998, 'Can the subaltern speak?', in C Nelson & L Grossberg (eds), *Marxism and the Interpretation of Culture*, University of Illinois Press, Urbana–Champaign, pp. 271–313.

Sreerama Murty, N 2012, 'Origin of social work profession in India', in I Ponnuswami & AP Francis (eds), *Professional Social Work Education: Emerging Perspectives*, Authorspress, New Delhi, pp. 82–107.

Vekataraman, J 1996, 'Indigenization process of alcoholism treatment from the American to the Indian context', PhD thesis, University of Illinois, Urbana–Champaign, IL.

World Bank 1990, *World Development Report, 1990: Poverty*, World Bank, Washington DC.

7

Developing culturally based methods of research

Ling How Kee and Christine Fejo-King

Introduction

Western research method is violent!

When Polly Walker, a Native American PhD candidate at an Australian university, gave a talk at a seminar on her research about conflict resolution between Aboriginal and white Australians, her opening statement (above) had many in her audience, mostly white Australians, flabbergasted (Walker 1996, pers. comm.; see also Walker 2006). How can a research method—a way of gathering data to generate knowledge—be conceived as 'violent'? How can such a statement about the nature of a research method even arise? Isn't the priority for all research students, and all researchers, to just get on with the business of choosing a research method suited for the topic of research?

For most students, the choice of research method is driven by questions of validity, reliability and generalisability. For Polly Walker, and students of Indigenous and non-Western backgrounds, the dominant Western research methodology is a reminder of professional imperialism (Midgley 1981, 2008) in which they have to conform to a certain standard of practice that is alien to their ways of being. Not only has Western culture been intricately linked to the way research has been conducted, but also the ways research questions are formulated and data is analysed are also embedded within the Western worldview. This chapter, jointly authored by an Aboriginal Australian (Christine Fejo-King) and a Malaysian of Chinese descent (Ling How Kee), shares our personal experiences of going through a journey of exploration that resulted in the development of an Indigenist/Indigenous theory of social work practice that enabled us to complete our research journey. We both went through strikingly similar experiences of feeling encapsulated in the Western research paradigm, finally breaking away from this encapsulation with insights on decolonising research methodology. We discuss different ways of decolonising research to develop culturally-based methods of inquiry before concluding the chapter with some recommendations for new reflexive research practice.

Our stories

In the tradition of many Indigenous cultures, tales of our personal experiences are woven into this chapter. Our key message is that research to develop an Indigenous theory of practice needs to be developed from an Indigenous research paradigm.

How Kee's journey

In 1996, I embarked on my PhD study on developing culturally appropriate social work practice in Sarawak in Malaysia (Ling 2001) at an Australian university. Having 13 years of practice behind me, I had come to this place to complete a PhD to qualify as a university lecturer to teach social work when I returned to Sarawak. I grew up in a culturally diverse region of Malaysia but it was in my early years of practice as a social worker after returning from Australia with a Bachelor of Social Work that the need to have an Indigenous practice theory dawned on me. However, I am constantly mindful that this theory has to incorporate the multicultural reality of Sarawak.

In the course of searching for a suitable methodology for my study, it became apparent to me that writings on culturally appropriate social work practice have not been accompanied by any examination or questioning of the research methodology used to develop social work knowledge. In other words, while Western social work knowledge may be queried, the mode of producing this knowledge was left unexamined; the applicability of Western research methodology for a non-Western context is left unquestioned.

In an article 'The search from within' (Ling 2004), I argued that Western research methodology is rooted in a certain cultural world view and that transplanting one cultural way of knowing to another context raises epistemological and methodological issues. I highlighted issues in relation to the problems of linguistic and conceptual equivalence, communication process and style, and the way human relationships are perceived in the context of Malaysia. I further posited that unravelling the epistemological base of social research is the first step in our quest to develop culturally appropriate practice. Only by breaking free from the 'professional encapsulation' (Pedersen 1994) that we have been socialised into during our training will we rediscover our Indigenous ways of knowing and ways of helping.

Christine's journey

My research journey began in earnest in 2005 when I wrote a paper entitled 'Decolonising research from an Australian Indigenous research perspective' (King 2005). In that paper I sought to share my reflections, as an Aboriginal research student examining the questions this process had raised for me, about how my research could be achieved within a culturally congruent and safe framework. These were central concepts for me, as I sought to find balance and harmony between theory and practice, the culture and knowledge base of the university and Aboriginal ways of knowing, being and doing.

The paper sought to privilege Australian Indigenous knowledge and ideologies by exploring paths that had been named by other Australian Indigenous researchers. In so doing, it identified decolonising research methodologies. By using a Western framework, I was trying to work within a framework that was totally alien to me, one that privileged Western knowledge and Western ways of doing and being. The Western framework is the social scientific legacy of a search for truth that has, from its earliest contact with my peoples, treated us as sub-human—the researchable 'other'—whose lives, laws, culture and society could be scrutinised, racialised, ignored, discounted and condemned by Western researchers simply because we did not fit into their understanding and expectation of the world (King 2005).

In 2007, I again spent some time critically reflecting upon the learning journey that I had taken since 2005. I explained the concepts I had struggled with, the new understandings and learning that had come from these struggles, and the ways in which this learning was being developed and incorporated into the final chapters of my thesis. One chapter of my thesis therefore illuminates my search for an Australian Indigenous ontology, an Australian Aboriginal epistemology and culturally congruent theoretical perspectives. These three were fundamental issues that needed to be answered before I could proceed with the research.

Western research methodology is rooted in a Western world view

A broad definition of different world views is offered by Charles Royal, a Māori man:

> A Western (Judaeo-Christian) view … sees God as external and in heaven 'above'; an Eastern view … focuses internally and concentrates on reaching within through meditation and other practices; and an Indigenous view … sees people as integral to the world, with humans having a seamless relationship with nature which includes seas, land, rivers, mountains, flora and fauna (cited in Cunningham & Stanley 2003, p. 403).

It is critical to understand the impact these differences have on non–Western peoples, as we negotiate living within two worlds, in which the Western world view dominates (Whyte 2005).

The Western world view is of man as the pinnacle of evolution—Western man, that is—along with the right to satisfy his wants (not just his needs) by plundering both the environment and other societies (since they are deemed to be of lesser value). Once Western colonising nations invaded other lands, they brought with them, and enforced, their laws, values and beliefs, which clash with those of the Aboriginal peoples (Kovach 2006; Martin 2008).

Dominant Western research methodology—specifically methodology originated from the positivistic paradigm—is rooted in a scientific paradigm that perceives knowledge as coming from objective reality, originating outside the self. Knowledge is discovered through detaching the self from the environment to observe and analyse reality objectively (Gowdy 1994; Weick 1991; Zimmerman 1989). Human knowing that is intuitive, sensory, tacit, and developed from doing, is devalued. Knowledge derived from these sources is disregarded (Sacco 1996; Saleebey 1994).

The Indigenous knowledge system based on the interconnectedness of all things is not accepted or respected as valid social science knowledge (Walker 2001). Indigenous researchers who, in their research process, acknowledge the interconnectedness with research participants and the community they are in, and the spiritual aspects of their inquiry, are often questioned and the data they collect deemed suspect. Christine's experience below illustrates the struggles Indigenous scholars encounter in the face of colonial processes within Western universities.

Christine's experience

Even as recently as 2010, my experience was of non-acceptance of Indigenous knowledge as an Indigenous researcher doing Indigenous research. It was not just a case of revealing aspects of my own tacit world and challenging my assumptions through the eyes of the 'other', but also a case of challenging my assumptions that others, particularly my non-Indigenous supervisors, were privy to my world and the tacit knowledge that is so much a part of it.

This was illustrated when, in writing up notes on the research I had undertaken in Tennant Creek in the Northern Territory, I spoke about sitting with a group of women who, although I had not met them before and am not blood-related, were all related to me through the kinship system. I wrote:

> This group of women agreed to be interviewed together as they sat in a circle on a ground sheet and a blanket under a big tree in the yard. The rain clouds were rolling in, the thunder was crashing in the background, the camp dogs were fighting, while the children ran around playing. I really felt like I was home in the Territory again and with my people, the music of the language was like a soothing breeze to my heart, I am home again.

When I showed this to my non-Indigenous supervisors, I was asked, 'What does this mean?' 'Why don't you go into more detail?' 'Why didn't you ask more questions?' I had forgotten that Aboriginal protocols, the understanding of sitting within a circle of cultural women all related through the kinship system, cuts across and through much of Western understanding so that when I was asked these questions I was taken aback. There is so much within Aboriginal culture that is unspoken based on the genuine acknowledgment and acceptance that is the natural right of all who live their lives within the bounds of the kinship system, and the spiritual nature and relatedness of the land, people and the elements.

When I spoke about the big tree in the yard, the rain clouds rolling in, the thunder crashing in the background, the camp dogs fighting and the children playing, I was reminded that my ancestors live in this land; that the earth, the sky, the plants, animals and human beings are all related; and that mother earth nurtures all. Also, having gone home to the Northern Territory after living in a drought-affected area, I felt that the thunder was the voice of my ancestors welcoming me home, with the wind on my face and the rain falling on me as their tears of welcome. All these things were acknowledged by all the women within the kinship circle with knowing smiles and nods.

Tacit knowledge, spiritual connections and relational self are not part of the Western research paradigm. Those with a Western world view have not used them as a standard part of their research and, until recently, have not supported research that incorporates them.

Research as a colonising project

The late eminent Malaysian social scientist Syed Hussein Alatas has long urged the 'emancipation of the captive mind' to break free from the intellectual imperialism scholars in the region have been subjected to in order to develop South-East Asian social science (Alatas SH 1972, 2000, 2002). He critiqued how Western scholars had created 'The myth of the lazy native' (Alatas 1977), propagating the view of the Indigenous peoples in the region as one of an indolent, dull, backward and treacherous native, requiring assistance to climb the ladder of progress. Social scientists in the region have long observed that concepts and theoretical terminology transplanted from a Western frame of reference are inappropriate when conducting studies with their own communities. Concepts such as time, modernity, self-esteem and independence are culturally based norms, which are either alien or differently interpreted in different cultures. Concepts and methodologies that can better account for Indigenous experiences are called for (Alatas SF 2000).

African American scholar Stanfield (1993, 1994) draws attention to the Western-centric paradigm that continues to dominate the creation and legitimisation of knowledge definition and production. This has resulted in marginalisation and even exclusion of culturally diverse interpretations of reality and human experiences. As argued by Afro-centric writers, a method of inquiry grounded in the interpretations of reality and ways of knowing of non-Western people remains underdeveloped (Asante 1987, 1988; Stanfield 1993, 1994).

Māori anthropologist Linda Tuhiwai Smith (1999), citing the filmmaker Merata Mita, has criticised the way the Māoris have been subjected to research in the same way as a scientist looks at an insect under a microscope. What is damaging is that 'the ones doing the looking are giving themselves the power to define' (Mita, cited in Smith 1999, p. 58). Similarly, Canadian academic Rosemary Clews (1999) cautions non-Indigenous researchers, coming from an expert position and conducting research among First Nations people, that their research can have a colonising effect.

Towards culturally based research methodology

Rigney (2001), an Australian Aboriginal researcher, discusses the historical movement of Australia's First Peoples from 'objects' of research to researchers themselves. He advanced an Indigenist philosophical framework in which he coined the term 'Indigenism', defined as:

> ... a body of knowledge by Indigenous scholars in the interest of Indigenous peoples for the purpose of self-determination. Indigenism is multi-disciplinary with the essential criteria being the identity and colonising experience of the writer. Similarly, by the term Indigenist I mean the body of knowledge by Indigenous scholars in relation to research methodological approaches (Rigney 2001, p. 1).

Indigenism and indigenist theory: insights from Christine

The methodology of my research is qualitative and based upon Aboriginal groundedness, which was developed in 2005 under the name 'Indigenous grounded research theory' as it is steeped in Aboriginal law, culture and spirituality. This methodology includes the wisdom of lived experience, cultural knowledge and insider perspectives and practices. To strengthen and frame this methodology, Indigenism and Indigenist theory were researched, validated and used as a means of progressing social work research and recommended as necessary knowledge for Australian social work education, theory and practice (King 2011).

In my exploration of Indigenism, there were a number of questions that I sought to answer: Who or what is an Indigenist? What is the definition of Indigenism? What is Indigenist theory?

In answering the first question, 'Who is an Indigenist?', I turned to the work of Ward Churchill (1996, 2002), who is of Creek and Cherokee descent and a long-time native rights activist, writer and public speaker, who describes himself as an Indigenist in the following way:

> By this I mean that I am one who not only takes the rights of Indigenous peoples as the highest priority of my political life, but who also draws on the traditions—the bodies of knowledge

---

and corresponding codes of value—evolved over many thousands of years by native peoples the world over. This is the basis on which I not only enhance critiques of, but conceptualize alternatives to, the present social, political, economic, and philosophical status quo. In turn, this gives shape not only to the sort of goals and objectives I advocate, the variety of struggles I tend to support, the nature of the alliances I'm inclined to enter into, and so on (Churchill 1996, p. 509).

These sentiments echoed in my heart, as they are the very ones I hold dear, so I felt that I had finally found a place for myself within the research field, from which I could move my thesis forward and complete it. This then led me into my next question, 'What is the definition of Indigenism?'

My research led me to the conclusion that Indigenism is a body of knowledge and way of working and doing things that was developed by Indigenous scholars and practitioners, both nationally and internationally, as a critical response to the experience of colonisation. It draws on traditions, bodies of knowledge and corresponding wisdom and values that have evolved over many thousands of years by the First Nations peoples of the world (Churchill 1996; Martin 2003; Rigney 2001; Sinclair 2007), and is based on Indigenous world views and ideologies. Indigenism aims to progress the interests of Indigenous peoples through achieving sovereignty, self-determination and culturally secure practice within the context of research.

Indigenist theory, then, is a theory of emancipation and empowerment developed by Indigenous academics and researchers, both nationally and internationally, and encompasses a paradigm shift that privileges Indigenous ways of knowing, being and doing (Martin 2003). It is an emerging theory that began to bloom about 12 years ago and has provided an opportunity for my research to contribute to its development.

Having said this, however, I believe that Indigenist theory is an example of an instance of theory catching up to practice. In Australia the inception of Aboriginal organisations—such as Aboriginal Health Services; the National Aboriginal Community Controlled Health Organisation; the Secretariat for National Aboriginal and Islander Child Care, which developed the Aboriginal child placement principle and more recently took leadership in developing Aboriginal cultural plans for Aboriginal children in out-of-home care; and even the inquiry into the removal of Aboriginal children from their families, more commonly known as the 'Stolen Generations'—are all grounded in Indigenism and Indigenist theory in practice.

To move on to the validation of Indigenism and Indigenist theory, I share the following two examples. First, to find the connections between my use of stories, learning circles and the connection of all things, I came across 'Indigenous cosmology' in the works of Raven Sinclair (2007), an Indigenous Canadian woman. Sinclair included concepts such as ceremonies and 'all my relations', which she identified as one of the most significant symbols of Indigenous cosmology. 'All my relations' captures the essence of Indigenous spirituality, illuminated by the following citation:

> 'All my relations' is first a reminder of who we are and our relationship with both our family and our relatives. It also reminds us of the extended relationship we share with all human beings. But the relationships that Native people see go further, the web of kinship extending to the animals, to the birds, to the fish, to the plants, to all the animate and inanimate forms that can be seen or imagined. More than that, 'all my relations' is an encouragement for us to accept the responsibilities we have within this universal family by living our lives in a harmonious and moral manner (King 1990, cited in Sinclair 2007, p. 89).

Another example was an Aboriginal protocol from my nation that involves the giving of gifts to those involved in my research as a way of recognising and valuing in some small way their contribution, our kinship connections and the concept of reciprocity. It was important that I acknowledge the central role of the cultural advisors, and of my ancestors, who continued to guide me and speak to me about how my research should progress. It was my ancestors who helped me to articulate culture. They also illustrated it for me, when needed, through dreams and visions. I honour them and thank them for the insights they provided. I was not alone in identifying and honouring spirituality within the research process, and it was interesting that Sinclair (2007) also spoke about the spiritual aspects of Indigenous research; in particular, the spiritual preparation, input and guidance she sought and received.

The methods used to complete my inquiry into the Aboriginal kinship system, and how it might act as a key to the future by influencing social work theory and practice in Australia, included a comparative study of the kinship system as understood by two Aboriginal nations within the Northern Territory. These were the Warumungu (desert people) and Larrakia (saltwater people). Culturally congruent interviews were undertaken as informed by the kinship system itself, using cultural advisors, Kriol language and inter-preters, and through the protocol of introduction.

Acknowledging the interconnections of culture and research: insights from How Kee

Based on a critical conceptualisation of culture and its interconnection with research and ways of knowing, I turned my research into a journey of discovery in which the method of inquiry was attuned to the culture of the informants. Affirmed by an understanding that practice and research mirror each other (Peile 1988, 1994), I adopted a reflective learning approach (Chambers 1986, 1995; Fook 1996) to allow issues of cultural appropriateness to unfold and so inform the development of a culturally appropriate social work practice.

Fang tang and *temu bual*

The Chinese words *fang tang*, meaning visit and talk, and the Malay words *temu bual*, meaning meet and chat, were used to convey the intention of my interviews to the informants. I also tried to convey the spirit of openness and humility by emphasising that I was there to learn from them. The format and place of the interviews—that is, either individually or in groups—were in accordance with the interviewee's preference.

The interviews resembled many of the everyday conversations in a community setting. An example of this was an interview with the family of an elderly woman. This was done in her home in a small village. The interview was continuously interposed with different members of the family coming in and out. The grandson and grandson-in-law came from the offices where they worked nearby, and a daughter, who lived only a few houses away, also came.

Another interview was with a group of 11 women whose children with disabilities were participants of a local community-based rehabilitation (CBR) centre. The interview coincided with the social gathering after the *gotong royong* (mutual help activities) for cleaning up and weeding the compound of the CBR centre. It was a very animated discussion amid food and drink, and the women talked openly and passionately about their experiences of help-seeking and being helped.

In both examples above, information gathering or discussion sessions conducted in a group or family setting was congruent with the local ways of interaction. This also indicates that one-to-one direct communication, typical of research methods and much social work interaction, may not be the norm; instead, researchers need to be aware of the metacommunicative patterns and processes in a community (Briggs 1986). For example, as an unmarried young Anglo-American conducting research in a Mexicano community in New Mexico, Briggs (1986) found himself in a position where he was expected to learn from the elders and to speak only when response was elicited. Similarly, in my interviews with older community leaders and elders, I have intuitively done more listening, allowing them to steer the direction of discussion and asking fewer questions than I have done in interviews with younger people. The social roles expected of younger and older people in a community may define the social interaction between them differently, and this is played out in a researcher–researched relationship.

In many non-Western cultures, relationship is not individualised, but is governed by a person's social position and roles in a network of interconnection. Also, the notion of a contractual relationship is alien to non-Western cultures. It is more difficult to enter into a community as a stranger to conduct research. There needs to be an extension of friendship and mutual exchange and reciprocity.

While I did not have the shared identity and bonding as in Christine's experiences, the interview processes were very much that of conveying acceptance and reciprocity, of attempting to establish a shared context and rules for interaction. This process reflected how the local ways of interaction were enacted, and included mutual attempts to 'make connections' with each other, to 'go with the flow' of the discussion, and to have food and drink along with discussion.

Making connections with each other was demonstrated by asking questions about each other's place of origin. I realised that it was important to answer questions pertaining to my personal background and show an interest in knowing what they had to say about themselves. I felt it was culturally appropriate to 'go with the flow' of the discussion since I was the one to 'visit and ask'. At times, this involved allowing the informants to diverge from the topic of discussion, even when the content seemed irrelevant. Sharing of food and drink was part of the interaction process between my informants and me. This is very much a part of observing the social etiquette of a particular community, which is important in establishing rapport between the two parties.

Giving voices to the knowledge holders

Our experiences of conducting research described above are likely to raise many questions; questions that confront researchers attempting to develop culturally based methods of inquiry. Is this research? How can this research method claim to be value-free? How can it be considered objective? Indeed, Indigenous Australian researchers who have been conducting research using life stories, oral histories and narratives have been 'discredited as value-laden, unscientific, or subjected to flawed memory' (Briskman 2007, p. 154).

In response to these questions, we draw inspiration from the work of Settee, a First Nation Canadian researcher, who positioned her research within a naturalistic inquiry. Settee states:

> Researchers position themselves in their research projects to reveal aspects of their own tacit world, to challenge their own assumptions, to locate themselves through the eyes of the 'other', and to observe themselves observing. This lens shifts the observer's gaze inward toward the self as a site for interpreting cultural experience. The approach is person-centred, unapologetically subjective, and gives voice to those who have often been silenced (2007, p. 117).

In advancing culturally based methods of research, giving voice to the research participants is a morally guided principle. The position of the research participants must be uplifted to that of the 'knowledge holders', a term used by Hart (2010), a Canadian First Nation academic from the Cree peoples, to describe participants. The term 'knowledge holders' recognises their expertise and knowledge, whereas the term 'participant' may leave the researcher as the expert and gives participants a lesser role.

The description 'knowledge holders' also fits with Wilson's (2008) argument that a shift in terminology enables a shift in understanding and ways of doing things, particularly around the ceremony that is embedded within research, or as he couches it, 'research is ceremony'. An example of what both Hart and Wilson refer to can be found within the concept of spirituality in research. Research can be identified as being a spiritual journey, a journey in which the ancestors of the researcher and the knowledge holders are invited to join, support and bless the research journey and all who enter it. This invitation also provides opportunities for ancestors to provide insights through dreams, visions and other guidance (King 2011; Sinclair 2007). This form of spirituality within Indigenous research offers a unique insight into some Indigenous research practices not widely written about or understood and which only emerge through a shift in research practice that honours and recognises the equality of knowledge holders within research.

From objectivity and subjectivity to reflexivity

The use of self and insider knowledge played a foundational role in our search for culturally congruent research methodology. The recurring question confronting us was the issue of objectivity versus subjectivity. We found it has been useful to move beyond the debate to that of a third position, that of reflexivity. Reflexivity is more than a state of self-reflectiveness. It refers to the capacity of the researcher self (the subject) to make the self the object of study. It acknowledges not only the presence of the researcher/subject but how researcher's subjectivity impacted on the researched/object, and the resultant impact on the researcher/subject. In other words, reflexivity entails a constant examination of the use of self, how we as researchers have impacted on the research process, how we have impacted on the informants and the resultant impact on ourselves.

Lakoff and Johnson (1980) argue that both objectivity and subjectivity are metaphors that provide ways of comprehending experiences and giving order to lives. Objectivity takes as its allies scientific truth, rationality, precision, fairness and impartiality. Subjectivity takes as its allies emotions, intuitive insight, imagination, humanness and art. What objectivity and subjectivity both miss is the way we understand the world through our interpretations of it and this is necessarily relative to our cultural conceptual systems. There is no absolute or neutral conceptual system from which we can frame our interpretations. Instead, understanding emerges from the interaction between subjectivity and objectivity. Each needs the other in order to exist (Lakoff & Johnson 1980).

Further, the argument between insider and outsider researcher, often framed in terms of an insider/subjective and outsider/objective dichotomised position, has understated the complexities involved in research. Indigenous researchers from around the world have illustrated that the insider/outsider binary does not do justice to the complex levels of relatedness that exist within insider positioning (Ergun & Erdemir 2010; Mafile'o 2009; Merriam et al. 2001). The analysis process of our research entailed situating the analysis in the third position of reflexivity arising out of the dialectic process of objectivity, the outsider position, and subjectivity, the insider position. Using an insider's knowledge, we interrogate social work and using social work knowledge, we take an outsider's view looking in. It is working on the dialectic between the insider's and outsider's views that 'the benefit of each can be achieved and the limits of each can be transcended' (Keesing & Strathern 1998, p. 476).

In research and practice, we constantly cross borders of cultures demarcated by ethnicity, age, dis/abilities and sexual orientation. Whether an insider or outsider, it is essential for the researcher to acknowledge and question how their status may shape the research experience and the construction of knowledge. Researchers coming to the task with different backgrounds and different perspectives will see different problems and pose different questions and perhaps discover different answers (Riessman 1994). The notion that a researcher is an objective detached knower is therefore untenable. Instead, the researcher is *in* and *an active part* of the event that they are investigating (Goldstein 1991, emphasis original). As such, a researcher must also acknowledge themself as a cultural being (Denzin & Lincoln 1994; Rosaldo 1989).

A culturally based method of inquiry must involve creating a space where the researcher and the knowledge holder come together, where the 'knower and the known interact and shape one another' and 'create understandings' (Denzin & Lincoln 1994, p. 13). Researchers are therefore catalysts; they elicit implicit knowledge or produce knowledge together with their informants (Peile 1994; Rudie 1993). A culturally based method of inquiry is, as with culturally appropriate practice, a negotiation of similarities and differences, of dialogic exchange in establishing relationship, rather than a mere application of culturally sensitive techniques.

Conclusion

Towards reflexive research practices

We would like to return to the opening statement of this chapter and reiterate that cultural imperialism and cultural abuse has permeated research on Indigenous peoples and non-Western peoples. A lack of recognition, until recently, of Indigenous sources of data and knowledge, such as oral tradition and spirituality, has marginalised Indigenous people and denigrated Indigenous knowledge. It is timely to forge a battle against the cultural abuse beyond the physical, social, mental and spiritual arena into the research and knowledge production realm, which is an equally colonising project.

We posit that research crossing cultural boundaries needs to be conducted within a research paradigm that is grounded in the world view and cultures of the local context. Social work researchers and practitioners, regardless of whether they are from Indigenous or non–Western backgrounds, need to break free of the 'professional encapsulation' (Pedersen 1994) to rediscover a way of knowing and being congruent with the cultures of the people we do research with. We offer the following as points to ponder and deliberate upon as we embark on a journey of discovery:

- rethinking research as about developing a way of knowing that respects and embraces differences
- reflecting on different ways of thinking about knowledge and engaging in other ways of knowing in order to search for an Indigenous research paradigm to uncover local knowledge
- supporting Indigenous research methodologies as an emerging and developing field that will be of interest not only to Indigenous and non–Western researchers, but also all social researchers
- exploring a research method in which the relationship between the researcher and participants is dialogical, and in which the process of enquiry allows for the possibility of research participants shaping a culturally appropriate way of knowledge generation
- using terms that acknowledge the expertise of research participants and uplift their position as 'knowledge holders'
- considering cultural nuances, protocols and concepts used in a different culture
- drawing on local patterns of communication; for example, participating in a dialogue in the *ruai* (verandah) or sitting in cultural circles
- exploring more deeply the possibilities of open communication by developing it, refining it and analysing the approach further as a local research method, or data collection method, in its own right, rather than naming it as a local version of focus group interviews or participatory research
- choosing locations that equalise power, such as a place of comfort for the client rather than the power base of the office
- thinking of not just the 'what' of research (the techniques), but more the 'how' of research (the process)
- doing research to elicit the views of research participants on their experiences of being researched and on their ideas of how knowledge could be shared and generated in the local Indigenous ways.

REFLECTIVE QUESTIONS

1 Describe some examples of research practices that can be considered a commission of violence to the people who are researched, especially to Indigenous peoples.

2 Do you agree that research methodology is rooted in a particular world view? Explain your answer.

3 Do you think there is a place for tacit knowledge and spiritual connections in research? Explain your answer.

4 What do you think of storytelling as a research method? What about the use of stories in social work research and theory development?

5 What are some culturally appropriate practice approaches that could be incorporated as part of a culturally congruent research methodology?

FURTHER READING

Ergun, A & Erdemir, A 2010, 'Negotiating insider and outsider identities in the field: "insider" in a foreign land; "outsider" in one's own land', *Field Methods*, vol. 22, no. 1, pp. 16–38.

Hart, MA 2010, 'Indigenous worldviews, knowledge, and research: the development of an indigenous research paradigm', *Journal of Indigenous Voices in Social Work*, vol. 1, no. 1, pp. 2–14.

King, C 2005, 'Decolonising research from an Australian Indigenous research perspective', unpublished paper presented at the 7th Indigenous Researchers Forum, Cairns, 29–31 August (available on request from <www.aiatsis.gov.au>).

Ling, HK 2004, 'The search from within: research issues in relation to developing culturally appropriate social work practice', *International Social Work*, vol. 47, no. 3, pp. 336–45.

Smith, LT 1999, *Decolonising Methodologies*, Zed Books, London and New York.

REFERENCES

Alatas, SF 2000, 'An introduction to the idea of alternative discourse', *Southeast Asian Journal of Social Sciences*, vol. 28, no. 1, pp. 1–12.

Alatas, SH 1972, 'The captive mind in development studies: some neglected problems and the need for an autonomous social science tradition in Asia', *International Social Science Journal*, vol. 24, no. 1, pp. 1–16.

Alatas, SH 1977, *The Myth of the Lazy Native*, Frank Cass, London.

Alatas, SH 2000, 'Intellectual imperialism: definition, traits, and problems', *Southeast Asian Journal of Social Sciences*, vol. 28, no. 1, pp. 23–45.

Alatas, SH 2002, 'The development of an autonomous social science tradition in Asia: problems and prospects', *Asian Journal of Social Science*, vol. 30, no. 1, pp. 150–7.

Asante, MK 1987, *The Afrocentric Idea*, Temple University Press, Philadelphia.

Asante, MK 1988, *Afrocentricity*, Africa World, Trenton, NJ.

Briggs, C 1986, *Learning How to Ask: A Sociolinguistic Appraisal of the Role of the Interview in Social Science Research*, Cambridge University Press, Cambridge.

Briskman, L 2007, *Social Work with Indigenous Communities*, Federation Press, Sydney.

Chambers, R 1986, *Normal Professionalism, New Paradigms and Development*, Institute of Development Studies, University of Sussex, Sussex.

Chambers, R 1995, *Poverty and Livelihoods: Whose Reality Counts?*, Institute of Development Studies, University Of Sussex, Sussex.

Churchill, W 1996, *From a Native Son: Selected Essays on Indigenism, 1985–1995*, South End Press, Boulder, CO.

Churchill, W 2002, *Struggle for the Land: Native North American Resistance to Genocide, Ecocide and Colonization*, City Lights, San Francisco.

Clews, R 1999, 'Cross-cultural research in Aboriginal rural communities: a Canadian case study of ethical challenges and dilemmas', *Rural Social Work*, 4, April, pp. 26–33.

Cunningham, C & Stanley, F 2003, 'Indigenous by definition, experience or world view', *British Medical Journal*, vol. 327, no. 7412, pp. 403–4.

Denzin, NK & Lincoln, YS (eds) 1994, *Handbook of Qualitative Research*, Sage, Thousand Oaks, CA.

Ergun, A & Erdemir, A 2010, 'Negotiating insider and outsider identities in the field: "insider" in a foreign land; "outsider" in one's own land', *Field Methods*, vol. 22, no. 1, pp. 16–38.

Fook, J 1996, *The Reflective Researcher: Social Workers' Theories of Practice Research*, Allen & Unwin, St Leonards, NSW.

Goldstein, H 1991, 'Qualitative research and social work practice: partner in discovery', *Journal of Sociology and Social Welfare*, vol. 18, no. 4, pp. 101–20.

Gowdy, EA 1994, 'From technical rationality to participating consciousness', *Social Work*, vol. 39, no. 4, pp. 362–71.

Hart, MA 2010, 'Indigenous worldviews, knowledge, and research: the development of an Indigenous research paradigm', *Journal of Indigenous Voices in Social Work*, vol. 1, no. 1, pp. 2–14.

Keesing, RM & Strathern, AJ 1998, *Cultural Anthropology: A Contemporary Perspective*, 3rd edn, Harcourt Brace, Philadelphia.

King, C 2005, 'Decolonising research from an Australian Indigenous research perspective', unpublished paper presented at the 7th Indigenous Researchers Forum, Cairns, 29–31 August (available on request from <www.aiatsis.gov.au>).

King, KC 2011, 'How understanding the Aboriginal kinship system can inform better policy and practice: social work research with the Larrakia and Warumungu peoples of the Northern Territory', PhD thesis, Australian Catholic University, Canberra.

Kovach, M 2006, 'Searching for arrowheads: an inquiry into approaches to Indigenous research using a tribal methodology with a Nêhiýaw Kiskêýihtamowin worldview', PhD thesis, University of Victoria, Canada.

Lakoff G & Johnson, M 1980, *Metaphors We Live By*, University of Chicago Press, Chicago.

Ling, HK 2001, 'Towards developing culturally appropriate social work practice: insights from a study of help-seeking and help-giving experiences in Sarawak, Malaysia', PhD thesis, University of Queensland.

Ling, HK 2004, 'The search from within: research issues in relation to developing culturally appropriate social work practice', *International Social Work*, vol. 47, no. 3, pp. 336–45.

Mafile'o, T 2009, 'Pasifika social work', in M Connolly & L Harms, *Social Work: Contexts and Practice*, 2nd edn, Oxford University Press, South Melbourne, Victoria.

Martin, KL 2003, 'Ways of knowing, being and doing: a theoretical framework and methods for Indigenous and Indigenist re-search', *Journal of Australian Studies: Voicing Dissent*, vol. 27, no. 76, pp. 203–14.

Martin, KL 2008, *Please Knock Before You Enter: Aboriginal Regulation of Outsiders and the Implications for Researchers*, Post Pressed, Teneriffe, Queensland.

Merriam, SB, Johnson-Bailey, J, Lee, M, Kee, YW, Ntseane, G & Muhamad, M 2001, 'Power and positionality: negotiating insider/outsider status within and across cultures', *International Journal of Lifelong Education'*, vol. 20, no. 5, pp. 405–16.

Midgley, J 1981, *Professional Imperialism: Social Work in the Third World*, Heinemann, London.

Midgley, J 2008, 'Promoting reciprocal international social work exchanges: professional imperialism revisited', in M Gray, J Coates & M Yellow Bird (eds), *Indigenous Social Work Around the World*, Ashgate, Aldershot, pp. 31–45.

Pedersen, P 1994, *A Handbook for Developing Multi-cultural Awareness*, American Counselling Association, Alexandria, VA.

Peile, C 1988, 'The unity of research and practice: creative practitioner research for social workers', in E Chamberlain (ed.), *Change and Continuity in Australian Social Work*, Longman Cheshire, Melbourne.

Peile, C 1994, 'Theory, practice, research: casual acquaintance or a seamless whole?', *Australian Social Work*, vol. 47, no. 2, pp. 17–23.

Riessman, CK 1994, 'Preface: making rooms for diversity in social work research', in CK Riessman (ed.), *Qualitative Studies in Social Work Research*, Sage, Thousand Oaks, CA.

Rigney, LI 2001, 'A first perspective of Indigenous Australian participation in science: framing Indigenous research towards Indigenous Australian intellectual sovereignty', *Kaurna Higher Education Journal*, no. 7, pp. 1–13.

Rosaldo, R 1989, *Culture and Truth: The Remaking of Social Analysis*, Beacon Press, Boston, MA.

Rudie, I 1993, 'A hall of mirrors: autonomy translated over time in Malaysia', in D Bell, P Caplan & WJ Karim (eds), *Gendered Fields: Women, Men and Ethnography*, Routledge, London.

Sacco, T 1996, 'Towards an inclusive paradigm for social work', in M Doel & S Shardlow (eds), *Social Work in a Changing World: An International Perspective on Practice Learning*, Arena, Aldershot.

Saleebey, D 1994, 'Culture, theory and narratives: the intersection of meaning in practice', *Social Work*, vol. 39, no. 4, pp. 351–9.

Settee, P 2007, 'Pimatisiwin: indigenous knowledge systems, our time has come', PhD thesis, University of Saskatchewan, Saskatoon.

Sinclair, R 2007, 'All my relations—native transracial adoption: a critical case study of cultural identity', PhD thesis, University of Calgary, Alberta.

Smith, LT 1999, *Decolonising Methodologies*, Zed Books, London and New York.

Stanfield II, JH 1993, 'Methodological reflections: an introduction', in JH Stanfield II & RM Dennis (eds), *Race and Ethnicity in Research Methods*, Sage, Newbury Park, CA, pp. 3–15.

Stanfield II, JH 1994, 'Ethnic modelling in qualitative research', in NK Denzin & YS Lincoln (eds), *Handbook of Qualitative Research*, Sage, Thousand Oaks, CA, pp. 175–88.

Walker, P 2001, 'Journey around the medicine wheel: a story of Indigenous research in a Western university', *The Australian Journal of Indigenous Education*, vol. 29, no. 2, pp. 18–21.

Walker, P 2006, 'Mending the web: sustainable conflict transformation between Indigenous and non-Indigenous Australians', PhD thesis, University of Queensland, St Lucia.

Weick, A 1991, 'The place of science in Social Work', *Journal of Sociology and Social Welfare*, vol. 18, no. 4, pp. 13–34.

Whyte, D 2005, 'Contesting paradigms: indigenous worldviews, Western science and professional social work', PhD thesis, University of Melbourne, Parkville.

Wilson, S 2008, *Research is Ceremony: Indigenous Research Methods*, Fernwood, Black Point, Nova Scotia.

Zimmerman, JH 1989, 'Determinism, science and social work', *Social Service Review*, vol. 63, no. 1, pp. 52–62.

PART 2

Approaches of working with culturally diverse groups and practice areas

8

Social work with marginalised Indigenous communities

Christine Fejo-King

Introduction

Social work practice with people from marginalised Indigenous communities needs to be located in a community context. This chapter will examine the cultural biases inherent in existing social work methods of service delivery, which go against the grain of minority Indigenous ways of help-seeking and help-giving through informal community networks. This chapter will promote a (re)turn to a greater community focus when working with marginalised Indigenous communities. Using a number of case studies of Indigenous communities in Australia, the chapter will highlight the divergence between the notion of traditional helping practices and professional social work, since professional social work sometimes marginalises and disempowers Indigenous communities.

Implicit in the discussion is acknowledgment of the local, Indigenous ways of helping within a community, and the need for social workers to strengthen and support the existing helping systems. The chapter will also situate power and control within the larger context of dominant social and political relations, thereby arguing for a power analysis approach in addition to cultural safety and an experiential learning approach to working with marginalised Indigenous communities.

Setting the scene

Before proceeding, it is useful to come to an agreed understanding about what is meant by culture, and by cultural bias, as these terms are used within this chapter. To enable a shared understanding, culture is defined as:

> the values, beliefs, norms, mores, and material artefacts that create a 'design for life'. Culture is both an ordering disposition for members of a society, and the everyday expressivity of its members, individually and collectively (Beilharz & Hogan 2008, p. 453).

Cultural bias then can be understood as 'a mental tendency or inclination, irrational preference or prejudice' (Collins Australian Concise Dictionary 2001), against, in this instance, the culture of Indigenous marginalised groups, as they are measured and judged with the dominant culture acting as the litmus test.

It is acknowledged that there are many marginalised groups and that each can be identified through various markers, such as religious background, race and ethnicity, immigrant and/or refugee status, indigeneity and sexual orientation, to name but a few. The struggles of these population groups relate to issues around their values, beliefs and ways of doing things, which do not always fit within the practices and norms of the nation that invaded and colonised their lands and is now dominant.

This chapter focuses in particular on the marginalisation of the Indigenous peoples of Australia. However, much of what is written here can be applied to other Indigenous groups, not just those invaded and/or colonised by Western powers. Each Indigenous group has a particular history and experiences, which add another layer of complexity to their lives. Invasion and colonisation have often resulted in the denigration and subjugation of Indigenous sovereignty, law, culture, values, knowledge, languages, and ways of help-seeking and help-giving.

Social work biases

Three biases embedded within social work theory and practice that can impact on service delivery will be introduced next: different world views, whiteness and wilful blindness.

World views

A broad definition of world views was provided in Chapter 7. While the ideas presented there were generalisations, the definition highlights some fundamental difference between three world views.

To successfully engage with Indigenous peoples, it is critical to understand the impact different world views have on Aboriginal and Torres Strait Islander and other Indigenous peoples as they negotiate living within sometimes conflicting world views, in which the beliefs, values and laws of the 'other' dominate (Whyte 2005). The world view of Indigenous peoples in general is one of relatedness and connectedness, with people being equal to, rather than more important than, all other parts of creation (whether living or inanimate). North American scholar Joanne DiNova focuses on connectedness in her discussion of Indigenous world views; in particular, on the idea that 'connectivity encompasses, infuses and constitutes everything, thus forming the foundations of classical Aboriginal thought' (2005, p. 6).

For Australian Aboriginal peoples, this connectivity is found within the kinship system, which is embedded within Aboriginal law, ways of knowing, being, doing and cultural protocols. This world view guides thought, action and reaction, impacting on the wellbeing and safety of children, families, clans and nations. As part of the world view, the beliefs, values and knowledge that comprise Aboriginal law have been developed specifically from this land and passed down through each succeeding generation.

In contrast, the dominant world view of non-Indigenous Australians in positions of power has, in the main, derived from the Western world view (see Chapter 7), which has meant that Indigenous world views and ways of knowing, being and doing are deemed to be of lesser value. It is important to recognise that the differences between the Western and Indigenous world views impact on Indigenous families in practical day-to-day situations, particularly with regard to the way professionals interact with Indigenous peoples and services are delivered.

Service deliverers in Australia—from within their Western world view and white standpoint—impose on Indigenous peoples with an expectation that they will conform to a Western:

- epistemology, or 'the study of the nature of thinking or knowing' (Wilson 2008, p. 33)
- axiology, or the 'ethics or morals that guide the search for knowledge and judge which information is worthy of searching for' (Wilson 2008, p. 34)
- ontology, or a 'theory of the nature of existence, or the nature of reality' (Wilson 2008, p. 33).

Service deliverers are then surprised when this does not happen. The Indigenous person is viewed to be non-compliant, and services are terminated. This can have devastating outcomes for the Indigenous person, their families and communities.

Whiteness

Whiteness is an assumption about the superiority of white society's world view and ideology, against which all others are judged to be of lesser value. This way of judging others is essentially racist. Peggy McIntosh (1988), in her seminal work *White Privilege: Unpacking the Invisible Knapsack*, demonstrated the invisibility of whiteness and white privilege when she introduced the concept of a knapsack of white privilege that was invisible but could be used at any time. She explained that she and other white people could take out and use the items within this knapsack to gain access or entry to privileged states that were not accessible to people of colour.

Whiteness in social work

Frankenberg (1993) raises three dimensions of white race privilege that play out in social work education theory, practice and service delivery:

- structural advantage
- a particular standpoint: 'a place from which white people look at ourselves, at others, and at society' (p. 1)
- whiteness in social work as 'a set of cultural practices that are usually unmarked and un-named' (p. 1).

These dimensions are discussed in greater detail below.

Cindy Blackstock, an Indigenous Canadian social worker, makes the following comments in reference to social work practice in Canada; however, her observations are just as relevant to social work in Australia.

> The notion of improving other people is endemic to social work. It is both a source of moral nobility and trepidation. It implies an ability to define accurately another's deficit, to locate its importance in his/her life, and assumes the efficacy of external motivations and sensibilities to change (Blackstock 2009, p. 31).

The goal of 'improving' others, especially Indigenous peoples, by making them more like white Australians, has been embedded within the ideology, policies and practices of this country for decades and has been progressed by social workers as they enacted the policies of their employing service, as illustrated by the Stolen Generations issue, which saw the fragmenting of Indigenous families from the 1800s to 2000 (Haebich 2001). Defining 'another's deficit' shows that individuals are viewed as having the problem, rather than society, and this lack of recognition can contribute to wilful blindness, which is unpacked next.

Wilful blindness

In the 1960s, psychologist Stanley Milgram conducted experiments to examine whether people would obey an instruction that they knew would hurt another person or group of people and, if so, why they would obey. He picked supposedly good people who had a high moral code. Milgram found that, in order to conform and to please the 'boss', almost all people would carry out actions that visibly caused grief and pain to others, without any emotional involvement on their part. Heffernan (2011) quotes Milgram as saying:

> Although a person acting under authority performs actions that seem to violate standards of conscience, it would not be true to say that he loses his moral sense. Instead,

it acquires a radically different focus. His moral concern now shifts to a consideration of how well he is living up to the expectations that the authority has of him (p. 113).

'Wilful blindness' is the term used by Heffernan to describe this phenomenon, because people in Milgram's experiments made a choice. Since the war crimes trials after World War II, and including white-collar crime today, obedience of employees to their superiors has not been considered a valid excuse for criminal activity.

This understanding of wilful blindness supports and furthers Frankenberg's (1993) three dimensions of white privilege within social work education theory and practice, and service delivery, and has, in the past, gone unmarked and unnamed. In fact, Milgram's results can be applied to everyone who was involved in the stealing/removing of Indigenous children (the Stolen Generations) for the last 200 years in Australia. These people saw the anguish of the parents and children as they tore the children from their mother's arms, and yet they still persisted. Why? This question is vital for social workers to consider, since social work has been the main profession involved in the removal of Aboriginal children from their families over the last 70 years (when social work first became a profession in Australia).

The actions of social workers in the Stolen Generations highlight how control was exerted, supposedly to show care (Calma & Priday 2011), but these actions had the opposite effect. This also supports Young's assertion that:

> As agents of the state, social work practitioners have been implicated in the control of marginalised people, contradictorily at the same time that they have worked towards emancipation and empowerment of those people under social work's social change and social justice functions (in Moreton-Robinson 2004, p. 104).

If nothing else, a statement such as Young's should have brought about a rigorous debate and change in social work practice. However, this did not happen, and this very lack of change should be questioned; otherwise, social work could find itself repeating actions similar to those carried out as part of the Stolen Generations, with social workers acting as agents of the state rather than as agents for change and social justice. Part of the reason for this lack of change can be found in the racism, stereotyping, wilful blindness and whiteness within social work, and the difference between professional social work versus traditional ways of help-seeking and help-giving, power and control.

Professional social work versus traditional ways of help-seeking and help-giving

This section explores what is meant by professional social work in Australia. It also explores what is meant by traditional Indigenous ways of help-seeking and help-giving and whether these are compatible and able to coexist. Professional social work can be positioned as another of Frankenberg's (1993) dimensions of white privilege that play out in social work education theory and practice, and service delivery, as professionalism is a particular standpoint or place from which social workers look at themselves, at others and at society.

What is professional social work in Australia?

The Australian Association of Social Work (AASW) has been working diligently for a number of years to have social work recognised as a profession within Australia. With this goal in mind, AASW's definition of social work in Australia has been aligned with that of the International Federation of Social Workers, developed in 2001:

> The social work profession promotes social change, problem solving in human relationships and the empowerment and liberation of people to enhance wellbeing. Utilising theories of human behaviour and social systems, social work intervenes at the points where people interact with their environments. Principles of human rights and social justice are fundamental to social work (AASW 2010, p. 7).

A number of questions arise from this definition, when viewed through the eyes of peoples who are not from Western backgrounds. These questions focus around social change, ways of problem-solving, human relationships, the empowerment and liberation of people to enhance wellbeing, human rights and social justice.

Who developed the theories of human relationships such as anthropology, sociology and psychology? And whose best interests have they served? Do these theories and practices coexist or meld easily when social work practice and service delivery meet the issues faced by Indigenous peoples? Do social workers really work to achieve social change, or do they work to bring about conformity to the dominant culture? These are not new questions, but they are an excellent way to provoke critical thinking.

What are traditional Indigenous ways of help-seeking and help-giving?

Indigenous peoples are fiercely loyal to their nations and clans, maintaining connections and ties even when they are living off-country in urban settings. This means that the tribal networks often extend nationally and internationally and can be tapped into as needs arise. This loyalty also extends to those who were removed from their homelands as part of the Stolen Generations. Most of them have, as a result, lost contact with their traditional networks and have had to build new ones. However, in their case, their loyalty is to the others who shared this experience with them and who were sent to the same missions and institutions. Traditional ways of help-seeking and help-giving have been maintained within these networks of kinship, reciprocity and care, usually guided by elders. This process ensures culturally congruent practice and cultural safety of all involved.

Culturally congruent practice means practice that 'fits' with the ways of knowing, being and doing of a particular group (Gibbs & Huang 2003). This kind of practice ensures the physical, spiritual and psychological safety of the Indigenous individual, family and/or community. It is a practice that is inclusive rather than exclusive of the values, beliefs, and everyday practices that have maintained the safety of a particular group for untold generations.

Power and control

Two examples of dominant social relations that offer insights through a power analysis approach to working with Indigenous peoples are shared below. First, we examine the political situation in Australia in terms of Indigenous Australians under John Howard, prime minister of Australia from 1996 to 2007, whose relationship with Indigenous Australians was very negative and strained during this time. In one meeting between Aboriginal leaders and John Howard, the Indigenous delegates disagreed so strongly with Howard that, as an act of defiance, they delivered one of the strongest insults that can be delivered by Indigenous Australians—they stood and turned their backs to him. The relationship between Howard and the Aboriginal people never recovered from that point.

This incident is important, as governments direct interactions with Indigenous peoples in either a positive or negative way through legislation, policy and practice, which impact on social workers and other service deliverers. The ways in which social workers fall in line with government policies and practices also fit with Frankenberg's (1993) three dimensions of white privilege and call into question whether social work is about assimilation or empowerment and social justice.

To illustrate how this can later play out, the Northern Territory Emergency Response is examined, along with some of the resulting impacts for Indigenous communities. It should be remembered that social work was one of the professions specifically named in relation to the Northern Territory National Emergency Response.

The Northern Territory National Emergency Response (2007)

The Northern Territory National Emergency Response was enacted by the Howard federal government as a result of allegations of widespread neglect, violence and sexual abuse being perpetrated against Aboriginal children in the Northern Territory in 2006. In response to these allegations, the Northern Territory government set up a broad enquiry to investigate what was happening to Aboriginal children across the Northern Territory. This government commissioned the *Ampe Akelyernemane Meke Mekarle 'Little Children are Sacred'* report (Wild & Anderson 2007) in an effort to find better ways to address child protection issues in remote Aboriginal communities within their jurisdiction.

The report found that Aboriginal people were not the only perpetrators; however, it could not 'definitely estimate the prevalence of various types of child sex offending, nor accurately identify the proportion of cases involving non-Aboriginals, Aboriginals, family member and others' (p. 60). The non-Indigenous perpetrators disappeared from the reports and media very quickly, leaving Aboriginal men to bear the brunt of the reprisal (Behrendt 2007).

The Australian Government declared a 'national emergency' on 21 June 2007. There were two stated aims of the intervention, the first dealing with protection of children and making communities safe (Brough 2007). The second, long-term aim was to create a better future for Aboriginal communities in the Northern Territory (Yu, Duncan & Gray 2008).

On 7 August 2007, the Howard government introduced emergency response legislation into the House of Representatives. This legislation consisted of three bills, which were passed on the same afternoon they were tabled, with in-principle support of the then opposition, the Australian Labor Party.

To enable the Northern Territory Emergency Response to proceed, the *Commonwealth Racial Discrimination Act 1975* was suspended and the anti-discrimination law in the Northern Territory was removed (Yu, Duncan & Gray 2008). In a quasi-military action, the Howard government deployed the military and police to specific Aboriginal communities to enforce this intervention. These forces were quickly followed by social workers, in a process that was similar to what happened with the Stolen Generations.

The Northern Territory intervention initially called for compulsory health checks on all Aboriginal children; control of all monies received by the Indigenous people in the form of pensions, unemployment benefits and other government support; control of land and repeal of permits that empower Aboriginal people to choose who could enter their land. The Human Rights legislation in the Northern Territory was amended by the Australian Government to enable these actions.

The compulsory health checks were quickly changed. However, the mental health of Indigenous communities still suffered greatly and stress was and is an ever-present companion.

This pattern of behaviour exhibited by an Australian government was not new. It mirrored what had happened in the past with the Stolen Generations, with the stealing of land, the massacres and other genocidal practices that have been happening since the invasion and colonisation of this land (Tatz 2006). Both the rights and the needs of Indigenous Australians were completely ignored to meet the political aspirations of a prime minister seeking another term of office (King 2007). This raises the issue of wilful blindness in that the government employees who invaded the Aboriginal communities carried out the policies of the government, despite the distress and bewilderment they saw on the faces of those whose lands and communities were invaded.

Returning power and control to Indigenous communities

From power and control exerted by others, we now move to returning the power and control to Indigenous communities, illustrating how professional social work can coexist with Indigenous ways of help-seeking and help-giving. The case studies below illustrate a (re)turn to greater community focus when working with Indigenous communities, how different approaches can be translated into practice and how professional social work can coexist with traditional help-seeking and help-giving through the practice of Indigenous social workers.

The impact on the ground of this political turmoil led to the particular case shared here about getting Christmas presents to children in remote Aboriginal communities in the year that the intervention was first implemented. It highlights the role of Indigenous social workers and the harnessing of Indigenous and non-Indigenous networks.

CASE STUDY 8.1

BRIGHTENING THE LIVES OF CHILDREN

The National Coalition of Aboriginal and Torres Strait Islander Social Workers has a very close relationship with a number of Indigenous doctors in the Northern Territory. Due to their concerns for the mental health of parents as a direct result of the NTER, in the lead-up to Christmas 2007, these doctors contacted the association to request help in getting Christmas presents to 16 000 children in a number of urban, rural and remote communities spread across the Northern Territory.

The NTER treated all Aboriginal families in receipt of welfare payments as economically dysfunctional and gave no recognition to families who had high levels of success in managing their income (*The Australian*, 4 July 2007, 'Editorial: beyond handouts'; Hinkson 2007). Income management prevented families from sharing resources because families were no longer given payments in the form of money. Instead, they were given a Basics Card that enabled them to purchase specific goods at certain shops, with a record being kept of all purchases made. Due to the imposition of this Basics Card on Aboriginal people in identified areas as part of the intervention, they could not save money for presents, or even ordinary shopping, as they would normally do at this time.

Combining networks, skills, contacts and people, the need was met using very little money and harnessing a lot of goodwill. The Christmas presents, which were mostly secondhand, were cleaned, wrapped and delivered to the communities prior to Christmas Day. Some of these communities had never celebrated this holiday or received presents before, so this was a special event in the lives of the children and their parents.

Achieving this goal went a long way to relieving the stress being experienced by parents and making the children happy. Meeting this goal was a great outcome, and what made it better was that no government was involved.

The second case study below also occurred in the Northern Territory, while the people were under control of the NTER. The intervention remains in place today, although the human rights legislation, with amendments, was reinstated.

NAIDOC BALL IN TENNANT CREEK, 2010

CASE STUDY 8.2

The elders group in Tennant Creek decided in 2010 that they would hold a National Aboriginal and Islander Day of Commemoration (NAIDOC) ball as a means of boosting the spirits of their community (also impacted upon by the NTER) by doing something that they had never done before, and giving their people something to look forward to. Once again, members of the community requested assistance from the National Coalition of Aboriginal and Torres Strait Islander Social Workers.

This chairperson was asked to do an interview on local radio in Canberra to talk up the ball, telling the community how it was something new and innovative for the Tennant Creek community, and to ask for assistance from the Canberra community. The people in Canberra were asked to provide clothing that no longer fitted them, as there are no shops in Tennant Creek where this kind of evening wear can be bought. They were also asked to donate shawls, jewellery, shoes and other accessories that they thought would help.

The response was amazing. People began to deliver bags of clothes, shoes, beautiful jewellery and other knick-knacks to the drop-off points. There was so much to be transported that Australia Post was approached, in line with their reconciliation action plan, to transport the goods from Canberra to Tennant Creek at no cost, which they agreed to do. The ball was a great success!

All the learning that informed the case studies came from Indigenous knowledge. While non–Indigenous social workers are not expected to know all the intricate details of working in culturally congruent and safe ways, if they take an open approach to working with marginalised Indigenous communities, successful outcomes can be realised. This could be achieved more in the future if social work students are required to complete at least one of their placements in an Aboriginal setting or community.

Conclusion

The power differentials that exist in the interactions between Indigenous peoples, governments, social workers and other service deliverers have been clearly illustrated throughout this chapter, as has the socioeconomic division between the Indigenous peoples and the dominant society. The cultural biases inherent in existing social work methods of service delivery, which often go against the grain of minority Indigenous ways of help-seeking and help-giving, are also clearly embedded deeply within the ways that the dominant Australian society interacts with Indigenous Australians, from the federal government to local governments.

This chapter has illustrated that what is needed when working with Indigenous peoples is a (re)turn to a greater community focus when working with marginalised Indigenous communities. It has also shown the value of Indigenous social workers and Indigenous social work associations as they connect professional social work and traditional helping practices. An experiential learning approach of working with marginalised Indigenous communities is recommended.

REFLECTIVE QUESTIONS

1   How can social work practice with people from marginalised Indigenous communities be located in a community context?
2   What is your world view and how might it impact on your practice?
3   In what ways does whiteness play a role in the theory and practice you are learning and what are the implications of this for your future practice?
4   Is the concept of wilful blindness something you have considered before? To what lengths would you go to meet the requirements of your workplace despite the visible distress of your clients?

FURTHER READING

Blackstock, C 2009, 'The occasional evil of angels: learning from the experiences of Aboriginal peoples and social work', *First Peoples Child & Family Review*, vol. 4, no. 1, pp. 28–37.
Heffernan, M 2011, *Wilful Blindness: Why We Ignore the Obvious at Our Peril*, Walker, New York.
Martin, KL 2008, *Please Knock Before You Enter: Aboriginal Regulation of Outsiders and the Implications for Researchers*, Post Pressed, Teneriffe, Qld.
Whyte, D 2005, 'Contesting paradigms: Indigenous worldviews, western science and professional social work', PhD thesis, University of Melbourne, Parkville.

REFERENCES

Australian Association of Social Workers 2010, *Code of Ethics*, 3rd edn, AASW, Canberra.
Behrendt, L 2007, 'The emergency we had to have', in J Altman & M Hinkson (eds), *Coercive Reconciliation: Stabilise, Normalise, Exit Aboriginal Australia*, Arena, North Carlton, pp. 15–20.
Beilharz, P & Hogan, T (eds) 2008, *Sociology: Place, Time and Division*, Oxford University Press, South Melbourne.

Blackstock, C 2009, 'The occasional evil of angels: learning from the experiences of Aboriginal peoples and social work', *First Peoples Child & Family Review*, vol. 4, no. 1, pp. 28–37.

Brough, M 2007, June 21, National emergency response to protect Aboriginal children in the NT, media release by Mal Brough, viewed 17 April 2013, <www.formerministers. fahcsia.gov.au/3581/emergency_21june07/>.

Calma, T & Priday, E 2011, 'Putting Indigenous human rights into social work practice', *Australian Social Work Special Issue on Australian Indigenous Social Work and Social Policy*, vol. 64, no. 2, pp. 147–55.

Cunningham, C & Stanley, F 2003, 'Indigenous by definition, experience, or world view', *British Medical Journal*, vol. 327, no. 7412, pp. 403–4.

DiNova, JR 2005, *Spiraling Webs of Relation: Movements Towards an Indigenist Criticism*, Routledge, New York.

Frankenberg, R 1993, *White Women, Race Matters: The Social Construction of Whiteness*, Routledge, Abingdon, UK.

Gibbs, JT & Huang, LN (eds) 2003, *Children of Color: Psychological Interventions with Culturally Diverse Youth*, 2nd edn, Jossey-Bass, San Francisco, CA.

Haebich, A 2000, *Broken Circles: Fragmenting Indigenous Families 1800–2000*, Fremantle Arts Centre Press, Fremantle, WA.

Heffernan, M 2011, *Willful Blindness: Why We Ignore the Obvious at Our Peril*, Walker, New York, NY.

Hinkson, M 2007, 'In the name of the child', in J Altman & M Hinkson (eds), *Coercive Reconciliation: Stabilise, Normalise, Exit Aboriginal Australia*, Arena, North Carlton, pp. 1–12.

King, C 2007, 'The Stolen Generations Alliance: a shift in focus or a refocusing', unpublished speech delivered at the ANTaR Conference, Canberra, 12–14 October.

McIntosh, P 1988, 'White Privilege: Unpacking the Invisible Knapsack', *Independent School*, Winter 1990, vol. 49, no. 2, pp. 31–36.

Moreton-Robinson, A (ed.) 2004, *Whitening Race: Essays in Social and Cultural Criticism*, Aboriginal Studies Press, Canberra.

Tatz, C 2006, 'The "doctorhood" of genocide', in CA Tatz, P Arnold & S Tatz (eds), *Genocide Perspectives III: Essays on the Holocaust and Other Genocides*, Brandl & Schlesinger, with the Australian Institute for Holocaust & Genocide Studies, Sydney, pp. 78–93.

Whyte, JD 2005, 'Contesting paradigms: Indigenous worldviews, Western science and professional social work', PhD thesis, University of Melbourne, Parkville.

Wild, R & Anderson, P 2007, *Ampe Akelyernemane Meke Mekarle 'Little Children are Sacred'*, Report of the Northern Territory Board of Inquiry into the Protection of Aboriginal Children from Sexual Abuse, Northern Territory Government, Darwin.

Wilson, S 2008, *Research is Ceremony: Indigenous Research Methods*, Fernwood, Halifax.

Yu, P, Duncan, ME & Gray, B 2008, *Report of the Northern Territory Emergency Response Review Board*, Attorney General's Department, Commonwealth of Australia, Canberra.

9

Social entrepreneurship: a culturally rooted approach to promoting social and economic justice

Peter J Mataira

Introduction

As the world has become more technologically sophisticated, culturally connected and economically dependent, the shift to a greater collective global identity has given us exigent cause to rethink what we mean by social and economic justice, diversity and social work itself. As a profession in search of new relevance, social work is at a crosswalk of change. Some, like Stoesz, Karger and Carrillo (2010), highlight the serious incongruence between social work's promise and its performance, which warrants cause for critical review of its professional standards and educational aims. Practitioners and educators across the globe are under no illusion that the profession is at the precipice of its own ethical and moral cliff. How it responds to social change and to social restoration amid complex cultural divisions and economic inequities has impelled it to consider new ways to reconcile the ideologies of welfarism and imperatives of global capitalism.

Rooted in the values of servitude and the dignity and worth of the individual and families, groups and communities, social work has to take the lead in the fight for economic human rights denied to the poor and the marginalised. The profession embodies the capacity to build networks and the potential to connect a range of disciplines and theories to formulate sustainable solutions to society's most pressing needs. For social workers working in the non-profit sector, diminishing resources and widening social and economic disparities have created immense and extraordinary challenges. It is patently clear that social workers alone will not solve the plight of the world's poorest or hungriest, or fix the family and community disintegration caused by natural or manmade disasters. It will be social workers, in collaboration with economists, farmers, health professionals, scientists and local elders, who will be achieving such goals: accountants are better at money matters, farmers are better at growing food, doctors at better at treating ailments, architects are better at building infrastructure and elders are better at cross-communicating and translating the local traditions of their communities. Those who work alongside social workers will perform social and economic development more expeditiously, expertly and sustainably.

This chapter thus makes the case that social workers are equipped to be social entrepreneurs and that social enterprises are effective organisational structures for achieving greater success outcomes, opportunities and improved structural designs, and are better suited to being able to work between the good intentions of government policy and the aspirations and interests of the community. Current social welfare and social and economic development programs are ill-equipped to respond to the growing complexities of global and local issues and to market forces. This then presents opportunities to build entrepreneurial leadership that fosters local social innovations and technology transfer and the potential to create sustainable families and communities. This chapter therefore argues why social entrepreneurship and non-profit social enterprise are essential to social work's search for relevancy and what cross-cultural practice means in the context of today's diverse economic realities.

A definition of social work that is not only realistic but also appropriate will have to take account of the roles that various kinds of other entrepreneurial stakeholders can and should play in addressing problems. Exposed to global markets, social workers operate within a precarious industrialised welfare complex in which helping the poor and marginalised and business enterprise are viable cohabiting dual-operating paradigms. Calls across the spectrum of human social services to move beyond organisational mission, vision, goal and objective statements to include more detailed analysis of key propositions such as program viability, partnership building, growth strategies, social marketing and branding are now central to greater fiscal and administrative efficiency. Indeed, to meet the challenge of overcoming global health inequalities and making foreign aid more effective, the United Nation's Millennium Development Goals set out its broad strategies to boldly resolve the health, education, environmental and economic inequities among the world's poorest in the most overpopulated developing countries (see <www.undp.org/content/undp/en/home/mdgoverview.html>).

For social workers, understanding the complex matrix of global and local forces—including conditions of cross-cultural exchange compounded by the transnational nature of capital markets and the impact of social technologies on communities—requires new areas of thinking in curriculum, including understanding concepts and theories that explain world systems, cross-cultural economics and social business. For social work, cultural diversity and global citizenry requires a reimagining of practice that encourages the profession to look beyond its silo fixation and frame issues in a wider, more pervasive, global relations context. Social work's purpose is to empower and enable the poor and marginalised, rooted in the values of service, justice, dignity, integrity and the worth of the individual, their families and their communities. Given the greater public interest in global market economics and the politics of nation-states, it is especially salient that social work focuses on globalisation and contemporary economic human rights issues.

Fostering social entrepreneurship—a culturally embedded practice

For the poor, especially in developing countries, social entrepreneurship is a vocation of necessity and not a job of choice. In efforts to maintain a living above subsistence, many rural poor in developing countries become social entrepreneurs. They typically go unnoticed because they do not engage in large-scale public relations work or have the necessary social technologies or language articulation to promote their ideas. In spite of this, they contribute in significant ways to the betterment of their local communities and, though they may not achieve a scale significant to trigger a paradigm shift, nevertheless their work has a profound and important impact on their respective communities. Contrary to popular belief, poor people do not seek charity; they strive to earn a living as best they know how. Given the necessary tools, resources and guidance they can develop into successful social entrepreneurs. Only when they can generate a consistent income to guarantee financial security, and their own families' economic stability, are they then willing to use their skills and resources to serve others in the community through their social enterprises.

The International Federation of Social Workers (IFSW) defines social work as a profession that:

> promotes social change, problem solving in human relationships and the empowerment and liberation of people to enhance well-being. Utilising theories of human behaviour and social systems, social work intervenes at the points where people interact with their environments. Principles of human rights and social justice are fundamental to social work (IFSW 2012).

While there is general agreement that the social work profession shares universal values across international datelines at one level, there are clearly idiosyncratic differences reflected in cultural practices and in the local critical discourse. But perhaps the most significant level of difference is in responses to specific local, regional and national concerns about changing economic and environmental impacts on land, agricultural production and community development. It is clear within the Asia–Pacific area that social work has been influenced by the rise of the industrialised Asian 'Tigers'—Hong Kong, Singapore, South Korea and Taiwan—and the United States as the dominant global powerhouse.

The idea of assimilating business ideals and welfare principles to resolve disparity gaps is a new concept to social work. The traditional business entrepreneur is skilled in recognising opportunities, exploring new ideas, advancing innovative approaches, mobilising resources, managing risk and building viable business enterprises. Douglas and Dubois (1977) and Hofstede (1984) first considered entrepreneurship in the context of culture, describing it as set of socially transmitted behaviours through which the values, norms and activities of a community's entrepreneurial activities are learned and transmitted though cultural stories, legends and metaphors (Gabriel 2000; Lounsbury, Tyler & Glynn 2011). Shapero and Sokel (1982) acknowledged this claim and saw cultural values as implicit to affecting level of risks and the ability to forge creative innovations evident in any prospering society. Busenitz and Lau's (1996) cognitive perspective of personal attributes and social context pointed to how cultural socialisation processes influence a person's intention to start a business. In this regard, economic activity is arguably contextual and culturally fashioned. It is an array of human and technical activities, 'networks', structures and processes all working together.

Historically, as Polanyi (1944) stressed, economic activity has always been embedded within the relations of pre-market societies as compared to today's more market-driven economies in which transactions are based principally on rationalised calculations of individual gain (Kuratko 2006). Perhaps a culturally 'embedded' understanding of entrepreneurship relates then to what Leibenstein (1968) saw as embedded activities involving the coordinating and carrying out of ongoing concerns that have important political, economic and human functions and, as Schumpeter (1934) added, the creation of activities where markets are not necessarily developed or well defined.

DiMaggio (1994) expanded Granovetter's (1985) and Leibenstein's (1968) initial work on embeddedness to include:

- *structural embeddedness*, which he saw as related to economic activities, outcomes and institutions affected by the overall structure of interacting networks
- *relational embeddedness*, which he saw as related to economic actions, outcomes and institutions affected by all its actors—including personal relations, kinship, and leadership
- *cognitive, political and cultural embeddedness*, which he saw in terms of a combination of all other important dimensions of economic activity. *Cultural embeddedness* included those shared cognitions, values, norms and expressive symbols that influenced and shaped economic activity and the quality of relationships to market institutions.

There is consensus among policy makers, educators and business leaders that entrepreneurship is about organising factors of production to make things happen, about creating new opportunities, and about developing new combinations of arrangements. To this point, state and federal governments are active in supporting local business through loans schemes, and entrepreneurship and financial capability training (see <www.sba.gov/>). According to the Schwab Foundation for Social Entrepreneurs (2008), social entrepreneurs create and lead organisations that catalyse 'social change through new ideas, products, services, methodologies and changes in attitude'. The Foundation goes on to say, '[S]ocial entrepreneurs create hybrid organizations that employ businesses methods—but their bottom line is social value creation. The ability to turn new ideas into concrete transformational solutions is the hallmark' (2008, p. 2).

Miller (1992) acknowledges the degree to which groups can become economic competitors and the degree to which group relations are adversarial or cooperative. When one group controls the economic means of another, it is obvious that the dependent group is more likely to be stigmatised. Sustaining and growing cultural capital is essential to economic development. If we determine culture as being the accumulation of customs, values and artefacts shared by people, then we can surmise cultural capital as that sense by which group consciousness and collective identity is harnessed (Franklin 2002). Yosso (2005) claims that cultural capital is a resource that advances the entire collective. Bourdieu (1986), who is credited for coining this term, 'cultural capital', sees it as the accumulation of cultural attributes including knowledge, skills and abilities owned and inherited by 'privileged groups in society'. Thus, how we define assets is determined by who has power and who is in control.

Bourdieu's classic work on cultural capital posits that it must be inherited or gained through formal education. Hence, what is taught becomes the dominant cultural paradigm. The net result of this creates what he calls the 'othering' or the 'nullifying' of Indigenous knowledge. Bourdieu's theory asserts the 'us' and 'them'— the culturally rich and poor—which leads to interpretations that expose his theory to white middle-class culture as the standard-bearer of all things and therefore all other forms and expressions of culture are judged to the contrary of this norm.

Yosso (2005) argues that marginalised communities possess large amounts of cultural wealth that manifest in various forms. She outlines these forms as aspirational, linguistic, familial, navigational and resistant capital. *Aspirational capital* is the ability to maintain hopeful, positive and resilient in the face of real and perceived barriers. This resilience is evidenced in the efforts of those in poverty-stricken areas in developing countries to take control of their economic destinies through initiating small-scale sustainable land-based enterprises. *Linguistic capital*, which includes intellectual and social skills, is attained through communication experiences in multiple languages. In developing countries, many people speak more than one language and typically teach their children traditions through storytelling, transmitting ancient principles through generations of time. Linguistic capital includes important visual cultural arts, music, dance and poetry, all of which are rich in traditional expression. *Familial capital* is cultural knowledge nurtured by and through family that carries a sense of who one is and a sense of place. This engages a community's sense of wellbeing. *Navigational capital* is skills gained by manoeuvring though social institutions. Historically, this is the ability to negotiate the seas, mountains, and geo-climate changes. Navigational capital today is the ability to assert individual agency within institutional constraints but also to connect with social networks that facilitate community navigation through place and space including schools, the job market, health care and judicial systems. *Resistant capital* is knowledge and skills fostered through oppositional behaviour that challenges inequality and injustice. This form of cultural capital (wealth) is grounded in the legacy of resistance to colonisation. Maintaining and passing on knowledge related to resistance is critical to survival.

Social enterprise—from conceptual model to organisational framework

The social enterprise phenomenon lies between the marketplace and government and is associated with the 'third sector' and the non-profit sector. The organisational structure that social enterprises adopt depends largely on the political economy of welfare provision, existing legal frameworks and the cultural and historical traditions of non-profit development in different countries. The social enterprise sector includes new typologies of organisations and traditional third-sector organisations refashioned and re-tooled as a result of entrepreneurial dynamics. The social enterprise aim is not to replace non-profits but rather to bridge these by focusing on entrepreneurial pathways for civic engagement and relevant initiatives that pursue social aims. Across many countries in the Organisation for Economic Co-operation and Development (OECD), social enterprises comply with the laws of the land and pursue social and economic goals with an entrepreneurial spirit. They engage in the delivery of social services and work integration services. They are also emerging in the provision of health, educational, cultural and environmental services. Fisher and Starr (2009) identify four critical questions for social enterprises that aim to create real, significant and sustainable change: Does the project have measurable and proven impacts? Are the impacts cost-effective? Will the impacts be sustained? Can the model be scaled and replicated?

From a comparative perspective, we can identify a set of key economic and social elements that help define social enterprises.

Economic criteria:
- Unlike traditional non-profits, social enterprises engage directly in the production and/or sale of goods and services.
- Social enterprises are voluntarily created and typically managed by groups of citizens. As a result, while they might receive grants and donations, they have a high degree of autonomy.

- The financial viability of social enterprises depends largely on the efforts of their members to ensure adequate financial resources are maintained; therefore, unlike most public institutions, they involve a significant level of economic risk.
- Activities carried out by social enterprises require a minimum number of paid workers, even if they may combine voluntary and paid workers.

Social criteria:

- Social enterprises are the result of an initiative by people belonging to the community or to a group that shares certain needs or aims. They must maintain this dimension in one form or another.
- Decision-making rights are shared by everyone through consensus voting. Although capital owners in social enterprises are important, decision-making power is not based on their capital investment.
- Social enterprises are, by and large, participatory insofar as those affected by their activities, the community, are represented and able to participate in the decision-making process. In many cases this strengthens democracy at the local level through economic activity.
- Social enterprises can include organisations that totally prohibit the distribution of profits and organisations such as cooperatives, which may distribute their profit only to a limited degree. Social enterprises avoid profit-maximising behaviour, as they involve a limited distribution of profit.
- Social enterprises pursue explicit goals that benefit the community and, by so doing, promote social responsibility.

A new paradigm for non-profit organisations

It is clear that the global crisis continues to generate widespread insecurity. While reactions to the crisis have exacerbated fears, the crisis has prompted donors and non-profit organisations to think more creatively and pragmatically. While the largest and most financially stable non-profits stand the best chance of surviving (Banjo & Kalita 2010), they generally provide services government is not equipped to deliver. Cost benefits fixed to program outcomes clearly appeal, as program costs precipitate and as communities in need increasingly become disenfranchised. Interest in social entrepreneurship, social marketing and social technologies is not only a viable way to monetise cost-savings, but also a practical way to improve efficacy. Indeed, it has become more imperative that non-profits generate evidence of success-related impact (Donaldson et al. 2011). As the global economy continues to engender volatility and uncertainty, donors are more prudent in their demands for tighter cost–benefit evaluations.

Financially unstable non-profits are at a higher risk of disappearing. Oftentimes small, community and culturally based programs fall into this category as they struggle to coexist alongside Western mainstream programs because they lack the empirical legitimacy needed to qualify for funding. Because of this, these non-profits tend to be more innovative and nimble to survive and more responsive to social needs in communities that have historically been ignored by mainstream social programs. The inverse relationship between a decline in human services and an increase in social problems represents a strange and threatening paradox that will ultimately deny services to large sectors of society.

Emerging from the fray is a reconceptualisation of program goals relating to social impact. With shortfalls in operating budgets and greater demand for accountability, non-profits are focusing more on primary prevention and systemic changes that will alter the rates and course of problem etiology. The maximisation of social impacts comprises multiple strategies aimed at addressing and preventing complex social problems and enhancing organisational capacity and sustainability (Gerring & Thomas 2011). Additionally, efforts to enhance program efficacy must involve investing in future leaders who possess a larger repertoire of skills related to strategy and vision, administration and entrepreneurship. Where vision outlines what a non-profit organisation desires to be and how it aims to get there, its mission expresses its purpose and how its leadership plans to achieve this. Values are what drive leaders in setting out priorities while providing a framework for decision-making. The strategy they employ is their roadmap for ensuring their organisation goes in the right direction.

Towards improved cost-effectiveness and accountability

Funding for philanthropic purposes is often restrictive and limited. As such, it is important to keep track of donor funds needed to produce a given impact. How much do the incomes of the local people rise for every dollar spent in poverty reduction? The social entrepreneur must strive to be cost-effective, optimising every dollar to produce the greatest benefit for the beneficiary (Angrist & Pischke 2010). Programs should also be evaluated to determine if they will be cost-effective into the future. Fisher and Starr (2009) offer additional advice:

> Cost-effectiveness is relative, so compare the project to other projects working to produce the same impacts in similar areas. If you have nothing to compare it to, then at least ensure that the effectiveness can be measured and that it feels reasonable to you.

A crucial question is whether the social initiative would be sustainable in the long run. What would happen to programs once the inflow of external funding stops? In an effective program, the initial positive impact should not fade away, but should continue to generate benefits even with scarce, decreasing funding. Fisher and Starr (2009) urge social entrepreneurs to continually ask the following questions: Will new technologies be used? Will they be used effectively? How will such technologies be replicated over time? Will new people want or have access to these technologies? Will businesses continue to prosper? And will new people be able to start new profitable businesses? Fisher and Starr (2009) assert that sustainable programs should have:

- a business model and a supply chain that continues to provide the required goods and/or services at a marginal profit (profit in this sense is revenue reinvested back into the program)
- a handover or succession provision whereby goods or services can be run by local government using tax funds; though viable, Fisher and Starr do point out this is not always sustainable as government support is not reliable
- an ability to build self-sustaining community processes that encourage solutions to local problems with little or continued external funding
- a plan set in place that works towards permanently eliminating the targeted problem it aims to resolve.

Muhammad Yunus, the founder of the Grameen Bank and co-winner of the 2006 Nobel Peace Prize, found a solution to the plight of the destitute of Bangladesh who were unable to acquire funds to start their own businesses: microcredit for the poor. He lent US$27 of his personal funds to a group of poor women, who quickly started a small sewing business that was able to generate enough income to help pay back their loan. More importantly, this helped them rise above poverty. The idea of the Grameen Bank was born. It sustained itself by charging interest on its loans and then recycling the capital to help other women start local entrepreneurial businesses (Martin & Osberg 2007). Having thus showed microcredit to be a sustainable method of combating global poverty, Yunus's work continues today to encourage organisations to adopt the Grameen model to combat a range of prevalent social and environmental problems, including workplace hazards, pollution, labour exploitation and poor sanitation. It, however, is not the be-all and end-all of local problems. There needs to be more collaborative efforts between bankers, government officials and the private business sector.

Critical synergy has to be created by harnessing local resources and the entrepreneurial talents of local people. Developing small businesses with the support of seed resourcing from social entrepreneurs from developed countries has more chance of sustainable growth. In an era of limited resources, branding a social cause and marketing are critical elements in resource generation. In many cases, social program personnel are preoccupied with daily operations or modestly go about their work without recognition. While it is seen as admirable and virtuous to not seek recognition for their important work, it is also critical to think in terms of promoting the good and effective work of social entrepreneurs for the sake of generating donations. It is imperative for human services to organise their activities in a more responsible, business-like manner; that they act wisely and strategically. For example, media presentations that send a clear public message (for example, ending poverty, reducing unwanted pregnancies) are invaluable taglines in resource development through promoting awareness, securing partnerships and attracting donors. Media presentations alone, however, do not guarantee resource sustainability. Those that develop mastery in marketing their social technologies and how they effect change stand a much better chance of surviving into the future.

Social entrepreneurship (Dees 1998; Martin & Osberg 2007) is a principal driver of providing essential economic relief to the poor. Developing innovative, value-added social activities that take into account cultural and local market forces and opportunities has wide appeal and interest as progressively more social workers and non-profit organisations reassess their deepening concerns about funding cuts to programs (Thompson 2002). As non-profits source alternative funding, they explore business and for-profit models that support their activities. In countries such as the Philippines, for example, for-profit philosophies and social entrepreneurship are

THE CONSUELO FOUNDATION

The Consuelo Foundation is a private operating foundation that serves to reduce and prevent abuses against the children and young people of the Philippines and Hawaii. Born in the Philippines in 1914, Consuelo Zobel Alger grew up in a prominent Manila family whose history dates back 400 years to the Spanish conquistador Juan Ponce de León. Her ancestors founded the Ayala Compañia, which is today recognised as one of the Philippines' foremost corporations, with vast business and financial interests in property development, banking, electronics and telecommunications. Renamed the Ayala Corporation in 1968, the company is recognised for its commitment to corporate social responsibility, and has a key role in the country's social and economic development.

The Consuelo Foundation was established in 1987 to enhance the welfare and improve the prospects of disadvantaged Filipino children and youth who are victims of abuse, street children, children of Indigenous people, and out-of-school youth. The Consuelo Foundation has four major program goals: to prevent child abuse and promote the recovery and reintegration of victims; to promote justice for disadvantaged children; to enhance the social and economic potential of out-of-school children and youth; and to promote appropriate education for Indigenous children and youth. Among its strategies are to:

- enhance the quality of social service, program sustainability and leadership development
- strengthen organisational capacity
- pursue its mission effectively and efficiently
- assist its partners in the use of progressive technology
- promote research, evaluation and integration of best and promising practices
- create a learning community both internally and externally among the board of directors, staff, partners and other organisations between both Hawaii and the Philippines.

See <www.consuelo.org> for further information.

CASE STUDY **9.1**

being integrated to fund local welfare programs (Duldulao 2012), as demonstrated in Case Study 9.1.

Social programs in the future will need to be focused on issues with a larger social impact, which is more likely to be achieved through collaboration, pooling resources, and layering prevention with intervention efforts. They will also need to develop more effective program designs that meet objectives and disrupt social forces that perpetuate chronic and intergenerational problems (Gertler et al. 2010). Government social programs, especially those in the United States, directed at marginalised, ethnic minorities and Indigenous peoples have been largely ineffectual in showing cost–benefit findings. Hence, new and innovative social technologies need to be synergistically crafted from the cultural characteristics and proclivities of those being served, an aim of the Harvard Project outlined in Case Study 9.2.

CASE STUDY 9.2

THE HARVARD PROJECT ON AMERICAN INDIAN ECONOMIC DEVELOPMENT

The Harvard Project on American Indian Economic Development (2010), through applied research and service, 'seeks to understand and foster conditions under which sustained, self-determined social and economic development is achieved among American Indian nations'. Core activities include research, education and the administration of a tribal governance awards program. At the heart of the Harvard Project is a systematic, comparative study of social and economic development occurring on American Indian reservations. Among its key results, the Harvard Project (2010) found that a number of things matter:

Sovereignty—when Native nations make their own decisions about what development approaches to take, they consistently out-perform external decision makers on matters as diverse as governmental form, natural resource management, economic development, health care, and social service provision.

Institutions—for development to take hold, assertions of sovereignty need to be backed by capable institutions of governance. Indian Nations do this as they adopt stable decision rules, establish fair and independent mechanisms for dispute resolution, and separate politics from day-to-day business and program management.

Culture—successful economies stand on the shoulders of legitimate, culturally grounded institutions of self-government. Indigenous societies are diverse; each nation must equip itself with a governing structure, economic system, policies, and procedures that fit its own contemporary culture.

Leadership—nation building requires leaders who introduce new knowledge and experiences, challenge assumptions, and propose change. Such leaders, whether elected, community, or spiritual, convince people that things can be different and inspire them to take action.

Knowledge-sharing with other social entrepreneurs

After assessing the impact of a social enterprise, the social entrepreneur will know whether it is successful or not. Success and failure is equally important because the social entrepreneur draws valuable lessons from both. More importantly, the manner in which social entrepreneurs share knowledge of what works and what doesn't with other social entrepreneurs will help them to achieve progress in their respective social projects. For Fisher and Starr (2009), successful models are those that, with a few modifications and adaptations, can be rescaled and replicated in a variety of different social contexts to address a similar problem. The Grameen model of poverty reduction, as an example, is successful not only because it is sustainable and cost-effective but also because it can be adapted to serve the needs of different communities with different sets of cultural and social needs. It is having access to financial services where none or nothing reasonable exists. If you are poor, have no credit and are unable to raise funds, microfinancing is a viable and attractive option. In fact, microfinance is being implemented in poor urban and rural communities in the United States.

Measuring social impact

It is important that social workers develop their confidence in understanding program accountability and the links between costs, inputs and outputs. Outcomes should be gauged against amount of money spent. There are ways to both measure desired change and demonstrate the extent to which outcomes are the results of planned interventions. This can be done adequately through empirically randomised trials or using simpler measurements such as comparative changes in control and experiment groups. Social entrepreneurs also know that past studies can be analysed and correlations between intervention and change made.

Impact evaluations have emerged as important tools to conduct such analyses. They assess the changes in the wellbeing of individuals and the extent to which change is attributable to a particular project, program or policy. At a broader level, the information generated can lead to a systematic practice evidence base that works. Rigorous project-specific impact evaluations force us to rethink assumptions about human behaviour and may bring to light some unexpected impact or consequence.

Arguably, very few impact evaluations collect or report on program costs and this represents a missed opportunity to gain greater insight into efficiency, budget allocations and concerns about sustainability. These operational objectives can be resolved by expanding the base of rigorous impact evaluations to replicate interventions that prove successful.

It is insufficient to simply measure impact. Scientific randomised trials involving control groups can be done to study the correlation between a particular social initiative and perceived social changes. Past studies of similar programs in similar contexts conducted by other non-profit enterprises could also be used.

Developing system-wide program evaluations

Well beyond accountability requirements, program evaluations are vital to the process of program development and finding best and promising practices, and serve as an important empirical element in promoting and marketing programs (Cabell 2011; Patton 2011). An effective approach to program evaluation involves establishing baseline measures of dependent variables, the application of valid measures and metrics, randomised clinical designs, and post-intervention follow-ups. Qualitative approaches, such as situational analysis (drawing together information from studies on discourse and agency; action and structure; image, text and context; history and the present to analyse complex situations) and discourse analysis, are also necessary in terms of eliciting specific programmatic aspects that don't readily lend themselves to quantification (Patton 2002, 2009). The less-tangible elements can be equally important in understanding the change process (Morelli & Mataira 2010) and the implementation of a comprehensive program evaluation process in a network of social organisations may require training of program personnel in data-gathering and data analysis.

New evaluation methodologies that capture essential program process and outcomes, as well as longitudinal impacts, are necessary to demonstrate the effectiveness of innovative practice. Standard evaluation methods may not be capable of apprehending unstructured and nebulous properties in relation to how they meet program objectives. Inappropriate measures will not register the more subtle and holistic qualities of a program and thus success will be indeterminate. There is a strong tendency to focus on the 'measureable', or that which is easily measured. A basic question that evaluators should pose is 'how do we measure what we value?'

A mix of qualitative and quantitative approaches offers a greater range of results that ultimately determine effectiveness across program sectors and in the near and long term (Donaldson et al. 2011; Gerring & Thomas 2011). Empirical data supporting program effectiveness, especially for ethnic and Indigenous populations, is critical to program sustainability (Mataira, Matsuoka & Morelli 2006; Patton 2009). Evidence of success can be leveraged to persuade donors to invest in the next phase of program development and replication. Attitudes towards evaluations are not always positive, as evaluations might detract from important programmatic activities and be seen as an exercise in futility. In such cases, programs need to reconceptualise the significance of evaluations in ways that extend beyond performance and compliance. Program personnel must realise the value of empirical data relative to a long-term process of program development, refinement through social research and development, and sustainability.

In many cases, program evaluations are community- and strength-based approaches that draw from historical factors including economic displacement and dispossession, environmental aspects, cultural predisposition and sovereignty (de Bruin & Mataira 2003; United Nations 2010). Such program evaluations in Hawaii focus on land-based therapeutic interventions, spirituality and connecting to ancestral lines for emotional strength and recovery (McCubbin & Marsella 2009; McGregor et al. 2003; Mokuau, Hishinuma & Nishimura 2001; Trask 1999). These innovations are anchored in a viable theory of change and lend themselves to process and outcome evaluations. As a part of a greater sustainability strategy, programs must encourage benefactors to think in terms of social investment in solutions that address specific problems, cultivate critical transference, reduce dependency and inspire a collective determination to eliminate root causes to social problems (Bonbright 1999). This is a departure from traditional notions of giving and charity that were not tied to accountability. This new strategy of social impact work encompasses investment capital in order to develop research, publications and solution-focused activities. The interface between program development, cultural studies, and economics is essential to the ongoing amelioration of social problems.

Sustainability and replicability

With limited donor funds it becomes too expensive to continue subsidising the same solution, in the same geographical area, in perpetuity. If we are to believe social work about valuing human diversity, evidence-based practice, research and development, professional identity and ethics, and understanding the dynamics of social and economic injustice, then social workers must understand how to leverage and leave sustainable solutions. Even with proven cost-effective impacts, it is important that practitioners know whether a project passes what Fisher and Starr (2009) refer to as 'the walk-away test'. Will the community continue to benefit? Will the project have in place the mechanisms to ensure that every new member of the community will benefit?

Creating sustainable effort is a challenging undertaking, but one that social workers should know and understand given that any realistic change requires a well-thought-out plan for sustainability and have built into the front end of the project an exit strategy. We should, however, be mindful not to associate impact sustainability with financial sustainability given that a non-profit organisation is measured not in terms of profitability but in its ability to effect change outcomes. An effective non-profit makes sound and efficient use of its donor funds to leave lasting results. Once it succeeds in one location, it aims to solicit support of additional donor funds to develop new high-impact and sustainable projects in that same location or expand into new locations.

It is important to develop a termination phase tied to revenue that may include future plans. It is imperative, therefore, to show whether a project's actual impact is cost-effective or not. As donor funds are often limited, it is necessary to know how much it takes to produce a given impact. Poverty reduction projects, for example, should know how much local incomes are increased for every donor dollar spent in the community. As cost-effectiveness is relative, comparing projects with others doing the same thing is an important benchmark. Fisher and Starr (2009, p. 2) declare 'if you have nothing to compare it to, then at least ensure that the cost-effectiveness can be measured and that it *feels* reasonable to you' (my emphasis).

Critical elements of replication are training and manualisation. The documentation of features and processes of a program serves to standardise it and provide a model and guide for replication. Trainers versed in the program can offer training services to those who are considering adopting it. While standardisation is an essential part of replication, there should also be flexibility built into any effort to emulate as context and conditions will vary. This largely depends on how effective local leaders are and their accountability to their community's ongoing need.

While donors reconceptualise their roles relative to social investors, they must also consider ways to enhance non-profit capacity building. Investing in a cause means that programs and organisations must be capable of effecting change for a sustained period. Organisations must, therefore, not only develop highly effective programs that systematically and incrementally change social conditions (McNamara 2008), but they must also focus on the sustainability of their organisation (Bowman 2011; Yunus 2010). Non-profits that focus on investing in human resources, information technology, fiscal management and evaluation have a much stronger position and are more likely to survive during tough economic times. Projects that show proven cost-effective impacts delivered in sustainable ways are important in demonstrating how can they be successfully replicated and scaled across to new settings, as shown in the example below.

Developing successful models for social change can be expensive and donors as well as non-profits know they cannot afford to simply duplicate models. Best practices can create cost-effective and sustainable impacts in different locations and under different conditions, and can also be used to address similar problems. In general though, scalable and replicable models for change are those that meet what Fisher and Starr (2009) call large-scale lasting change by meeting the following criteria. The model must be:

- systematic enough to be distilled to an easily understood methodology
- simple enough that it can then be replicated
- flexible enough to be adapted to new situations and new problems
- not depend for its success on the unique circumstances of the project—that is, not depend on a unique local institution, a unique local market opportunity, a local government figure or a charismatic leader, as none of these can be replicated elsewhere.

NA HAKU

Na Haku is an after-school youth entrepreneurship program operating on the north shore of Oahu in Hawaii providing an 8-week entrepreneurial training, business mentoring and risk-taking experiential course to Grade 11 and 12 students. It has gained the support of local community leaders, business owners as well as non-profit organisations providing family and youth services in the area.

Na Haku was established in 2010 by a local social worker who was herself a small business owner and social entrepreneur in response to high levels of family unemployment and poverty. She devised a curriculum that incorporated the richness and diversity of local Hawaiian culture and Asian and Pacific Island values. The idea of developing a program that empowers young people through culture and entrepreneurship lay in its replicability of the theory that preparing today's students for success and leadership in the global marketplace is the most important responsibility in education.

Providing young local people with guidance and opportunity at this most critical time in their educational journey can have a profound impact. Entrepreneurship is an important tool to achieving these (N Mozo 2012, pers. comm., 30 January).

Supporting capacity development

Traditional donors typically provide seed resources to develop and replicate social programs and, as a general rule, do not typically invest in organisational infrastructure or capacity building. Yet non-profits need to be stable and sustainable in order to continue to operate and deliver their programs to their respective populations (Hummel 1996). Investing in organisational capacity and social capital is critical to long-term sustainability. In affluent economies, non-profits that rely primarily on contracts and grant funds are at a high operational risk due to declining public resources. Furthermore, grants tend to be program-focused, providing minimal administrative coverage. Overhead or indirect fees from external funding sources will become scarce, thus reducing the administrative capacity of organisations. The scope of services and the ability to take risks through innovative social technologies will certainly be in decline. In less affluent economies, the risks are not as significant; however, the ability to remain stable and sustainable relies less on grants and more on self-reliance and economic resilience.

After assessing impact, social entrepreneurs share knowledge of what works and what doesn't with other social entrepreneurs to help them achieve progress in their respective projects. Successful models for social change can be relatively expensive and cannot be easily reinvented every time. The best projects are those that, with a few modifications, can be rescaled and replicated in a variety of contexts. The Grameen model, as mentioned, has proven to be successful not only because it has been sustainable and cost–effective, but also because it can readily be adapted to serve the needs of different communities worldwide.

Creating networks of local and international donors

Generally speaking, non–profits are ineffectual in framing and promoting their programs and the positive effects principally because they have little or no experience in social marketing and cause branding. Moreover, prevention programs have generally not attempted to monetise cost savings in terms of their ability to run the programs (Gupta, Verhoeven & Tiongson 2003). Effective prevention substantially reduces expense requirements for programs designed to provide services to the poor, and the premise behind social impact bonds is to give investors a return from cost savings.

Branding a cause and marketing social programs are a critical means of bringing greater community awareness to the issues and soliciting support for the continuation and expansion of programs (Baines et al. 2003). Professional consultants—microfinance trainers, community organisers, program evaluators—can be instrumental in providing the types of service, training and knowledge needed to advertise issues and design public relations strategies to garner monetary donations and social capital. Articulating inspiring stories of recovery, producing significant results and employing social media to draw a large audience are critical to engaging prospective donors.

As costs are negligible, setting up an appealing, user–friendly website offering easy-to-access information—such as blogs that provide updates and trend information; an interactive Facebook group page; and promotional videos depicting program designs, goals and inspiring life stories—will become elements that can inspire future giving. Other mechanisms, including donor community building and volunteerism, will likely increase in–kind giving also. In a number of developing countries, volunteer tourism, internships and promotional tours are growing as effective ways to gain notice and cultivate global support. Although these tend to be viewed positively, they can produce feelings of antipathy among local people.

Conclusion

Non–profit organisations that can act entrepreneurially to position themselves in a changing global economy will fare better than those that lack adaptability (Wei-Skillern et al. 2007). The fact that donors are now holding social programs to higher levels of accountability means the non–profit sector is having to act more responsibly and show the extent to which donor funds impact on success. As we gravitate into the realm of social investing and business planning, performance will be held at a premium. Donors want to see results that make sound social benefit and business sense (Notcull & Ratcliffe 2012).

As we look to social technologies, improved efficiencies and new leadership, innovation and sustainability will become important organisational goals. The critical role of leadership in championing change will determine long-term sustainability. As economics becomes more culturally symbiotic there will be increased pressure to correlate impact with expenditure. Social entrepreneurship presents not only as a viable way to monetise cost-savings in terms of reducing social problems but also as a mechanism to shape and improve efficacy. As the global recession continues to stir volatility, clearer fiscal, programmatic and organisational decision-making is in order. This will go a long way to building enhanced approaches to the social impact and outcomes of non-profits.

As the OECD report 'A new vision of growth and wellbeing' (2012) concluded, the idea of an inclusive vision of wellbeing for both advanced and emerging economies—one that recognises new challenges, new opportunities and new sources of innovation—must aim at improving the total quality of life for everyone. Sharing knowledge, building collaborations and establishing support systems will be a critical factor in this. Where sustainability builds capacity, capacity then fosters leadership, innovation and technology that coalesce to solve problems. For social workers, social entrepreneurship emerges as a critical practice that will give the profession greater relevancy in its fight for social and economic justice.

REFLECTIVE QUESTIONS

1   This chapter discusses entrepreneurship as an activity that is 'embedded' into social, political, cultural and economic life. What do you think embeddedness means? What examples from your own community can you share about embedded entrepreneurial practices?

2   Reflect on the various capitals (aspirational, cultural, linguistic, etc.) discussed by Yosso. Do you think these are useful concepts in helping to think about or initiate a social enterprise in your community? How?

3   The Schwab Foundation on Social Entrepreneurs defines social entrepreneurs as leaders who can catalyse social change through business methods to create social value. What are your views about this definition? How could social value be harnessed and used in this way to strengthen your community?

4   Discuss how a social enterprise achieves sustainability. Review Fisher and Starr's four questions. Could these help establish social enterprises in your community?

5   Non-profits are beginning to focus more on impact evaluation studies to help improve program efficiencies and their chances of securing future funding. What are your views about doing impact studies? How can they help improve a non-profit's chances of generating new revenues?

6   Do you think social work programs should teach courses in social entrepreneurship? What may be some of the challenges for students and for social workers?

FURTHER READING

Bornstein, D 2007, *How to Change the World: Social Entrepreneurs and the Power of New Ideas*, Oxford University Press, New York.

Elkington, J & Hartigan, P 2008, *The Power of Unreasonable People: How Social Entrepreneurs Create Markets that Change the World*, Harvard Business Press, Boston.

Korten, DC 2010, *Agenda for a New Economy: From phantom wealth to real wealth*, 2nd edn, Berrett-Koelher, San Francisco.

Sherraden, MS, & Ninacs, WA (eds) 1998, *Community Economic Development and Social Work*, The Hawthorne Press Inc., New York.

Yunus, M 2003, *Banker to the Poor: Micro-lending and the Battle Against World Poverty*, Public Affairs, New York.

REFERENCES

Angrist, JD & Pischke, J 2010, 'The credibility revolution in empirical economies: how better research design is taking the con out of econometrics', *Journal of Economic Perspectives*, vol. 24, no. 2, pp. 3–30.

Baines, JW, McClintock, W, Taylor, N & Buckenham, B 2003, 'Using local knowledge', in HA Becker & F Vanclay (eds), *The International Handbook of Social Impact Assessment: Conceptual and Methodological Advances*, Edward Elgar, Cheltenham, UK, pp. 26–41.

Banjo, S & Kalita, SM 2010, 'Once robust charity sector hit with mergers, closings', *Wall Street Journal*, 2 February.

Bonbright, D 1999, 'Sustainability: the grantmaker's paradox', *Alliance Magazine*, December.

Bourdieu, P 1986, 'The forms of capital', in JG Richardson, *Handbook for Theory and Research for the Sociology of Education*, Greenwood, Westport, CT, pp. 241–58.

Bowman, W 2011, 'Financial capacity and sustainability of ordinary non-profit', *Nonprofit Management and Leadership*, vol. 22, no. 1, pp. 37–51.

Busenitiz, L & Lau, CM 1996, 'A cross-cultural cognitive model of new venture creation', *Entrepeneurship Theory and Practice*, vol. 20, no. 4, pp. 25–39.

Cabell, S 2011, 'Learning what works: best practices in program evaluation', DIPNOTE: US Department of State Official Blog, 13 January, viewed 27 August 2012, <http://blogs.state.gov/index.php/site/entry/best_practices_program_evaluation>.

de Bruin, A & Mataira, P 2003, 'Indigenous entrepreneurship', in A de Bruin & A Dupuis (eds), *Entrepreneurship: New Perspectives in a Global Age*, Ashgate, Aldershot, pp. 169–84.

Dees, J 1998, *The Meaning of Social Entrepreneurship*, Center for the Advancement of Social Entrepreneurship, Fuqua School of Business, Duke University, Durham, NC.

DiMaggio, P 1994, 'Culture and economy', in N Smelser & R Swedberg (eds), *The Handbook of Economic Sociology*, Princeton University Press, Princeton NJ.

Donaldson, C, Baker, R, Cheater, F, Gillespie, M, McHugh, N & Sinclair, S 2011, 'Social business, health and wellbeing', *Social Business*, vol. 1, no. 1, pp. 17–35.

Douglas, S & Dubois, B 1977, 'Looking at the Cultural Environment of international marketing', *International Journal of Market Research*, vol. 12, Winter, pp. 102–9.

Duldulao, GA 2012, 'Social entrepreneurship and sustainability in three cases of non-governmental organizations in the Philippines: a case study', Masters thesis, University of Hawai`i Manoa.

Fisher, MJ & Starr, K 2009, *Real Good, Not Feel Good: A Brief Guide to High-Impact Philanthropy*, viewed 27 December 2012, <http://realgoodnotfeelgood.org>.

Franklin, VP 2002, 'Introduction: cultural capital and African-American education', *The Journal of African-American History*, vol. 87, Spring, pp. 175–81.

Gabriel, Y 2000, *Storytelling in Organizations: Facts, Fictions and Fantasies*, Oxford University Press, New York.

Gerring, J & Thomas, G 2011, 'Quantitative and qualitative: a question of comparability', in B Bertrand, D Berg-Schlosser & L Morlino (eds), *International Encyclopedia of Political Science*, Sage, London.

Gertler, P, Martinez, S, Premand, P, Rawlings, LB & Vermeersch, CM 2010, *Impact Evaluation in Practice*, World Bank, Washington DC.

Granovetter, M 1985, 'Economic action and social structure: the problem of embeddedness', *American Journal of Sociology*, vol. 91, no. 3, pp. 481–510.

Gupta, S, Verhoeven, M & Tiongson, E 2003, 'Public spending on health care and the poor', *Health Economics*, vol. 12, no. 8, pp. 685–96.

Harvard Project on American Indian Economic Development 2010, *About the Harvard Project, Overview*, viewed 27 December 2012, <http://hpaied.org>.

Hofstede, G 1984, *Culture's Consequences*, Sage, London.

Hummel, JM 1996, *Starting and Running a Nonprofit Organization*, Center for Non-Profit Management, University of St Thomas, University of Minnesota Press, Minneapolis, MN.

International Federation of Social Workers 2012, *Definition of social work*, <http://ifsw.org/policies/definition-of-social-work>.

Kuratko, DF 2006, *Entrepreneurship: Theory, Process, Practice*, 7th edn, Thomson South-Western, Mason, OH.

Leibenstein, H 1968, 'Entrepreneurship and development', *The American Economic Review* papers and proceedings, vol. 58, no. 2, pp. 72–83.

Lounsbury, M, Tyler, W & Glynn, M 2011, 'Legitimizing nascent collective identities: coordinating cultural entrepreneurship', *Organization Science*, vol. 22, no. 2, pp. 449–63.

Martin, RL & Osberg, S 2007, 'Social entrepreneurship: the case for definition', *Stanford Social Innovation Review*, Spring, pp. 28–39.

Mataira, PJ, Matsuoka, JK & Morelli, PT 2005, 'Issues and processes in Indigenous research', *Hūlili: Multidisciplinary Research on Hawaiian Well-being*, vol. 2, no. 1, pp. 35–46.

McCubbin, LD & Marsella, A 2009, 'Native Hawaiians and psychology: the cultural, and historical context of indigenous ways of knowing', *Cultural Diversity and Ethnic Minority Psychology*, vol. 15, no. 4, pp. 374–87.

McGregor, DP, Morelli, PT, Matsuoka, JK & Minerbi, L 2003, 'An ecological model of wellbeing', in HA Becker & F Vanclay (eds), *The International Handbook of Social Impact Assessment: Conceptual and Methodological Advances*, Edward Elgar, Cheltenham, UK, pp. 108–26.

McNamara, C 2008, *Field Guide to Nonprofit Program Design, Marketing and Evaluation*, Authenticity Consulting, LLC.

Miller RL 1992, 'The human ecology of multiracial identity', in M Root (ed.), *Racially Mixed People in America*, Sage, Newbury Park, CA, pp. 24–30.

Mokuau, N, Hishinuma, E & Nishimura, S 2001, 'Validating a measure of religiousness/spirituality for Native Hawaiians', *Pacific Health Dialog: Journal of Community Health and Clinical Medicine for the Pacific*, vol. 8, no. 2, pp. 407–16.

Morelli, PT & Mataira, PJ 2010, 'Indigenizing evaluation research: a long-awaited paradigm shift', *Journal of Indigenous Voices in Social Work*, vol. 1, no. 2, pp. 1–12.

Notcull, K & Ratcliffe, T 2012, 'The narrative of impact: it's not just the numbers', *Alliance Magazine*, vol. 17, no. 3, p. 52.

Organisation for Economic Development and Cooperation 2012, 'A new vision of growth and well-being', *OECD Observer*, no. 290/291, p. 11.

Patton, MQ 2002, *Qualitative Research and Evaluation Methods*, Sage, Thousand Oaks, CA.

Patton, MQ 2009, 'Connecting evaluation to what people know' (guest editorial), *Aotearoa New Zealand Evaluation Association Newsletter*, September 2009, pp. 5–9.

Patton, MQ 2011, *Developmental Evaluation: Applying Complexity Concepts to Enhance Innovation and Use*, The Guilford Press, New York.

Polanyi, K 1944, *The Great Transformation: The Political and Economic Organizing of Our Time*, Rinehart, New York.

Schumpeter, J 1934, *The Theory of Economic Development*, Harvard University Press, Cambridge, MA.

Schwab Foundation for Social Entrepreneurship 2008, *Schwab Foundation for Social Entrepreneurship Activities Report 2006–2008*, Schwab Foundation, Geneva.

Shapero, A & Sokol, L 1982, 'The social dimensions of entrepreneurship', in C Kent, D Sexton & KH Vesper (eds), *Encyclopedia of Entrepreneurship*, Prentice Hall, Englewood Cliffs, NJ, pp. 72–90.

Stoesz, D, Karger, HK & Carrillo, TE 2010, *A Dream Deferred: How Social Work Education Lost its Way and What Can Be Done*, Aldine Transaction, New Brunswick.

Trask, H 1999, *From a Native Daughter: Colonialism and Sovereignty in Hawai`i*, University of Hawai`i Press, Honolulu.

Thompson, J 2002, 'The world of the social entrepreneur', *International Journal of Public Sector Management*, vol. 15, no. 5, pp. 412–31.

United Nations Economic and Social Council 2010, 'Indigenous principles: development with culture and identity in the light of the United Nations Declaration on the Rights of Indigenous Peoples', discussion paper for *Permanent Forum on Indigenous Issues*, Ninth Session, New York, 19–30 April, viewed 17 April 2013, <www.un.org/esa/socdev/unpfii/documents/E.C.19.2010.17EN.pdf>.

Wei-Skillern, J, Austin, JE, Leonard, H & Stevenson, H 2007, *Entrepreneurship in the Social Sector*, Sage, Thousand Oaks, CA.

Yosso, T 2005, 'Whose culture has capital? A critical race theory discussion of community cultural wealth', *Race, Ethnicity and Education*, vol. 8, no. 1, pp. 69–91.

Yunus, M 2010, *Building Social Business: A New Kind of Capitalism that Serves Humanity's Most Pressing Needs*, Public Affairs Books, New York.

10

Cultural safety with new and emerging communities: older refugee experiences of health and welfare services in Australia

Nirmala Abraham and Jennifer Martin

Introduction

New and emerging communities have been arriving in Australia since World War II as humanitarian entrants. These communities are small in numbers and have very low use of mainstream health and welfare services. They have fled their countries of origin, many having witnessed atrocities in their homeland and en route to Australia. Experiences of loss, trauma and grief suggest that they would benefit from specialist support and assistance appropriate to their settlement needs but few actually receive such services. For many new and emerging communities the initial settlement experience is very challenging and is further complicated due to limited skills in English, loss of networks, financial difficulties, lack of confidence and shame.

In this chapter, the lens of cultural safety is used to explore the resettlement experiences of refugees and asylum seekers in Australia with a focus on the experiences of refugees from Somalia. Cultural safety acknowledges the political, economic and social factors that impact upon migration and resettlement experiences and service responses. The main features of cultural safety are presented, followed by a discussion of the defining characteristics and needs of new and emerging communities. A case study is used to present research findings on the experiences of elderly refugees from Somalia who have resettled in the north-western suburbs of Melbourne,

Australia. This research was conducted in 2011 by Nirmala Abraham for a Master of Social Work thesis under the supervision of Jennifer Martin at RMIT University (Abraham 2012). This chapter draws together Nirmala's research findings on the Somali community and Jennifer's research on cultural safety.

Through the lens of cultural safety, it is argued that government and policymakers must move beyond misconceptions of refugees and asylum seekers as social problems, or not in need of services because they do not ask for them. Culturally safe and inclusive health and welfare service models must be developed for all, not just the cultural majority, to improve access to services for people of all nations. Opportunities for meaningful community participation are required to assist with resettlement and to promote positive health and wellbeing.

Cultural safety

In the late 1980s, Irihapeti Ramsden, a Māori student nurse, developed the concept of 'cultural safety' in response to concerns about the negative experiences of Māori patients when using health services in New Zealand. Cultural safety was to become a nursing response to bicultural interactions between Māori and other New Zealanders. Ramsden (1990, 1993, 2002) argues that nursing care is unsafe if the person is alienated, humiliated or discouraged from accessing necessary care. The focus of cultural safety moves beyond the notion of cultural competence, or cultural practices, to focus on the political, economic and social context impacting upon the individual's lived experience and health status. Cultural safety has its underpinnings in critical social theory and is characterised by reflective and reflexive practices that acknowledge unequal power relationships. Williams describes cultural safety as:

> An environment that is safe for people: where there is no assault, challenge or denial of their identity, of who they are and what they need. It is about shared respect, shared meaning, shared knowledge and experience of learning, living and working together with dignity and truly listening (1999, p. 212).

According to Ramsden, for ethical practice to occur nurses are 'not to blame the victims of historical process for their current plight and examine their own realities and the attitudes that they bring to each new person they encounter in practice' (2002, p. 85). The aim is to encourage a shift in thinking beyond cultural characteristics of particular groups to issues of institutional racism and discrimination in the healthcare system (Ramsden 2002). Cultural safety considers the client's perspective as the norm rather than the culture of health care. Doutrich et al. (2012, p. 143) assert that an understanding of power differences and personal biases can 'help challenge victim-blaming responses by health care providers'. It is through incorporating these new understandings in healthcare practices that culturally safe care is provided.

Today, the emphasis of cultural safety is on improving access to health services for people of all nations. In 2009 the Australian Medical Council incorporated standards on cultural safety and competency for accreditation for medical education and training (Australian Medical Council 2009). Ewen (2011) argues that cultural competence and cultural safety are problematic concepts when used for accreditation purposes for medical practitioners and proposes cultural literacy as a preferred approach. According to Ewen,

> cultural literacy is a set of skills whereby health professionals can recognise the need to obtain, process, understand and be responsive to cultural factors that are relevant to their patient within the broad range of contexts within which they might practise (2011, p. 69).

It is argued in this chapter that cultural safety is far more than a skill set but rather is concerned with praxis that embodies both process and outcome, providing a critical lens for analysing power relationships within healthcare systems (Josewski 2012; Ramsden 1993). McEldowney and Connor (2011) have further developed the notion of cultural safety as an 'ethics of care', informed by collaborative relationships and generic competence within a collectivist framework.

Cultural safety has been used by Indigenous populations around the world including in New Zealand, the United States, Canada and Australia. Using a cultural safety lens to examine the healthcare system in Canada, Smye and Browne (2002) have illustrated the inadequacies of the 'illness model' in meeting the needs of Aboriginal people, highlighting the negative impacts of colonisation and assimilation policies and practices. Bourque Bearskin's (2011) Canadian study of cultural competence and cultural safety in relation to nursing ethics identifies three dimensions of cultural safety: the profession, organisation and client. She stresses the importance of the worker–client relationship that 'honours Indigenous people's connection to self, others, the environment and the universe' (2011, p. 548). It is through respectful relationships focused more on the needs of the client than the health professional that professional knowledge and practices are further developed and enhanced (Bourque Bearskin 2011). Brooke (2011) emphasises the importance of individual and collaborative approaches that consider care for the person, family and community. In accordance with the principle of client-centred care, the decision rests with the client as to whether the care received is considered culturally safe (Darlington 2011).

Frankland, Bamblett and Lewis (2011) advocate the promotion and strengthening of cultural safety in Aboriginal communities. They assert that 'the diminishing of cultural safety in Australia occurs though a lack of respect and recognition of the positive aspects of Aboriginal culture and its centrality in creating a sense of meaning and purpose for Aboriginal peoples' (Frankland, Bamblett & Lewis 2011, p. 27). In her study of the needs of Aboriginal and Torres Strait Islander clients residing in aged-care facilities in Australia, Brooke (2011) stresses the importance of cultural safety principles being maintained across a culturally competent workforce. Anderson et al.'s (2011) Australian study of loss and bereavement for employees and managers in Aboriginal health and education services in South Australia and New South Wales revealed practices that were considered to be culturally safe and supportive. These included having non-judgmental and understanding managers and colleagues who had flexible interpretations of policy guidelines, particularly in relation to bereavement leave. During the 12-month study period, over half of the Aboriginal respondents attended seven or more funerals with a third going to between 12 and 30 funerals. Having a community of Aboriginal colleagues was also important for cultural safety in Anderson et al.'s study, as this provided familiarity and shared knowledge and experience of issues related to grief and loss. Anderson et al. (2011) recommend a review of organisational policies and guidelines regarding bereavement leave, in consultation with Aboriginal staff, to ensure that appropriate support is provided and that staff feel culturally safe.

Commenting specifically on the nursing profession in New Zealand, Day (2012) questions whether employment and contractual arrangements that occur within a dominant Western biomedical framework empower Māori health providers to deliver services that are truly culturally safe. For change to occur, she emphasises the importance of increased political awareness and advocacy campaigns and 'voice' to influence policy formulation and directions. Josewski (2012) highlights the personal and professional risks associated with speaking up for workers employed by government-funded services. Cultural safety redirects the focus from worker–client interactions to critical scrutiny of power relations in health care and the dominant influences of biomedical, colonial and neo-liberal ideologies. The increased application of neo-liberal ideologies in health care directs attention to efficient and expedient business practices. This can result in the silencing of community voices as they are absorbed into the dominant mainstream heathcare system. Organisations that propose programs to address social contextual factors in local communities that do not produce measurable short-term cost-effective outcomes are not likely to be supported in such an environment.

Wilson (2012, p. 18) describes health as a 'socio–cultural construction influenced by the culture within which we are raised, the subsequent cultures we interact with, and the interactions we have with others'. She identifies a need for increased culturally appropriate and responsive services into the future as communities continue to grow in diversity. This view is supported by the International Federation of Social Workers (IFSW), which considers health a fundamental issue of human rights and social justice, with governments held responsible for ensuring access to services for all. Social workers in all settings are called upon to articulate and advocate for social understandings of health and the roles of social workers in bringing about health improvements for individuals, families, communities and populations. The IFSW (2012) asserts that

> All people have an equal right to enjoy the basic conditions which underpin human health. These conditions include a minimum standard of living to support health and a sustainable and health promoting environment. All people have an equal right to access resources and services that promote health and address illness, injury and impairment, including social services.

This social model of health underpins the World Health Organization's (2008) social determinants of health and the United Nations development agenda. In an address at the United Nations conference on Sustainable Development for the Post-2015 Development Agenda, Sha Zukang (2012), Under-Secretary-General for Economic and Social Affairs, highlighted the importance of human rights, with particular attention on economic, social and cultural rights, and rights of participation. He reminded delegates to be mindful that 'no one size fits all' and called for development that reflects new and emerging challenges.

New and emerging communities: refugees and asylum seekers

In Australia, the term 'new and emerging' is used to describe communities that are small in numbers and are emerging into the aged-care service sector. Numerous definitions are used for new and emerging communities, the most comprehensive of which is provided by the National Ethnic and Multicultural Broadcasters' Council (NEMBC):

> A "new and emerging community" is any ethnic community that has experienced a significant percentage increase in the number of people arriving in Australia in the past fifteen years. These communities are relatively small and may experience one of the following: high levels of unemployment, English language barriers, low-income status or other social factors that could be defined as special needs (2013, p.147).

New and emerging communities have been identified as a priority for government funding, with many arriving as refugees and asylum seekers (Multicultural Affairs Queensland 2007). However, effective service delivery has been hindered by a lack of shared understandings and agreement on conceptual definitions and terminology used, with 'small' and 'new' often used interchangeably. This is coupled with scarce data available on the health and welfare needs of specific communities and low requests for services. This is often misinterpreted as lack of need. Early intervention models of service delivery are supported by government for optimum outcomes. These services are generally located in mainstream services and are underutilised by members of new and emerging communities who have migrated as refugees and asylum seekers (Department of Human Services 2008).

Refugees migrate due to well-founded fears of persecution in their countries of origin and cannot return safely. The main need of refugees is for a place to stay permanently, and to remain away from the place of persecution. Often refugees have fled in circumstances that have not allowed time for adequate preparation, arriving in the country of migration with few or no belongings. Most migrants will experience varying degrees of disorientation, often referred to as 'culture shock'. However, this is often greater for refugees and asylum seekers who have arrived with few resources and have experienced torture and trauma prior to and during migration and resettlement. The experience of loss and grief is often immense, with many refugees having lost family and close friends and witnessed human rights atrocities.

The United Nations High Commissioner for Refugees (UNHCR) highlights the complexities of reception and integration of refugees into the host society. According to the UNHCR:

> Integration requires pre-departure preparation; the active participation of refugees in all stages of the process; opportunities for language training, skill development, and employment; the support of communities in the resettlement process, including the availability of services tailored to vulnerable groups; and the coordination and engagement of all relevant Government authorities, particularly at the local level (2012, p. 12).

Refugees are a broadly definable group with diverse racial, ethnic, cultural and religious backgrounds. This diversity is reflected in the United Nations' definition of the term 'refugee'. Clear understanding of current national and international human rights laws, conventions, agreements and polices is required. These include relevant United Nations conventions, particularly the 1951 Convention relating to the Status of Refugees and the 1967 Protocol relating to the Status of Refugees (the Refugees Convention). Article 1A(2) of the 1951 Convention applies to any person who:

> owing to well-founded fear of being persecuted for reasons of race, religion, nationality, membership of a particular social group or political opinion, is outside the country of his [sic] nationality and is unable or, owing to such fear, is unwilling to avail himself of the protection of that country; or who, not having a nationality and being outside the country of his former habitual residence, is unable or, owing to such fear, is unwilling to return to it (UNHCR 1951, p. 14).

Conventions, legislation and policies governing other areas will also be relevant, including international conventions on political, economic, social and cultural rights as well as those relating to inhumane treatment including torture and trauma. Migration legislation will determine migration status, with different types and categories of migration determining eligibility for services. However, other areas of legislation will also be relevant, such as for income security, education, health and employment. This legislation will govern the amount and type of income support, entitlements to health and welfare services, recognition of overseas qualifications, eligibility for English language classes, enrolment as a local student and ability to legally participate in paid employment.

The Somali refugee experience

During the civil war between 1988 and 1994 many people fled Somalia to escape persecution. Corruption, banditry and looting were prevalent, with the government and military unable to meet the population's basic needs of sustenance, safety and security. Many people were subjected to extreme poverty. Female-headed households and children were particularly vulnerable and there were increased numbers of reports of women being assaulted, raped and murdered (UNDFW 2004). Approximately 300 000 people remain internally displaced within Mogadishu, the capital city of Somalia. Many of those who have escaped live in refugee camps in Africa in Kenya, Mombasa and Ethiopia. Dadaab in Kenya is the largest refugee camp in the world, with over 463 000 Somalis (Refugees International 2012). Ongoing security is a major daily concern for those in the camps where the daily lived experienced is one of further hardship, trauma and fear.

Somalis have predominantly sought refuge in Britain, Canada, Netherlands, Sweden, Finland and Australia. The poor conditions in Somalia led to the United Nations establishing a transition plan for Somalia, aimed at supporting the reconstruction and development of Somalia to address critical issues such as human rights, gender inequality and HIV/AIDS prevention and treatment (United Nations 2007).

The majority of Somalis in Australia have arrived as humanitarian entrants since the late 1990s; most are Sunni Muslims. The traumatic circumstances prior to migration of war and famine have exacerbated the challenges of resettlement and this is further complicated by a lack of knowledge of English, with some migrants having never attended school. The most recent Australian community profile data reveals that in 2006 there were 4310 Somalis living in Australia, with 2.3 per cent aged 65 years or older (Australian Bureau of Statistics 2008). Over half of this number (2624) lived in Victoria compared with 242 in 1991 and only 12 in 1981 (MRCNW 2004). The next highest population of 630 is in Western Australia, with 580 Somalis living in

New South Wales and 260 in Queensland (Australian Bureau of Statistics 2008). The highest proportion of this new and emerging population resides in the northern suburbs of Melbourne, where a study was recently conducted by Victoria Police. Figures released by Victoria Police in mid-2012 indicate that Somali-born Victorians were five times more likely to commit crimes than members of the general population (Oakes 2012). However, Adam Bandt, Deputy Leader of the Australian Greens, attributes this to racism against Somalis. He sees Somalis as victims rather than perpetrators, looking more broadly at social indicators that reveal unemployment rates of 47 per cent within the Somali community of Victoria (Bandt, quoted in Oakes 2012). In March 2013, a watershed case saw Victoria Police settle a civil case of racial discrimination due to profiling and targeting Afro-Australian men (Chadwick 2013).

Barriers for the Somali elderly in accessing health and welfare services

Elderly Somali people have low rates of utilisation of mainstream health and welfare services in Australia. As members of the Somali community age, it is necessary to identify their health and welfare needs early so that culturally safe services can be provided to them. This will potentially lead to overall improvements in quality of life and avoid them becoming a burden on government resources. In 2011 Nirmala Abraham conducted a study in the northern suburbs of Melbourne to investigate the barriers for the Somali elderly in accessing these services and to gain a greater understanding of their health and welfare needs (Abraham 2012). An exploratory research design was chosen, with a study sample of 60 respondents. A total of 36 individual interviews were conducted with mainstream and ethno-specific workers. Respondents were selected using a key indicators approach. Six interviews were conducted with general practitioners, aged-care workers, social workers, bilingual support workers, community leaders and religious leaders. Two gender-specific focus groups were formed with 12 members in each. Bilingual workers were considered most appropriate for conducting the focus groups as they led the discussions and encouraged participation through established trust.

All Somali participants in the study were aged 65 years and over. This age was chosen as it is the age for eligibility for services under the Australian Government Home and Community Care (HACC) program. It is important to note that refugees and asylum seekers are eligible for HACC services (Department of Health 2011). A limitation of the study was that it excluded younger community members who identified as elderly.

Questions and discussions focused on the four main areas of knowledge, access, barriers and cultural appropriateness of mainstream health and welfare services. Data collected from the interviews and focus groups was analysed according to the identification of common patterns, themes and experiences. Themes that evolved from respondents' stories were pieced together to develop a picture of their shared experiences. These themes have been categorised under the headings of political, economic and social context, as these are main areas of consideration for cultural safety.

Political context

Respondents commented that they were not provided with any verbal information about aged-care services on their arrival in Australia. Assistance was provided initially with housing only. One of the respondents describes his experience:

> When I arrived in Australia only in the beginning the government gave us a temporary home. After a few days they started looking for another house for us. No one told us anything about Australian services. We had no help. We were waiting for our children to help us.
>
> Abdi

As humanitarian entrants, Somali immigrants were acknowledged by the Australian Government as having been persecuted and having experienced considerable loss, trauma and grief. However, very limited support was provided to the immigrants on arrival, and no follow-up assistance was provided to manage their mental health and wellbeing needs in a new country, with their language limitations and limited knowledge of basic Australian service systems. A major issue for respondents was the continuing impact of traumatic pre-settlement experiences, including extensive displacement. There was also a deep sense of grief for family members who were lost or killed during the years of political unrest in Somalia. The Somali women felt that due to their recent traumas associated with the war, they required social activities to make them forget the sadness in their lives. Dalmar kept herself busy as a way of coping with ongoing trauma:

> After coming to Australia I am always busy looking after my family. Sometimes I feel so sad when I think of what happened to my husband and brothers. I don't know whether I will see them again. I need to change my mind and go out of the house to forget these things.
>
> Dalmar

General practitioners working with the Somali community raised concerns that many elderly members were vulnerable to mental illness due to past experiences of loss, trauma and grief, yet services were not provided to them. Both Somali women and men accessed local hospitals, health centres or local general practitioners with whom they are familiar, but only when they had become severely ill. HACC services provided by the government, including home care, personal care and respite, were only used as a last resort. In some cases, there was a reluctance to see a doctor, especially because of English limitations and an inherent fear of Western medication. In the case of the older women, it was necessary for them to be seen only by female medical practitioners or allied health workers and to have separate waiting areas and services provided in their own language. One respondent describes the difficulties she experienced as a Somali woman seeking medical assistance:

> When I go to the health centre there is no separate room and I have to wait with men too until my appointment and I am not comfortable. I don't know what they say about my treatment because I don't understand.
>
> Amina

Council services such as meals-on-wheels were not considered suitable for most Somali older people as Western-style meals were not familiar and were considered culturally inappropriate. Meal preparation did not conform to religious beliefs and halal requirements, deeming this service culturally inaccessible. Somali women complained that limited programs were funded that were appropriate to their ageing needs and that even though they had raised concerns regarding more sustainable group-based programs, there was no response from government.

Culturally it was considered shameful for children to allow their elderly parents to be looked after by outsiders. A Somali religious leader reported that some elderly members of the community, who were educated and were aware of services, did not share this information with other non-educated elderly community members. He indicated that they believed it was the duty of the Australian Government to ensure that information was provided to the Somali community. He also stated that often due to shame associated with accessing government services this information was not dispersed to people outside the immediate family. This view was supported in the following comment by one respondent:

> In Australia we feel ashamed to ask for help from the government as it will spoil my family's name in the community. People will talk that my children do not look after me.
>
> Nadifa

Economic context

The majority of the elderly Somali respondents surveyed were dependent on family and social security payments from the government as their main source of income. The civil war in Somalia resulted in major loss of established assets and this, compounded by the costs associated with becoming refugees, had left many Somali respondents with minimal assets or financial resources.

Most of the elderly Somali respondents had what they considered to be inappropriate living conditions in public housing, often high-rise accommodation, provided by the government. Religious and cultural rules forbade them, and younger family members, from acquiring bank loans and mortgages to purchase homes. This was compounded by high levels of unemployment. Life in Somalia was considered much healthier than in Australia as there respondents had lived in large homes, enjoyed sea air and eaten fresh food. Inappropriate housing was seen as a contributory factor for an increased incidence in diseases such as high cholesterol, heart disease, arthritis and diabetes in the elderly Somali community. Preferred foods were too costly and respondents were concerned that changes to diet were having a detrimental effect on their health. Labaan commented:

> In Mogadishu we ate more fish but in Australia we cannot afford to buy fish all the time because it is very costly and we have too many bills to pay for other things.
>
> Labaan

Somali men and women wanted to access healthy recreation activities such as swimming and exercise programs organised by local government leisure centres but the costs of these activities meant they were often not affordable. Erastro lamented:

> In Somalia old people can walk a lot and go and visit family and also can swim in the sea but in Australia we are afraid to walk too far from our home. We want to join the gym and also go swimming but it is too costly and government does not help us even though we are old. I miss Somalia but I cannot go back.
>
> Erastro

A community welfare worker stated that Somali men liked to attend men's social group activities and enjoyed networking with other men from the community to socialise, discuss the political situation in Somalia and share stories. It was suggested that if the local council would provide a meeting room on a weekly basis, it would support Somali men to come together to reduce their social isolation and loss of identity.

Older Somali men wanted paid employment and to actively participate in and contribute to the community rather than rely upon government handouts. Some of them believed they were capable of working for local councils to improve service provision for the Somali community and wanted to be considered for such positions. Specific concerns regarding elderly Somali men were raised during the interviews in relation to their limited capacity to gain employment because of language barriers and lack of recognition of their qualifications. This often led to social isolation and depression. One respondent described this dilemma.

> Arriving as an older person in Australia our basic needs were met but not our social needs. We have integrated into the society but we don't work. We don't go to school. It is very difficult.
>
> Ghedi

Social context

Most elderly Somalis had low levels of education in their own language. The Somalis had inherited a verbal culture that did not possess a written dialect. Many of these elderly did not speak or understand English. The complexity of learning English, particularly written language, was simply beyond many of them in their old age. Women respondents had particularly low literacy levels. Older women did not see that learning English was vital to their roles as mother, grandmother or wife. They depended upon their children to assist with communication with service providers and government authorities, as one woman commented.

> I am scared to pick the telephone up when I am alone at home because my children have gone to work, I don't understand what they are saying.
>
> Ayanna

Somali men were better educated than women. However, many elderly Somali men were not fluent in English. According to Roble:

> In the Somali culture men are educated and women are not encouraged to participate in formal education and must learn all the housework.
>
> Roble

Workers and community leaders identified HACC group activities, including social support and planned activity groups run by bilingual workers, as culturally appropriate, yet few Somalis knew about these services or accessed them. More Somali men were aware of services than women. The explanation for this was that in Somalia a male child had more opportunities for education than a female child. However, these men did not have a sound knowledge of health and wellbeing services due to language barriers. A Somali social worker commented:

> They depend on their children and grandchildren to access services, and are often supported by members of the community to attend appointments and pay bills.
>
> Korfa

Older Somalis provided care for their grandchildren and helped with the day-to-day chores to assist the family, as younger family members tried to establish themselves in their new home country. Many did not drive or use public transport and could not speak English. They depended on family or members of the community to support them with trips to their places of worship, shopping and attending appointments.

In Somalia, men and women considered themselves old at a much younger age, 55 years old, than the mainstream Australian community. This was attributed to them being obliged to acquire adult responsibilities at a much earlier age, as observed by one woman:

> In Somalia women get children early and take care of the elderly, and their family, and become grandparents early and take care of our grandchildren too.
>
> Aziza

It was not uncommon for a Somali man or woman to be a grandparent when they were in their early 40s as a result of getting married in their teens or early 20s. The experiences of teenage parenting and war trauma, and traditional family roles, meant that they were perceived by the Somali community as elders at a much younger age. Living in Australia was also seen to have accelerated the ageing process as Western diseases became more prevalent. General practitioners interviewed who have worked closely with the Somali community reported on low Vitamin D levels and obesity leading to serious long-term health concerns, including osteoporosis, among elderly Somalis. Ayan commented:

> Older Somali people get old quickly in Australia as we get western diseases as many Somalis suffer from high cholesterol, heart disease, arthritis and diabetes.
>
> Ayan

The Somalis in the study had generally become less active and more isolated in the community compared to their lifestyle in Somalia. This was attributed to being Muslims living in a predominantly non-Muslim community. Respondents identified social isolation as one of their main concerns. Those who did use these services were provided with opportunities to meet others from the Somali community and this helped reduce feelings of social isolation. These services also provided increased access to information and knowledge about aged-care and other health services. Some female respondents participated in healthy activities, such as swimming and yoga, when run for women only. The group activities also gave women an opportunity to pray together, discuss the Koran and talk about common issues affecting their community. Social outings increased knowledge of the Australian environment and indirectly created links to mainstream services such as local councils, health centres and local hospitals.

Policy implications

Cultural safety provides a useful theoretical lens that moves beyond the notion of cultural competence, or cultural practices, by focusing on the political, economic and social contexts that impact upon lived experience and health status. This approach stresses human rights, with particular attention to economic, social and cultural rights, and rights of participation. In the study of the Somali community, the lack of prior substantive research on the resettlement experiences and needs of the community, as well as scarcity of government data, contributed to this community being a low priority or invisible to healthcare policymakers and practitioners. Members of the community had scant knowledge of available services or how to access these.

The Somalis in the study were not considered to be culturally safe as they experienced alienation within mainstream health and welfare services. When services were not accessed, the assumption formed by some mainstream service providers was lack of need. This gives rise to consideration of the issue of 'voice', central in the cultural safety literature, in influencing policy formulation and directions. It also questions the notion of whether dominant Western models of mainstream service delivery are appropriate for all. A lack of consultation and reliance on family as intermediaries has meant that the voices of elderly Somalis have been silenced, even though concerns have been raised by health practitioners about health risks for older members of the community. This includes mental health vulnerabilities due to past experiences of loss, trauma and grief, compounded by a lack of English and social isolation.

The focus of cultural safety on praxis, including both process and outcomes, highlights the importance of reflective and reflexive practices that acknowledge unequal power relationships that can lead to overt and covert discriminatory practices. It is through incorporating these new understandings in healthcare and social services practice that culturally safe care is provided. Survey respondents expressed a strong preference for culturally appropriate services, including bilingual support workers, medical practitioners and allied health staff. They wanted gender-specific services and to be able to communicate verbally in their own language. Cultural safety places an emphasis on improving access to services for people of all nations, emphasising the centrality of open and inclusive consultation processes that reflect the voices of the people. In the Melbourne study when concerns that services did not cater to the community's cultural needs and service preferences were expressed to government, there was no response.

From a cultural safety perspective, an ethics of care develops that is informed by collaborative relationships and generic competence within a collectivist framework. This approach highlights the importance of worker–client relationships that are participatory, respectful, non-judgmental and promote understanding and trust. An emphasis is on familiarity, shared knowledge and experiences within communities. The study findings suggest that some ethno-specific services provided by bilingual workers were considered very appropriate to the community's needs and more of these services were wanted. Engaging bilingual workers, who spoke the respondents' language and understood their religious and cultural requirements, created a pathway for these elderly participants to access knowledge of health and wellbeing services.

Cultural safety highlights concerns when measures are focused on service priorities. The increased use of neo-liberal ideologies in health care and social services direct attention to efficient and expedient business practices silencing community voices as they are absorbed into the dominant mainstream systems. If this focus remains, it is unlikely that the service models preferred by the Somali community will be supported.

Conclusion

Cultural safety draws attention to political, economic and social factors that influence the development and provision of service models and evaluative frameworks and measures. A major paradigm shift is required from dominant service models that privilege narrow service-efficiency measures tailored to mainstream communities to those that recognise and celebrate diversity and value client health and wellbeing satisfaction outcomes. A consistent theme in the literature on cultural safety and in the Melbourne study findings on the health and welfare needs of older Somalis is the importance of community consultation and collaboration. This requires careful listening to the voices of community members, with mainstream and ethno-specific services working together to achieve optimum outcomes.

The study findings support the cultural safety argument that there is a need for increased culturally appropriate and responsive services into the future as communities continue to grow in diversity. This poses a major challenge for social workers to engage appropriately with new and emerging communities to articulate and advocate for culturally safe service responses, at all stages of the resettlement process and including all levels of government, especially at the local level. A focus is required beyond the narrow misconception of new and emerging communities as social problems to be managed. A new paradigm is required that is characterised by welcoming attitudes and generosity of spirit; an understanding of loss, trauma and grief; and the provision of appropriate health and welfare services. The case study of the Somalis highlights the importance of providing opportunities for full community participation to support the rebuilding of fragmented lives in peace and harmony to develop a sense of identification and belonging in the new homeland, Australia.

REFLECTIVE QUESTIONS

1   Whose perspective is privileged by a cultural safety approach?
2   Who should decide if services received are culturally safe? What should this decision be based upon?
3   What does institutional racism and discrimination look like?
4   Can culturally safe services be provided to new and emerging communities within a dominant Western biomedical framework?
5   How can social workers influence governments to create culturally safe environments for members of new and emerging communities?

FURTHER READING

Day, L 2012, 'Journeying to a new understanding of cultural safety', *Kai Tiaki: Nursing New Zealand*, vol. 18, no. 4, pp. 14–15.
Doutrich, D, Arcus, K, Dekker, L, Spuck, J & Pollock-Robinson, C 2012, 'Cultural safety in New Zealand and the United States: looking at a way forward together', *Journal of Transcultural Nursing*, vol. 23, no. 2, pp. 143–50.
Frankland, R, Bamblett, M & Lewis, P 2011, '"Forever business": a framework for maintaining and restoring cultural safety in Aboriginal Victoria', *Indigenous Law Bulletin*, vol. 7, no. 24, pp. 27–30.
Josewski, V 2012, 'Analysing "cultural safety" in mental health policy reform: lessons from British Columbia, Canada', *Critical Public Health*, vol. 22, no. 2, pp. 223–34.

REFERENCES

Abraham, N 2012, 'What are the barriers for Somali and Assyrian Chaldean communities in accessing mainstream health and welfare services?', Masters thesis, RMIT University, Melbourne.
Anderson, M, Bilney, J, Bycroft, N, Cockatoo-Collins, D, Creighton, G, Else, J, Faulkner, C, French, J, Liddle, T, Miller, A, Miller, J, Quinell, L, Stewart, B, Sutton, P, Thomas, C,

Trindall, C, Wilson, J, Malin, M & Moller, J 2011, 'Closing the gap: support for indigenous loss', *Australian Nursing Journal*, vol. 19, no. 10, pp. 25–7.

Australian Bureau of Statistics 2008, *People of Australia*, cat. no. 2891.0, ABS, ACT.

Australian, Medical Council 2009, *Assessment and Accreditation of Medical Schools Standards and Procedures*, AMC, ACT.

Bourque Bearskin, RL 2011, 'A critical lens on culture in nursing practice', *Nursing Ethics*, vol. 18, no. 4, pp. 548–59.

Brooke, N 2011, 'Needs of Aboriginal and Torres Strait Islander clients residing in Australian residential aged-care facilities', *Australian Journal of Rural Health*, vol. 19, no. 4, pp. 166–70.

Chadwick, V 2013, 'Victoria police settle racial harassment case', *The Age*, 18 February.

Darlington, A 2011, 'Raising a critical consciousness for the reformation of health care culture', *Canadian Journal of Respiratory Therapy*, vol. 47, no. 3, pp. 6–12.

Day, L 2012, 'Journeying to a new understanding of cultural safety', *Kai Tiaki: Nursing New Zealand*, vol. 18, no. 4, pp. 14–15.

Department of Health 2011, *Guide to Asylum Seeker Access to Health and Community Services in Victoria*, State Government of Victoria, Department of Health, Melbourne.

Department of Human Services 2008, *Refugee Health and Wellbeing Action Plan 2008–2010*, State Government of Victoria, Department of Human Services, Melbourne.

Doutrich, D, Arcus, K, Dekker, L, Spuck, J & Pollock-Robinson, C 2012, 'Cultural safety in New Zealand and the United States: looking at a way forward together', *Journal of Transcultural Nursing*, vol. 23, no. 2, pp. 143–50.

Ewen, S 2011, 'Cultural literacy and Indigenous health in medical education', *Focus on Health Professional Education: A Multidisciplinary Journal*, vol. 13, no. 1, pp. 69–74.

Frankland, R, Bamblett, M & Lewis, P 2011, '"Forever business": a framework for maintaining and restoring cultural safety in Aboriginal Victoria', *Indigenous Law Bulletin*, vol. 7, no. 24, pp. 27–30.

International Federation of Social Workers 2012, *Policies: Health*, at <http://ifsw.org/policies/health>.

Josewski, V 2012, 'Analysing "cultural safety" in mental health policy reform: lessons from British Columbia, Canada', *Critical Public Health*, vol. 22, no. 2, pp. 223–34.

McEldowney, R & Connor, M 2011, 'Cultural safety as an ethics of care: a praxiological process', *Journal of Transcultural Nursing*, vol. 22, no. 4, pp. 342–9.

Migrant Resource Centre North West Region (MRCNW) 2004, *Somali Born Profile*, Migrant Resource Centre North West Region Inc., Melbourne.

Multicultural Affairs Queensland 2007, *New and Emerging Communities in Queensland: A Profile and Needs Analysis of New and Emerging Communities in Queensland*, Department of the Premier and Cabinet, Queensland.

National Ethnic and Multicultural Broadcasters' Council 2013, 'New and Emerging Communities', NEMBC, viewed 17 April 2013, <www.nembc.org.au/info_pages_nembc.php/pages_id/147>.

Oakes, D 2012, 'African youth crime concern', *The Age*, 20 August.

Ramsden, I 1990, 'Cultural safety', *The New Zealand Nursing Journal: Kai Tiaki*, vol. 83, no. 11, pp. 18–19.

Ramsden, I 1993, 'Cultural safety in nursing education in Aotearoa New Zealand', *Nursing Praxis in New Zealand*, vol. 8, no. 3, pp. 4–10.

Ramsden, IM 2002, 'Cultural safety and nursing education in Aoteraroa and Te Waipounamu', PhD thesis, Victoria University of Wellington, New Zealand.

Refugees International 2012, 'Where we work: Somalia', Refugees International, <http://refugeesinternational.org/where-we-work/africa/somalia>.

Sha Zukang 2012, 'Welcome remarks by Mr Sha Zukang, Under-Secretary-General for Economic and Social Affairs, Secretary-General of the 2012 UN Conference on Sustainable Development', Briefing with UN delegates on Post 2015 Development Agenda, New York, 28 February, viewed 17 April 2013, <www.un.org/en/development/desa/usg/statements/post-2015-development-agenda-2.html>.

Smye V & Browne, A 2002, 'Cultural safety and the analysis of health policy affecting Aboriginal people', *Nurse Researcher*, vol. 9, no. 3, pp. 42–56.

United Nations 2007, *Transition Plan for Somalia, 2008–2009*, Version 3, UN, New York.

United Nations Development Fund for Women 2004, *Gender Profile of the Conflict in Somalia: Women, War, Peace Organization*, UNDFW, New York.

United Nations High Commissioner for Refugees 1951, 'Convention and Protocol Relating to the Status of Refugees', UNHCR, Geneva, viewed 18 April 2013, <www.unhcr.org/3b66c2aa10.html>.

United Nations High Commissioner for Refugees 2012, *UNHCR Projected Global Resettlement Needs 2013*, UNHCR, Geneva.

Williams, R 1999, 'Cultural safety—what does it mean for our work practice?', *Australian and New Zealand Journal of Public Health*, vol. 23, no. 2, pp. 212–14.

Wilson, D 2012, '20 years of cultural safety: how far have we come?', *Kai Tiaki: Nursing New Zealand*, vol. 18, no. 4, p. 18.

World Health Organization 2008, *Closing the Gap in a Generation: Health Equity through Action on the Social Determinants of Health*, Commission on Social Determinants of Health Final Report, WHO, Geneva.

11

End-of-life issues: perspectives in multicultural societies

Rosaleen Ow

Mum, why are people born, then live and die?

Question from a ten-year-old boy in Singapore

Introduction

The question of the meaning of life and death will confront every individual at some point in their journey on earth. The question above was asked by my son one evening many years ago and it set me thinking about the 'why' in life and death and the process of meaning-making as people experience each of these life events. This chapter focuses on the last part of the question about death and dying. Are there universals and specifics in the meanings that people create about the end of life and the care they would like to receive? What are the issues and normative expectations involved and do people respond to them in a similar manner? Social work practice in the field of death and dying spans a range of settings that include healthcare services such as hospitals, hospices and nursing homes, as well as non-healthcare settings: for example, home-care and family service centres in the community. What, therefore, are 'good' formal and informal carers? While death and dying are generally perceived as associated with the elderly, there is an increasing awareness that pediatric palliative care needs to be addressed in a more explicit manner (*The Straits Times*, 16 April 2012, p. B2).

According to the World Health Organization (WHO) (2012), the rapid ageing of the world's population between 2000 and 2050 will result in the doubling of the population over 60 years old from about 11 per cent to 22 per cent, increasing from 605 million to 2 billion. The number of people aged 80 years and older will quadruple in the same period to almost 400 million. By 2050, it is projected that 80 per cent of older people will live in low- and middle-income countries, with Chile, China, and the Islamic Republic of Iran having a greater proportion of older people than the United States. The number of older people in Africa will grow from 54 million to 213 million. While these figures are indicators of improving global health, the magnitude of the global increase in the number of older people means that health care for the elderly will become more urgent and addressing end-of-life issues in every society will also become more prominent.

The general theoretical framework that is adopted in this chapter in understanding the issues that surround death and dying, and the responses to these issues by the individual and the family, is the ecological perspective of practice. Adapted from Bronfenbrenner's (1979) model of human development, the holistic view of the person-in-environment in the ecological model has been widely used in social work practice (Germain 1991). The ecological conceptualisation embracing the person-in-environment presents an easily understood way of showing the coexistence and mutual responses or transactions between the person and the environment, including both social systems and physical (non-human) elements such as the built environment.

Human functioning in the ecological model of practice is viewed from many levels of human interaction. An individual's behaviour is understood in terms of the dynamic interaction between the person's innate capacity and the *microsystem* (family), the *exosystem* (immediate social institutions such as the school and neighbourhood), and the *macrosystem* (wider societal environment), such as the cultural and economic context in which the person is located. Apart from its ability to provide a holistic framework for assessment, goal-setting and intervention, the ecological model is able to incorporate other theories for practice such as spirituality.

The onset of a life-threatening illness not only affects the patient but also the family and its environs. Reciprocal relationships among the different systems described in the ecological model reflect the reality of the experiences of death and dying. Family caregivers have a major role in providing care to a sick relative especially in close-knit rural communities and in societies where interdependence among family members is a social norm. In life-threatening illnesses, apart from the medical care of patients, one of the main areas of concern is the quality of life for both the patients and their family. In addition, the nature of a person's relationship with friends, peers and care institutions also has an important influence on the perception of what issues may confront the patient at the end of life. Societal and culture-specific values and beliefs are often perceived as the bedrock in the development of normative expectations regarding what constitutes a 'good' death, and will be major considerations in the assessment of and goal-setting and intervention in the care of persons who are terminally ill. As such, this chapter explores the concept of a 'good death', whether there are universal expectations people have about how to prepare for and what to do near the end of life and whether there are culture-specific norms. The chapter ends with some thoughts on the implications of these cultural norms for advance care planning.

End of life and the concept of a 'good death'

Discourse on what is a 'good death' has been of interest since the palliative care movement began and Walters (2004) wrote that the concept of a 'good death' can be viewed as developing over three stages. First, the pre-modern concept of a good death was mostly religious in nature, emphasising the ability to die in peace with God and man. To some extent, this emphasis has continued in the Roman Catholic need for a priest to conduct the last rites for the believer prior to the event of death. Subsequently, with the rise of medical science, death is managed as something to be avoided, resisted or postponed and its existence denied as much as possible. The third stage is the impact of palliative care on the world: death and how a person dies are perceived as within the individual's control. Death as a subject of conversation is no longer taboo and a good death may include palliative care and euthanasia as an option.

End-of-life issues within the control of the individual, the family and society include expectations regarding the process of dying and the event of death itself, and are embedded in the beliefs of the individual, the family culture and the norms acceptable to the society in which the death and dying take place. Not every society will experience these three stages in similar degrees, and normative expectations about a good death will be part of an existing cultural paradigm. Individuals facing death and their carers develop their sense of cohesion about the experience from cultural scripts derived from various sources such as religion, medicine or psychology (Seale 1998).

End-of-life issues, normative expectations and universal concerns

As issues related to death and dying became more open to public discussion, there have been numerous articles in the printed media. From such sources, it is possible to cull some normative expectations that may be universal in nature. Bosma, Apland & Kazanjian (2010) concluded, after reviewing 15 qualitative studies on hospice palliative care, that while the role of culture is significant, there appeared to be three major universal themes:

- attending to the physical, psychosocial and spiritual aspects of death and dying
- the presence of care professionals who demonstrate knowledge and expertise as well as respect and compassion
- the availability of a range of resources to alleviate the burden of end-of-life care.

These three themes encompass a number of issues that are associated with a 'good death' experience and are discussed below.

First, the juxtaposition of silence and openness is commonly debated in medical care. Physicians generally do not openly confront their dying patients with their impending death. It seems less difficult to maintain hope than to dash it. However, social scientists such as psychologists, sociologists and social workers favour openness with such patients in order to help them with the psychosocial and spiritual aspects of the process and facing the event itself. Death and dying is both an individual and a social experience. Openness is believed to empower the patients, caregivers and families to face death and to provide care for the patients in a balanced and appropriate manner. Dying with dignity becomes an important aspect of research and service development in end-of-life care.

Second, the process of dying is as important as the event of death. In fact, 'All healthcare professionals must fully understand the importance of living well until death' (Altilio & Otis-Green 2011, p. 18). Quality of life and not just quantity has become an important end-of-life issue. Apart from open acknowledgment of the imminence of death, some other common possible indicators of a good quality of life in the process may include the opportunity for a person to live out their last days and die at home (Gott et al. 2004), for personal growth along the journey and to be able to exercise personal preferences in physical and social care and to articulate future preferences such as for funeral rites and care of personal assets. The physical and psychosocial environment may also have an impact on the patient's quality of life in the process (Rowlands 2008).

Third, expectations of what constitutes a good death may include appropriate and well-managed pain control of the symptoms of the illness and at the point of death. A patient quoted in Gott et al. (2008, p. 1116) asked, 'Is it going to be painful? I'm frightened of pain, I'm no hero, so it's just not knowing what's going to happen … so that's about the only concern I have, not am I going to die, but how am I going to die'. A worry such as this causes anxiety and distress and is an end-of-life issue of universal concern.

Fourth, in recent years, spirituality has been considered an important part of the holistic view of personhood and an important aspect of multicultural practice. Haw and Hughes (1998, p. 156), in a report on education for the 21st century, surmised that 'diversity in religion and spirituality is specifically linked to multi-cultural and multi-faith contexts' and affects every aspect of daily living. All humans can be said to be spiritual beings reflected in their beliefs, values and behaviours. Spirituality influences the mental, physical and emotional health of people and is particularly important to people whose taken-for-granted plans for living are shaken by the imminence of death and who need to reconstruct their identity and value.

Spirituality is not identical with religion but the two concepts can be related and share some common characteristics. Religion is defined as a set of formalised rituals and traditions in which a higher being/force is the focus and is supported by an established belief system that the believer adheres to or aspires to (Cashwell & Young 2005; Frame 2003; Hodges 2002). Spirituality, on the other hand, seems to be more nebulous and has defied a concrete definition as it appears to be a more intensely personal spiritual experience than found in institutionalised religion. The 1995 Summit on Spirituality described spirituality as:

> the infusion and drawing out of spirit in one's life ... moves through the individual toward knowledge, love, meaning, hope, transcendence, connectedness, and compassion ... includes one's capacity for creativity, growth, and the development of a value system ... encompasses the religious, spiritual and transpersonal (quoted in Gold 2010, p. 5).

Frankl's (1974, 1985) book *Man's Search for Meaning*, about life in a Nazi concentration camp, was one of the earliest examples of such an intense personal experience of living and meaning-making in the midst of suffering. Hence, one of the expected norms related to care in death and dying is the spiritual aspect of meaning-making for the here and now or the future and after-life.

Fifth, from the perspective of the ecological model of practice, the involvement of formal and informal carers in decision-making and implementing care plans with the patient is another important end-of-life issue. What are the desired norms about pain and symptom management, advance care planning, place of care and place of death, use of life support and the debate on medical futility, which in a sense counters the spirit of palliative care? Diagnosis and care are closely intertwined, and medical care interfaces with psychosocial care in seeking the best care outcome for the patient. The social worker mediates between formal and informal carers and is also part of a subsystem that influences the attention given to different issues in end-of-life care. The social worker's professional and personal feelings and anxieties are also important issues to be addressed in end-of-life care. Being able to accept their own feelings about mortality will enhance the social worker's ability to help the patient die in a sensitive and culturally appropriate context and the bereaved to cope with the traumatic experience.

Culture-specific responses within the universal concerns

What is meant by a 'good death'? Many healthcare and social work articles operationalise this concept as a set of quality-of-life goals; for example, a pain-free death, dying with dignity, awareness and open acknowledgment of imminent death, death at home surrounded by family and friends, being finished with 'unfinished business' and articulation of wishes regarding funeral rites and so on (Clark 2002). How are these expressed in different cultural contexts?

Communication about death

The literature suggests that openness to the patient about imminent death is more helpful than silence. A recent review of 13 studies (Innes & Payne 2009) found that while open communication and sharing of prognostic information is common there is variability in the type of information desired by patients and the quantitative prognostic information. While patients wanted some general prognostic information there is less certainty about the desirability of detailed or unequivocal information. For example, in Singapore, not talking about death or preparation for death seems to arise more from a societal taboo than fear or superstitions. The social taboo may be associated with the wish not to create negative emotions in people and reflects the mutual consideration that individuals, including patients, have for each other in a collectivist environment (Chan & Yau 2009). In a study of health workers in an Indian palliative care facility, it was reported that collusion was a common phenomenon as the 'false promise of "curing" can be construed as a form of "caring", as both a method of coping for the health assistant and as a way of giving hope to the patient' (Loiselle & Sterling 2012, p. 253). In societies where interdependence and collectivist approaches to decision-making are the norm, prognostic discussions require careful negotiation of individual and family wishes as to whether realism or hope will add to a better quality of life for the patient.

Hirai et al. (2006) hypothesised that because of differences in cultural backgrounds, especially the involvement of the family in making decisions related to individual members, Japanese concepts of a good death will be different from those in Western societies. Although exploratory in nature, the study by Hirai et al. (2006) found that the top attribute of a 'good death' is freedom from physical and psychological pain, followed by having a good family relationship, dying at one's favourite place or environment, and having a good relationship with medical staff. Other attributes found in a non-Western concept of a good death—such as maintaining hope, having a fighting spirit, maintaining a sense of control, maintaining dignity, and being prepared for death—were also identified. Since Japanese families may have higher cohesiveness and more control over decisions about care than Western families, autonomy and maintaining control may thus be perceived as less important by the patients themselves (Slingsby 2004). It is also interesting to note that the least indicated item in the study was 'having faith'. Japanese religions do not emphasise 'faith' with being in a protective relationship with a higher being or god compared to other non-Western religions such as Hinduism and Islam.

Zen Buddhism and the Shinto Indigenous religion of Japan have coexisted since Shintoism became the state religion from the Meiji period. Zen Buddhism is about 'coming face-to-face with yourself, in a very direct and intimate way' (O'Brien 2012), emphasising meditative quietness and inner peace rather than a dependent relationship with a higher force. Shintoism has no absolute dogma about right or wrong and believes that nobody is perfect. It is an optimistic and proactive religion with the belief that humans are fundamentally good and that evil is caused by evil spirits. Wellbeing is sought through keeping evil spirits away with appropriate rituals at the Shinto shrines or a home altar. Wedding ceremonies are generally held in Shinto style but since death is perceived as a source of evil and impurity, funerals are generally Buddhist style and there are few Shinto cemeteries in Japan (japan-guide.com 2012). Therefore, depending on the beliefs rooted in a person's spirituality within the cultural paradigm of the event, the behavioural responses to end-of-life issues related to what is a good death may differ among individuals and their families. While awareness of cultural elements is important in deciding the nature of care and pre- and post-death behavioural norms, professional discretion and attention to individual differences are still very important.

On another front, Jalland (2002), in a social and historical review of Australian ways of death from 1840 to 1918, concluded that death in Australia has always been a diverse and individual experience with no single model being the most appropriate. The Christian way of death declined rapidly in the colony, mainly due to a lack of clergy in the early days, and traditions quickly waned. In contrast, experiences of death and Australian bush burials in rural areas adapted by early immigrants are more enduring. Unaffected by British traditions, the bush culture of death was drawn from the land, personal experiences and responses to the unique environment in Australia. According to Jalland (2002, p. 5), the bushman's view of death played a significant role in the development of a distinctively Australian secular way of death that had been transmitted into the 20th century. A typical characteristic was a stoical acceptance that death was inevitable and to be met without fuss. Death was not seen as anything other than the will of God until the later part of the 20th century. With the development of medical science and the possibility of prolonging life, death became increasingly seen as a medical failure. According to a study of cancer patients in their final year of life in Australia (Kellehear 1990), a good death involved having a good social life, the creation of openness, social adjustment to and personal preparation for death and final farewells.

In contrast, the Aboriginal culture of death over 40 000 years is more complex and communal. Death weakens the social fabric of the community and ceremonies and rituals are crucial in helping survivors express their sorrow and reorient towards the future. Beliefs about the after-life are varied but generally the concept of eternal dreaming is fundamental to the Aboriginal view of the world and a person's relationship to their environment, and is reflected in the concern for the performance of ceremonies and rituals in the process of dying and death. Responses to death and dying are social and spiritual in nature, concerned with the here and now and the future.

Dying as a spiritual process

One aspect of a good death that Western literature does not emphasise is the process of dying free from pain as a spiritual process that is not just medical in nature. In many non-Western societies, understanding and coping with suffering and pain lie in the tension between the body and soul and the impact of spiritual beliefs on present behaviours. For instance, in India, embodied in Hinduism is the concept of karma—the belief that behaviours in past lives have an impact on present lives—which has remained strong in spite of the diversity of religions and subcultures. Further suffering may be necessary to clear off the negative karma accumulated over many lifetimes (Loiselle & Sterling 2012, p. 251). Similar beliefs are found in Taoism (retribution) and Buddhism (karma and rebirth). Mindfulness of care providers to the notion of pain relief at the end of life from the medical, individual and collective perspective, and the integration of personal and collective experiences of care in the dying process is crucial (Fong 2009).

The Chinese are said to have had the most successful and continuous culture and traditions over four millennia. Regardless of where Chinese people are in the world, philosophies and beliefs embedded in ancestor worship, Taoism, Confucianism, Buddhism and traditional Chinese medicine have influenced how they live. A synthesis of these philosophies and beliefs becomes the bedrock for a particular definition of death and dying. For example, a study among Chinese-Australians (Yeo et al. 2005) suggested that the respondents used mainly supernatural explanations for the cause of cancer such as retribution (Taoist philosophy), misfortune, bad luck and destiny. For non-believers these are perceived as mere superstitions.

In Singapore, a predominantly Chinese society, 33.3 per cent of the population professes to be Buddhist and 10.9 per cent followers of Taoism (Ministry of Community Development, Youth and Sports 2011). Preparation for death and dying is slowly gaining acceptance through formal exposition of the subject in Buddhist institutions and temples. Venerable Sangye Khadro (2010) prefaced her lecture and book *Preparation for Death and Helping the Dying* by defining two major problems that people in general have about the issue of death and dying. One is the belief that death is a fearful and horrible experience and the other is a flippant attitude that ignores the reality and significance of the death and dying experience. Both these attitudes can lead to neglecting attention to end-of-life issues that can help decrease fear and produce a sense of peace when the event appears.

A study of healthy Chinese individuals aged 65 years and over in Singapore showed that older people do have thoughts about a good death, and a quick, pain-free and natural death is still generally considered the ideal (Chan & Yau 2009, p. 232). Quoting from the authors' respondents, we can also see an association between faith and the fulfilment of the ideal:

> I always thank God that I'm able to walk. I just pray to God that I don't want to be paralyzed. Pain is quite a terrible thing [that] human beings cannot bear. You have no escape. It's so unbearable that you just don't know what to do.
>
> Mrs B

> I pray to Buddha not to let me be sick or lose my ability to walk [I want to] die in an easy way, like in my sleep.
>
> Mrs G

In response to questions on a good death and dying experience, Venerable Sangye Khadro (2010) taught that there are four essential tasks in living and dying that can assist in achieving this goal. One is to understand and transform from believing that suffering is something that can be avoided to accepting that problems and painful experiences are an inevitable part of life and therefore learn to cope with them. Second is to maintain healing and positive relationships with people, with forgiveness meditation as one method of achieving this state of mind. Third is associated with preparing spiritually for death, emphasised in all religious traditions, so that it becomes a reflexive response in every situation in life, including experiences of suffering in the dying process. Last is finding meaning in life, which becomes more important as one becomes less capable and closer to death and has to depend on others more and more.

'Painful and frightening experiences that occur at the time of death and afterwards are the results of negative actions, or karma' according to Venerable Sangye Khadro (2010, p. 13). Hence, to achieve nirvana, the freedom from the curses of rebirth to this earth, a person's thoughts during their last moments, whether good or evil, will influence their rebirth and affect the journey towards nirvana, the complete freedom from the cycle of life and death. Therefore, among the Chinese–Buddhists, at the point of death it is important for carers to focus on the patient's state of mind and help the dying to have positive thoughts. Reciting the *sutra* (Buddhist religious texts) for example, is said to help generate peace of mind and facilitate the transition positively to the next cycle of life towards nirvana (Hsu, O'Connor & Lee 2009, p. 163).

In addition, the Tibetan tradition of Buddhism teaches that there are eight stages in the process of dying. Care professionals are generally cognisant of the first four stages of physical weakening that culminate in the declaration of clinical death, when the breath stops and there is no movement in the brain or circulatory system. However, according to Buddhism, death has not yet taken place because consciousness is still in the body. Consciousness must fully dissipate before real death occurs. How long these final stages take is believed to depend on the preparation of the deceased. Thus, the body cannot be moved immediately after clinical death nor crying and negative distractive words be expressed in front of the body to enable the person to leave this world in peace. The best practice therefore is to leave the body without interference for several hours, or even days, when possible to enable the final stages of death to be fully completed. Such beliefs continue even among those who have migrated to a non–Chinese society, causing conflict, as expressed in the following quote:

> My father told me that when he died I should wait for eight hours before contacting authorities. The ambulance officer told me I could keep my father at home for about two hours. I felt guilty about not being able to implement my father's last wish (Campbell, Moore & Small 2000, p. 68).

Given the structure of hospitals and nursing homes in urban settings, concerns have been expressed about the lack of space for a family to stay with a dying patient, especially to be there at the point of death (Munn & Zimmerman 2006; Wilson & Daley 1999). Privacy for bereaved families to grieve after death and the discreet removal of the deceased from the building (Komaromy, Sidell & Katz 2000; Moss, Braunschweig & Rubinstein 2002) are also generally lacking. Should care facilities in future be constructed in a more culturally accommodating manner and not just meet the needs for medical care?

In a modern hospital setting, leaving the body for a few hours in the ward may not be possible but in Taiwan, for example, hospitals providing palliative care services have a special room in the hospital as a quiet place for the body where close relatives can commune and say prayers after clinical death had been declared. Dying at home may therefore have a special cultural meaning for Chinese patients and their families (Hsu, O'Connor & Lee 2009). The fear of being a 'burden' to children may affect articulation of the parents' wishes, but the children's death preparation for parents and often elaborate funeral arrangements resonates with the concept of filial piety among the Chinese. In Singapore, it is considered appropriate and filial for the family to hold a wake for several days at which priests are engaged to chant or perform ceremonies involving immediate family members that will help the deceased to transit well into the next life (Tong 2004).

The question therefore remains as to whether modern care systems can cater to the needs arising from varying cultural views of death and dying in addition to the needs of medical care. For example, should a mortuary be just a place for keeping the body until it is ready for burial? Could its use be also extended to providing a space for sending off the spirit and the soul in a culturally appropriate manner when required? Are there more creative uses of space to meet the needs of bereaved families at the point of death?

Role of complementary and alternative medicine

In the discussion on culture and end-of-life issues, the debate on the role of alternative complementary and spiritual medicine comes to the fore. Sparber et al. (2000) conducted a descriptive survey in the United States of 100 patients with HIV/ AIDS to identify and characterise patterns of use of complementary and alternative medicine (CAM). The findings showed that a variety of CAM therapies were used to cope with the disease and the challenges of treatment and clinical trials. In a similar study, Cho et al. (2006) investigated the prevalence and perceived benefit of CAM among a cohort of HIV-positive patients in the United States. CAM use was reported to be high, and more conventional CAM, such as exercise, diet and vitamins as well as prayer and meditation, were perceived to be effective for improving a general sense of wellbeing. In Singapore, it is reported that cancer patients often ask medical doctors whether the use of complementary treatments together with chemotherapy will compromise kidney and liver functions and also the effectiveness of CAM (Pang 2012). In an attempt to answer these questions, the National Cancer Centre in Singapore conducted a study of 357 patients with cancer, comprising both CAM users and non-CAM users. The findings showed that CAM use was associated with a reduction in hospitalisations and requirement for antibiotics and was not associated with significant changes in hepatic and renal function (Chan et al. 2012). However, due to the limited sample size and the lack of homogeneity in cancer types and stages of treatment in the sample, a better-designed prospective study to confirm these findings is needed.

India also has numerous systems of alternative medicine that are often linked with spirituality and these systems are reflected in pre-death and post-death ceremonies and rituals that may conflict with medical care. For example, customs and rituals for a dying person are reported to include putting the person on the ground and not the bed, pouring holy water into the person's mouth and chanting hymns. Such practices often take precedence and overlook the risk of aspiration and interference with respiratory efforts made for the person (Chaturvedi 2012). Among the culture-based healing traditions in Hawaii, for example, *lomilomi* or therapeutic massage is used by patients of all ethno-cultural backgrounds to manage distressful symptoms related to medical treatment (Bushnell 1993, cited in Anngela-Cole, Ka'opua & Yim 2011).

Conclusion

Implications for advance care planning and palliative care

Those engaged in palliative and end-of-life care perceive culture as having two dimensions (Clark 2012). One dimension consists of beliefs, values, behaviours and inclinations that exist among groups of people. The other aspect involves a material dimension found in objects, artefacts and practical inventions; for example, sprinkling 'holy' water over a dying person. In addition, in every end-of-life care situation, there is the interface between the culture of the patient and families comprising mainly lay knowledge and the culture of the professional care systems based mainly on knowledge synthesised from disparate sources of evidence (Green 1999). Culture, therefore, has to be addressed from these different perspectives. Is there really a universal concept of a good death in end-of life care? Studies have so far shown that end-of-life issues may be common but the response to these issues is not a case of one size fits all. Differences exist across cultures and there may even be diversity within a culture. The possible conclusion at this point may be that reflected by Venerable Sangye Khadro (2010), which is to encourage whatever teachings and practices the patients are familiar and comfortable with in order to provide confidence and hope.

Students as well as practitioners were reported to have acquired cultural competency through both formal (education and training) and informal (observations of everyday life) means in a study by Kwong (2009). As such, it seems essential that students and junior social workers be engaged in some formal supervision for culturally relevant practice in working with issues that involve a high level of cultural sensitivity. In the same study, Kwong (2009) postulated that developing cultural competency is an integrative process that includes firstly being able to engage service users in a safe and trusting environment followed by clinical and cultural assessment that involves using client knowledge, cultural knowledge and clinical knowledge to assess needs or problems to be managed. Problem conceptualisation arises from the clinical–cultural assessment and is the basis for a culturally sensitive direction for intervention. In social work supervision of practitioners working with end-of-life issues, sensitivity to the cultural dynamics in communication and belief in the interface between the healthcare provider, the patient and the family is essential.

Shouldn't more be done, therefore, to ensure that every social work professional be given an opportunity for formal training and supervision in culturally competent practice, especially in the areas of palliative care and end-of-life issues?

REFLECTIVE QUESTIONS

1   How complementary are religious ethics and medical ethics?
2   How useful are complementary or alternative cures in the face of medical futility?
3   To what extent do social factors affect decisions about the process of care for the dying and the death event; for example, availability of social support network, access to societal resources, age and gender issues?
4   In the medicalisation of death and dying, how would you manage the interface of the service users' spiritual and philosophical worldviews and those of the professional caregivers in planning and receiving care?

FURTHER READING

Altilio, T & Otis-Green, S 2011, *Oxford Textbook of Palliative Social Work*, Oxford University Press, Oxford.

Chan, CLW & Chow, AYM (eds) 2006, *Death, Dying and Bereavement: A Hong Kong Chinese Experience*, Hong Kong University Press, Hong Kong.

Fielding, R & Chan, CLW 2000, *Psychosocial Oncology and Palliative Care in Hong Kong—The First Decade*, Hong Kong University Press, Hong Kong.

Kellehear, A 2000, *Death and Dying in Australia*, Oxford University Press, South Melbourne.

Knapp, C & Thompson, L 2012, 'Factors associated with perceived barriers to pediatric palliative care: a survey of pediatricians in Florida and California', *Palliative Medicine*, vol. 26, no. 3, pp. 268–74.

REFERENCES

Altilio, T & Otis-Green, S 2011, *Oxford Textbook of Palliative Care*, Oxford University Press, Oxford.

Anngela-Cole, L, Ka'opua, LS & Yim, Y 2011, 'Palliative care, culture, and the Pacific Basin', in T Altilio and S Oyis-Green, *Oxford Textbook of Palliative Care*, Oxford University Press, Oxford.

Bosma, H, Apland, L & Kazanjian, A 2010, 'Cultural conceptualizations of hospice palliative care: more similarities than differences', *Palliative Medicine*, vol. 24, no. 5, pp. 510–22.

Bronfenbrenner, U 1979, *The Ecology of Human Development: Experiments by Nature and Design*, Harvard University Press, Cambridge, MA.

Campbell, D, Moore, G & Small, D 2000, 'Death and Australian cultural diversity', in A Kellehear (ed.), *Death and Dying in Australia*, Oxford University Press, South Melbourne.

Cashwell, CS & Young, JS 2005, 'Integrating spirituality and religion into counseling: an introduction', in CS Cashwell & JS Young (eds), *Integrating Spirituality and Religion into Counseling: A Guide to Competent Practice*, American Counseling Association, Alexandria, VA.

Chan, A, Tan, HL, Ching, TH & Tan, HC 2012, 'Clinical outcomes for cancer patients using complementary and alternative medicine', *Alternative Therapies in Health and Medicine*, vol. 18, no. 1, pp. 12–17.

Chan, CKL & Yau, MK 2009, 'Death preparation among the ethnic Chinese well-elderly in Singapore: an exploratory study', *Omega*, vol. 60, no. 3, pp. 225–39.

Chaturvedi, SK 2012, 'Ethical dilemmas in palliative care in traditional developing societies, with special reference to the Indian setting', *Journal of Medical Ethics*, vol. 34, no. 8, pp. 611–15.

Cho, M, Ye, X, Dobs, A & Confrancesco, J Jr 2006, 'Prevalence of complementary and alternative medicine use among HIV patients for perceived lipodystrophy', *Journal of Alternative and Complementary Medicine*, vol. 12, no. 5, pp. 475–82.

Clark, D 2002, 'Between hope and acceptance: the medicalisation of dying', *British Medical Journal*, vol. 324, no. 7342, pp. 905–7.

Clark, D 2012, 'Cultural considerations in planning palliative and end of life care', *Palliative Medicine*, vol. 26, no. 3, pp. 195–6.

Fong, XK 2009, 'How perceptions about medically diagnosed terminally-ill cancer patients and their palliative care social workers believe is a good death influence decisions in palliative care', thesis, National University of Singapore.

Frankl, VE 1974, *Man's Search for Meaning: An Introduction to Logotherapy*, Better Yourself Books, Allahabad Saint Paul Society, Allahabad.

Frankl, VE 1985, *Man's Search for Meaning*, Washington Square Press, New York.

Frame, MW 2003, *Integrating Religion and Spirituality into Counseling: A Comprehensive Approach*, Thomson Brooks/Cole, Pacific Grove, CA.

Germain, C 1991, *Human Behavior in the Social Environment: An Ecological View*, Columbia University Press, New York.

Gold, JM 2010, *Counseling and Spirituality: Integrating Spiritual and Clinical Orientations*, Pearson Education, New Jersey.

Goldsteen, M, Houtepen, R, Proot, IM, Abu-Saad, HH, Spreeuwenberg, C & Widdershoven, G 2006, 'What is a good death? Terminally ill patients dealing with normative expectations around death and dying', *Patient Education and Counseling*, vol. 64, no. 1, pp. 378–86.

Gott, M, Seymour, J, Bellamy, G, Clark, D & Ahmedzai, S 2004, 'Older people's views about home as a place of care at the end of life', *Palliative Medicine*, vol. 18, no. 15, pp. 460–7.

Gott, M, Small, N, Barnes, S, Payne, S, Parker, C, Seamark, D, Gariballa, S 2008, 'Older people's views of a good death in heart failure: implications for palliative care provision', *Social Science and Medicine*, vol. 67, no. 7, pp. 1113–21.

Green, JW 1999, *Culture Awareness in the Human Service: A Multi-ethnic Approach*, 3rd edn, Allyn & Bacon, Boston, MA.

Haw, GW & Hughes, PW (eds) 1998, *Education for the 21st Century in the Asia-Pacific Region: Report of the Melbourne UNESCO Conference*, Australian National Commission for UNESCO, Canberra, Australia.

Hirai, K, Mayashita, M, Morita, T, Sanjo, M & Uchitomi, Y 2006), 'Good death in Japanese cancer care: a qualitative study', *Journal of Pain and Symptom Management*, vol. 31, no. 2, pp. 140–7.

Hodges, S 2002, 'Mental health, depression and dimensions of spirituality and religion', *Journal of Adult Development*, vol. 9, no. 2, pp. 109–15.

Hsu, CY, O'Connor, M & Lee, S 2009, 'Understanding of death and dying for people of Chinese origin', *Death Studies*, vol. 33, no. 2, pp. 153–74.

Kwong, MH 2009, 'Applying cultural competence in clinical practice: findings from multicultural experts' experience', *Journal of Ethnic and Cultural Diversity in Social Work*, vol. 18, no. 1/2, pp. 146–65.

Innes, S & Payne, S 2009, 'Advanced cancer patients' prognostic information preferences: a review', *Palliative Medicine*, vol. 23, no. 1, pp. 29–39.

Jalland, P 2002, *Australian Ways of Death: A Social and Cultural History, 1840–1918* eBook), American Council of Learned Societies and Oxford University Press, Melbourne, New York.

Japan-guide.com 2008, 'Shinto', viewed 17 April 2013, <www.japan-guide.com/e/e2056. html>.

Kellehear, A 1990, *Dying of Cancer: The Final Year of Life*, Harwood, Melbourne.

Komaromy, C, Sidell, M & Katz, JT 2000, 'The quality of terminal care in residential and nursing homes', *International Journal of Palliative Nursing*, vol. 6, no. 4, pp. 192–200.

Loiselle, CG & Sterling, MM 2012, 'Views on death and dying among health care workers in an Indian cancer care hospice: balancing individual and collective perspective', *Palliative Medicine*, vol. 26, no. 3, pp. 250–6.

Ministry of Community Development, Youth and Sports 2011, *Singapore Social Statistics in Brief*, Strategic Planning, Research and Development Division, Singapore.

Moss, M, Braunschweig, H & Rubinstein, R 2002, 'Terminal care for nursing residents with dementia', *Alzheimer's Care Quarterly*, vol. 3, no. 3, pp. 233–46.

Munn, J & Zimmerman, S 2006, 'A good death for residents of long-term care: family members speak', *Journal of Social Work in End-of-Life Palliative Care*, vol. 2, no. 3, pp. 45–59.

O'Brien, B 2012, 'Zen 101: Zazen and Zenspeak', About.com Guide, viewed 17 April 2013, <http://buddhism.about.com/od/chanandzenbuddhism/a/zen101_2.htm>.

Pang, M 2012, 'Alternative medicine may help cancer patients', *The Straits Times*, 14 June, Home p. B1.

Rowlands, J 2008, 'How does the environment impact on the quality of life of advanced cancer patients? A qualitative study with implications for ward design', *Palliative Medicine*, vol. 22, no. 6, pp. 768–74.

Sangye Khadro 2010, *Preparation for Death and Helping the Dying*, 3rd edn, Kong Meng San Phor Kark See Monastery, Singapore.

Seale, C 1998, 'Theories and studying the care of dying people', *British Medical Journal*, vol. 317, no. 7171, pp. 1518–20.

Slingsby, BT 2004, 'Decision-making models in Japanese psychiatry: transitions from passive to active patterns', *Social Science and Medicine*, vol. 59, no. 1, pp. 83–91.

Sparber, A, Wootton, JC, Bauer, L, Curt, G, Eisenberg, D, Levin, T & Steinberg, SM 2000, 'Use of complementary medicine by adult patients participating in HIV/AIDS clinical trials', *Journal of Alternative and Complementary Medicine*, vol. 6, no. 5, pp. 415–22.

Tong, CK 2004, *Chinese Death Rituals in Singapore*, RoutledgeCurzon, London.

Walters, G 2004, 'Is there such a thing as a good death?', *Palliative Medicine*, vol. 18, no. 5, pp. 404–8.

Wilson, SA & Daley, BJ 1999, 'Family perspectives on dying in long-term care settings', *Journal of Gerontological Nursing*, vol. 25, no. 11, pp. 19–25.

World Health Organization 2012, '10 Facts on Ageing and the Life Course', viewed 17 April 2013, <www.who.int/features/factfiles/ageing/en>.

Yeo, SS, Meiser, B, Barlow-Stewart, K, Goldstein, D, Tucker, K & Eisenbruch, M 2005, 'Understanding community beliefs of Chinese-Australians about cancer: initial insights using an ethnographic approach', *Psycho-Oncology*, vol. 14, no. 3, pp. 174–86.

12

International adoption: policy and practice issues

Jayashree Mohanty

Introduction

International adoption, also referred to as intercountry or transnational adoption, is no longer an anomaly and has touched many families around the world. Around 29 000 children are placed for international adoption every year (Selman 2012), although the number has declined significantly in recent years. While the major sending countries for international adoption are China, Russia, Guatemala, Ethiopia, Haiti, South Korea, Colombia, Ukraine and Vietnam, the major receiving countries are the United States, France, Italy, Spain, Canada, the Netherlands and Sweden. International adoption has received both positive and negative reactions from the public. Opponents often argue that it presents risks. They claim that internationally adopted children will be deprived of the opportunity to know and have access to their birth families and their racial, ethnic, cultural and national groups of origin (Hollingsworth 2003). Lack of knowledge and contact with racial and ethnic backgrounds may create feelings of marginality and negatively affect the children's psychosocial adjustment (Mohanty & Newhill 2011). The practice of international adoption is also perceived as a lucrative and largely unregulated business (Smolin 2010). Other issues associated with international adoptions are inadequate information about the children's socio-familial backgrounds, and unreliable medical and developmental histories.

This chapter describes some of the practice challenges and the roles of social workers in both sending and receiving countries in protecting the best interests of internationally adopted children. For practitioners working in this area, knowledge of policy and practice issues is crucial when providing support to the adoption triangle.

Factors that contribute to international adoption

Numerous factors contribute to the placement and adoption of children internationally. The factors for sending countries can include gender and cultural bias, poverty, political upheaval, civil war, natural disasters and domestic policies in the sending countries. Political upheaval in Romania during 1989 when the president, Nicolae Ceaușescu, was deposed and executed, followed by media coverage of the 100 000 children in state orphanages, boosted the availability of children for adoption internationally. In South Korea, strong emphasis on family structure is a barrier for illegitimate or mixed-race children to be accepted by society. For example, the birth of a child is registered in the child's father's name (Wilkinson 1995) and, in situations where the mother has never married or is divorced, the child becomes 'a legal and social nonentity' (Wilkinson 1995, p. 174). China's one-child policy, which began in 1979 to curtail excessive population growth, meant that children, mostly girls, became available for international adoption (Hollingsworth 2003). The general preference for male children in countries such as China and India has also contributed to the availability of girls for international adoption. Family poverty in developing countries is another reason for the placement of children internationally. Many children come from countries with higher infant mortality rate and lower per capita gross national product (GNP) than that of receiving countries (Selman 2002).

For receiving countries, the factors can include decline in the number of healthy infants available domestically for adoption, many domestic children available for adoption being older and often with siblings, concerns about the lingering effects on children of state care, and emphases on open adoption (when the biological and adoptive families have access to varying degrees of information and contact before and/or after the placement of the child; Berry 1993). The shorter period required to adopt internationally, confidential adoption and the opportunity to adopt same-race children are other factors that contribute to international adoption (Hollingsworth 2003). Older, single and/or gay and lesbian prospective parents who have been discriminated against by birth mothers in domestic adoption often prefer international adoption. Further, African-American social workers' statements against interracial placement within the United States have deterred many parents from adopting domestically. In 1972, the National Association of Black Social Workers (NABSW) strongly advocated same-race adoptions for African-American children. The main concern was that white parents may not be able to provide black children with the skills they need to survive in a race-conscious society (Silverman 1993).

International adoption policy

The Hague Convention on the Protection of Children and Co-operation in Respect to Intercountry Adoption in 1993 endorsed international adoption as a practice. The Convention recognised that a child, for the full and harmonious development of their personality, should grow up in a family environment in an atmosphere of happiness, love and understanding. The third provision of the preamble suggests that to provide a child with a permanent family, international adoption should be placed ahead of foster or institutional care in the child's country of origin. Chapter 11 of the

Convention (Articles 4–5) delineates the requirements for intercountry adoptions. An adoption can only take place if the competent authorities of the country of origin determine that the child is adoptable, that an international adoption is in the child's best interests, and if the competent authorities of the receiving country have determined that the prospective adoptive parents are eligible and suitable to adopt. So far 89 countries have ratified the Convention. The Hague Convention provides a legal framework for the protection of children as well as the interests of their birth parents and their adoptive parents. The adoption process differs depending on whether the adoption occurs within and from convention or non-convention countries. In general, prospective adoptive parents have more protection when adopting from convention countries. Accredited agencies in convention countries assure prospective adoptive parents that they have knowledge of the special issues and expertise needed to conduct intercountry adoptions competently.

Policy and practice issues in international adoption

In this section, discussion centres on some key issues associated with international adoption, such as the wellbeing of older children, rights of birth mothers and the importance of ethnic and racial socialisation opportunities for internationally adopted children. The role of sending and receiving countries involved in international adoptions is also highlighted. Some of the comments and suggestions made here might not apply to all sending and receiving countries. Although the issues discussed may be relevant to domestic transcultural and transracial adoption, the focus is on international adoptions that are often transracial and/or transcultural.

Older children and international adoption

The characteristics of children available for international adoption have changed in recent years. Such children used to be mostly infants, girls, and from Asian countries (Selman 2012; United Nations 2009). In recent years, growing numbers of older and special needs children have been placed for international adoption. The reasons for such change may be attributed to improved child welfare systems in countries such as China and South Korea, increased interest in domestic adoptions in sending countries and dwindling fertility rates in South Korea (Selman 2009). Given this new mix of children, both receiving and originating countries need to play a greater role in protecting the best interests of these children.

For international adoptees, the risk factors for later adjustment include older age at adoption and the experiences of institutionalisation before adoption. Studies have shown that children who are adopted at a later age are more vulnerable to psychological maladjustment (Hjern, Lindblad & Vinnerljung 2001; Verhulst, Althaus & Versluis-Den Bieman 1990). These children are more likely to demonstrate developmental delays (O'Connor et al. 2000). With later age at placement, there is concern that children are more likely to have spent time in institutional care or orphanages, and institutional experience has been associated with increased developmental and behavioural challenges (Ryan & Groza 2004). Most sending countries have policies that encourage international adoption as an alternative to institutional care for older children. However, it is not clear that international adoption serves the best interests of these children.

What alternative placement options are available for older children who need families in the country of origin? If intercountry adoption is indeed the best solution for children in institutional care, then the eligibility criteria for adopting older children and the support systems for adoptive parents need to be assessed. Agencies in receiving countries must guarantee pre-adoption and post-adoption services to the adoptive parents and post-adoption services to older adoptees if these placements are to continue. Pre-adoption services can include preparing adoptive parents for the challenges posed by children raised in institutions, assessing adoptive parents' motivation to adopt, and mobilising resources within the community and family networks. Parents who understand and deal with the challenges of raising older children may provide nurturing and loving family environments in which those children can grow and develop competently and overcome complex emotional and developmental needs (Palacios et al. 2009). In fact, a growing body of evidence suggests that the parent–child relationship is a more significant risk factor for increased behavioural problems than a history of institutionalisation (Groza, Ryan & Cash 2003; Versluis-den Bieman & Verhulst 1995).

Originating countries may also consider providing interventions to help socialise older children into family living. One such intervention may be short-term foster care in the state of origin once children are eligible for international adoption. This short-term care would allow children to be familiar with staying in home care and improve their family relationships and connectedness. While fostering can be a useful intermediate phase, social workers need to be cautious about the attachment and separation issues related to moving children. For agencies and social workers in sending countries, there may be challenges in implementing this intervention. In some sending countries, fostering may not be a preferred care for children deprived of family environment. For others, recruiting foster families who can provide a safe and supportive home for these children and the lack of resources available to adoption placement agencies are the real challenges. In order to increase the adoption success for older children, it is important that the central authority of the sending countries ensure that the older children living in institutions are socialised into family care before they are adopted internationally. Another intervention that social workers in sending countries could use would be to start preparing a 'lifebook' as soon as the child enters the institution. This lifebook could document the caretakers' experience in raising the child, and provide photos taken with caretakers, photos taken at orphanages, information about childhood taken during relinquishment of the child, and if the child was abandoned then information about how the child was found. This information may help adoptees in resolving identity issues and to feel whole.

Another issue relates to how soon children can be made available for international adoption. Many sending countries have stringent policies that ultimately result in children staying in institutions for long periods before they are declared adoptable through intercountry adoption. Different countries apply a reconsideration period, during which biological parents can consider their decision to relinquish the child for adoption, differently. In the case of India, the reconsideration period is two months (Central Adoption Resource Authority 2004). In addition, Indian adoption agencies are also required to provide evidence that they have tried to find suitable Indian parent(s). In such cases, understanding domestic adoption situations in sending countries, such as by gaining information about who adopts and the characteristics of children that domestic parents prefer, may be helpful in developing policies that allow children to be available for international adoption in a timely manner that meets their needs.

Rights of birth parents in international adoption

Intercountry adoption allows adoptive children the immediate benefits of a family, but for birth families adoption is a loss. Many birth families relinquish their children under severe economic, social and cultural conditions. Women in poor countries, particularly single mothers, have fewer options in finding alternative care for children they are unable to care for and most children are relinquished to adoption by single mothers. There have been instances where financial advantage was used to induce impoverished birth parents to surrender their children. Often, the birth parents are not involved in the child's placement and are never even asked about their wishes for the child. In some cases, the birth parents do not know whether their child has been placed out of the country. The question for us to consider is, do the birth parents have the right to choose the type of adoption they want? Although the emphasis in domestic adoptions in many Western countries is on the rights of birth parents, birth families have few rights in international adoptions.

One of the best practices in international adoption is to provide counselling services to birth parents during the adoption process. Adoption laws in most sending countries (for example, India) mandate counselling services to birth mothers during relinquishment; however, there is no standard procedure for these services. Further, the services are not always provided by professional counsellors, and in some cases where services are provided, it is hoped that the birth mothers will relinquish their children. Therefore, it is important to develop a step-by-step procedure for pre-relinquishment counselling, including recording the outcome of each counselling session. Questions to consider should include the following:

- How many pre-relinquishment counselling sessions should be provided to birth parents?
- Should the services be provided by independent professional counsellors?
- Are birth parents well informed about the consequences of their relinquishment?

Documented evidence of pre-relinquishment counselling should serve as part of the informed consent submitted when declaring the child available for adoption. This procedure will help the birth parents to feel that they have thoroughly explored all options before making adoption plans. It may also help to curb fraudulent practices in international adoption, such as coercing or forcing birth parents to relinquish their children. When biological parents choose to keep their children, support should be provided in the form of sponsorship for the children's education and health care. Above all, when addressing birth parents' rights in adoption, originating countries need to reduce the social stigma attached to illegitimacy or single motherhood. With increasing awareness there will be fewer abandoned children, and parents who are not able to care for their children will be able to make informed decisions about the best interests of those children.

Very little is known about birth parents' experiences after relinquishment and the care they wish for their child. It is important that the voices of birth parents in originating countries be heard in the adoption community, and social workers can play an important role in conducting this practice-based research. Further, there have been growing concerns of abusive practices in international adoption, specifically obtaining children illicitly. To ensure that intercountry adoption adheres to the principles of the Hague Convention, originating countries also need to develop protective measures even before the child enters the adoption process.

In addition, many parents still accept a child or children based on minimal, inaccurate or incomplete information about who they are adopting. Adoptive families are built on trust and faith in the other people involved in the process, all of whom are expected to have the welfare and safety of the child at heart. The joy of adopting a child is invariably mixed with the sadness of the life-changing decisions made by biological parents, social workers, judges, government officials and sometimes even the child. Adoptive families have to put their trust in strangers and have faith that the unknown details about their child's birth or medical history will not hurt them. And when a child's health is challenged, parents would do anything to try to help them. However, this is sometimes more difficult for adoptive families than for biological families. Pre-relinquishment counselling may also help in generating viable information about family medical histories. Some birth mothers might not be aware of their own, their spouse's or partner's or their extended family's medical history. Social workers providing pre-relinquishment counselling should make concentrated efforts to acquire information about interests, skills and medical histories that might ultimately help to meet the unique needs of internationally adopted children.

The following case study highlights the importance of family medical histories in international adoption.

The importance of family medical history in adoption is well recognised. In most domestic adoptions in Western countries, medical records of the child and the social history of the birth parents pertaining to the child are available to prospective adoptive parents. However, in international adoption, such information is not available. Further,

CASE STUDY 12.1

IMPORTANCE OF FAMILY MEDICAL HISTORIES

Nandita was adopted when she was four years old from India by a white Caucasian family in the United States. She was a happy, healthy child, friendly and outgoing, and a favourite at the small orphanage where she had lived since shortly after her birth. Her sweet smile could brighten a room and warm hearts. She was small but healthy. Her adoptive parents learned as much as they could about her life before they left to start their lives together in the United States. Nandita transitioned to day care about a month after arriving home. The program was designed for children who were learning English as a second language (English Language Learners, or ELL), and she loved the adventures of school and spending time with other children.

Initially, Nandita thrived in the program. She was happy and her English improved, but after a year, her teachers said that they had more trouble understanding her than the other ELL students in her class. They identified speech delays, so Nandita started speech therapy. During the next few years, she had trouble with reading, writing and learning that was not related to her ELL status. She was approved for special education classes and occupational therapy. Nandita loved school, despite the challenges.

During this time, Nandita developed a puzzling set of medical problems, but getting medical help was frustrating. She saw an array of doctors and specialists, who treated her for minor problems, but medical tests for other conditions were negative. Something was wrong, but they couldn't figure it out. Finally, Nandita saw a neurologist, who found that she had mild hypotonia and a mild neuromuscular disorder. He ruled out fetal alcohol syndrome and identified prematurity as the most likely cause. He advised her parents to continue special education classes and therapy (speech and occupational) to address her delays.

Things went well for several years. Over time, the special education services at school helped Nandita learn, but she didn't catch up with her peers. She continued to struggle with reading, writing and maths, but she still loved school. By her early teens, her muscle symptoms became worse. The doctors made many attempts to treat her pain, but nothing worked. They desperately needed more information about Nandita's birth family, but that information was unavailable. Without that information, they couldn't make progress and finally had to give up.

certain diseases are endemic to a particular locality, region and people. Without this information, doctors face unique challenges in assessing and diagnosing a child's health conditions properly. In Nandita's case, having access to her family medical history might have made it possible for her doctors to diagnose and treat her disorder, which would make a major difference in her life. Since most of her family history is still a mystery, she will probably continue to struggle with unexplained pain and injuries for the rest of her life, with limited treatment options from her doctors.

For social workers, the question is how to collect this information creatively? How can you involve extended family members during this process? The challenge for social workers is that some of these children are abandoned and therefore no records are available and, in other cases, the birth parents might not be aware of the illnesses in their family or be unwilling to reveal such information to adoption workers. Some advocate introducing certain aspects of open adoptions in intercountry adoption, such as sharing information and/or developing contact between adoptive and biological parents after the placement of the child. Until now no standard of practice protocol has been developed in this regard.

Adoptive parents and the importance of providing opportunities for ethnic and racial socialisation

Ethnic and racial socialisation refers to the ways parents prepare their children to feel pride in their ethnic and racial identity, help them to succeed in the mainstream culture and prepare them to be aware of discrimination and prejudice (Boykin & Toms 1985). Research has generally shown that providing opportunities for ethnic and racial socialisation influences the adoptee's developmental and psychological wellbeing, including ethnic identity development and self-esteem (Basow et al. 2008; Evan B Donaldson Adoption Institute 2009; Mohanty, Koeske & Sales 2006; Yoon 2000). The Hague Convention emphasises connecting internationally adopted children to their birth cultures. Social work professionals encourage adoptive parents to socialise children to their ethnic cultures in the belief that children's knowledge about their ethnic and racial background will enhance their developmental and psychosocial adjustment. Hence, many adoptive parents actively look for opportunities for their children to participate in cultural activities. Although the attitudes of adoptive parents may differ according to the degree of importance they place on maintaining their children's ethnic culture, most adoptive parents socialise children to a range of cultural activities such as eating ethnic foods, watching videos, reading books, developing relationships with other children from their countries of origin, attending cultural camps and visiting their birth countries. By doing so, they assist their children in absorbing racial and ethnic origins into the process of developing their identities.

Most parents emphasise socialising their children to their culture of origin when they are young. Such efforts tend to decline when children reach pre-adolescence or adolescence, when parents discover that their adolescent children are unwilling to participate, even if they were willing to when they were younger. During adolescence, children need parental support in resolving the dual issues of their adoptive and ethnic heritage. Social workers should encourage parents to provide support that is developmentally appropriate. Such support could include connecting children to online support groups and encouraging them to maintain connections with children from other adoptive families or with children from their birth cultures via email, telephone or letters. Recent studies emphasise providing opportunities for racial socialisation (Mohanty & Newhill 2011). Preparing children to be aware of discrimination and prejudice may help adoptees take active stances toward prejudice and discrimination. Racial socialisation requires a certain level of awareness and knowledge about racial differences on the part of adoptive parents. Therefore, it is important that parents recognise that internationally adopted children who grow up in Western cultures are exposed to and internalise various biases and stereotypes toward other people who are different. Adoptive parents must openly explore their own biases and prejudices toward other racial and minority groups; this is important because parents inevitably transmit their own attitudes, values, ways and skills through the socialisation of their children.

Much attention has been paid to parental support for ethnic and racial socialisation when children are young. With the increasing number of older children available for international adoption, social workers have a greater responsibility of counselling parents about how to provide such socialisation support to older children and what socialisation efforts are effective in facilitating older children to adapt to their adoptive country while maintaining their ethnic culture. When internationally adopted children enter new countries, they leave behind familiar cultures, languages and communities, which could create stress for older children. In the early stages of their placement, such children may have ambivalent feelings towards their new families, environments and countries. Like any other new immigrant children, they may also struggle to adapt to their new countries without the support of familiar people and friends they had in their home countries. For parents, the challenge is not only how to maintain a child's ethnic culture, but also how to socialise the child to become competent in participating in the majority culture. Parents need to have patience and should be careful not to add more pressure to children, which might exacerbate their risk of psychological stress.

One suggestion is for parents to stay in touch with the social workers in placement agencies and encourage their children to speak to those social workers. This might help adoptees to transition from institutional to family care more easily. It is equally important that adoptive parents provide their children with opportunities to establish relationships with other adoptees from the same orphanage or who speak the same language. Older children should also be prepared for the move in the institution itself.

Telling children about the new countries, their cultures and traditions, watching videos and learning the language may help them to adapt to the new countries. For example, pre-existing knowledge about English language has been associated with more positive outcomes for immigrant children, including more positive education experiences (Rumbaut 1997). Policies need to be developed to provide these opportunities to older children in the placement agencies in sending countries for smooth transitions from institutional care to permanent homes. Social workers in sending countries play an important role in facilitating this transition. For many children, this is the first time they are experiencing a home environment, so they might not understand the norms, values and customs of the new family. Even if some children have experienced living in home care, they might still have difficulty adapting to their new family environments. As Palacios et al. (2009) suggest, social workers in receiving countries should provide services to help children during the first phases of their integration into new families and new countries rather than in the later stages of adoptive family life.

Finally, although Asian countries have traditionally been sending countries, low fertility and marriage rates in Singapore and Japan have resulted in these countries receiving children from other Asian countries. In contrast to those in Western countries, most international adoptions in Singapore are same-race adoptions. Most adoptive children come from countries such as China, Indonesia, India and Malaysia, reflecting the ethnic groups in Singapore. However, we have little information about how these children are faring in Singapore. What are the cultural needs of international adoptees who are racially similar to their adopted parents? When parents and children are racially similar and belong to the majority race, is it important to socialise international adoptees to their ethnic culture? In what ways do parents support their children in developing healthy identities, including adoptive and ethnic identities? Few studies have been conducted on the importance of the ethnic socialisation of same-race children in international adoption.

Scherman and Harre (2008) found that Eastern European children adopted into New Zealand homes were interested in their ethnic culture and that parental support for ethnic socialisation enhanced their development of bicultural identities and identification with both their birth culture and New Zealand culture. A growing body of evidence suggests the need for ethnic identification and cultural pride arises for individuals whose culture and identity are denigrated by the mainstream (Phinney 1991; Smith & Carlson 1997). Recent anecdotal evidence in Singapore suggests that there is prejudice against certain immigrant groups. For example, even though a child placed with Chinese Singaporean parents may be from the People's Republic of China (PRC), if society devalues individuals from the PRC, then the child might not feel comfortable identifying with their birth culture and could be subjected to bias and discrimination. Therefore, it is important that parents provide support for ethnic socialisation to help their children develop positive identities and self-esteem.

Providing opportunities for ethnic socialisation may validate children's feelings that their parents respect their countries of origin and care for their cultural needs.

Role of social workers in international adoption

The *Guide to Good Practice* (Hague Conference on Private International Law 2012) states that developing collaborative working relationships between social workers in sending and receiving countries will ensure that children placed internationally have secure and happy family lives. In practice, what mainly happens is that social workers in sending and receiving countries work independently, one side ensuring that the child is adoptable and the other side ensuring that the parents are eligible to adopt. This lack of collaborative partnership results in inaccurate and incomplete information about the child, incomplete family and medical histories, and a lack of confidence on the part of social workers in sending countries about the suitability of adoptive parents to raise the child. With the increasing number of older and special needs children available for international adoption, there is a bigger challenge for social workers to think about how and in what areas they can develop collaborative partnerships. For example, social workers in sending countries may reject home study reports based on the fact that parents have had mental illnesses or have gone through divorces, and so on. In that case, proper communication is important because it allows social workers in both countries to gain confidence in each other and resolve practice differences. There is also a need to train social workers in sending countries about adoption issues and what the best practice models are, and to create opportunities for social workers in both receiving and origin countries to share their practice expertise and knowledge in forums. Social workers need to share the responsibility for the placement of children and work collaboratively to serve the best interests of those children.

Conclusion

International adoption has specific risks and advantages for the adoptive triangle. For the biological parents, the risks seem to outweigh the advantages in that the biological mothers' rights are curtailed and there is little chance of eventually reuniting with the children they have relinquished. For the adoptee, international adoption may provide a better socioeconomic environment, but the different cultural environment may pose unique challenges to psychosocial development. For the adoptive parents, the challenge includes dealing with adoption-related issues including potential medical issues and connecting children to their birth cultures. Although international adoption is an immediate solution that may appear to be in the best interest of children, it should not be a long-term solution for the sending countries. Those countries need to develop better child protection measures to ensure that children are well cared for in their own environments.

REFLECTIVE QUESTIONS

1   What alternatives to international adoption could be used to place children who need a family within their country of origin?

2   Is it important for originating countries in Asia to ensure that children retain their cultural and ethnic identity? Explain your answer.

3   What aspects of open adoption can we introduce to intercountry adoption? What are the risks to and benefits for the adoption triangle?

4   Do you think that placing children in a cultural context similar to their own enhances their wellbeing? Explain your answer.

FURTHER READING

Hollingsworth, LD 2003, 'International adoption among families in the United States: considerations of social justice', *Social Work*, vol. 48, no. 2, pp. 209–17.

Lee, RM 2003, 'The transracial adoption paradox: history, research and counseling implications of cultural socialization', *The Counseling Psychologist*, vol. 31, no. 6, pp. 711–44.

Mohanty, J & Newhill, C 2008, 'A theoretical framework for understanding ethnic socialization among international adoptees', *Families in Society*, vol. 89, no. 4, pp. 543–50.

Selman, P 2009, 'The rise and fall of intercountry adoption in the 21st century', *International Social Work*, vol. 52, no. 5, pp. 575–94.

REFERENCES

Basow, SA, Lilley, E, Bookwala, J & McGillicuddy-DeLisi, A 2008, 'Identity development and psychological well-being in Korean-born adoptees in the U.S.', *American Journal of Orthopsychiatry*, vol. 78, no. 4, pp. 473–80.

Berry, M 1993, 'Risks and benefits of open adoption', *The Future of Children*, vol. 3, no. 1, pp. 125–38.

Boykin, AW & Toms, FD 1985, 'Black child socialization: a conceptual framework', in HP McAdoo and JL McAdoo (eds), *Black Children: Social, Educational, and Parental Environments*, Sage, Beverly Hills, CA, pp. 33–51.

Central Adoption Resource Authority 2004, 'Guidelines for in-country adoption 2004', Ministry of Women and Child Development, Government of India, viewed 17 April 2013, <www.adoptionindia.nic.in/guide_in_country.htm>.

Evan B Donaldson Adoption Institute 2009, *Beyond Culture Camp: Promoting Healthy Identity Formation in Adoption*, New York.

Groza, V, Ryan, SD & Cash, SJ 2003, 'Institutionalization, behavior and international adoption: Predictors of behavior problems', *Journal of Immigrant Health*, vol. 5, no. 1, pp. 5–17.

Hague Conference on Private International Law 2012, *Accreditation and Adoption Accredited Bodies: General Principles and Guide to Good Practice. Guide No 2 under the Hague Convention of 29 May 1993 on Protection of Children and Co-operation in Respect of Intercountry Adoption*, Family Law, Bristol.

Hollingsworth, LD 2003, 'International adoption among families in the United States: considerations of social justice', *Social Work*, vol. 48, no. 2, pp. 209–17.

Hjern, A, Lindblad, F & Vinnerljung, B 2001, 'Suicide, psychiatric illness, and social maladjustment in intercountry adoptees in Sweden: a cohort study', *The Lancet*, vol. 360, no. 9331, pp. 443–8.

Mohanty, J, Koeske, G & Sales, E 2006, 'Family cultural socialization, ethnic identity, and self-esteem: web-based survey of international adult adoptees', *Journal of Ethnic and Cultural Diversity in Social Work*, vol. 15, no. 3–4, pp. 153–71.

Mohanty, J & Newhill, C 2011, 'Asian adolescent and young adult adoptees' psychological well-being: examining the mediating role of marginality', *Children and Youth Services Review*, vol. 33, no. 7, pp. 1189–95.

O'Connor, TG, Rutter, M, Beckett, C, Keaveney, L, Kreppner, JM 2000, 'The effects of global severe privation on cognitive competence: extension and longitudinal follow-up. English and Romanian Adoptees Study Team', *Child Development*, vol. 71, no. 2, pp. 376–90.

Palacios, J, Roman, M, Moreno, C, Leon, E 2009, 'Family context for emotional recovery in internationally adopted children', *International Social Work*, vol. 52, no. 5, pp. 609–20.

Phinney, JS 1991, 'Ethnic identity and self-esteem: a review and integration', *Hispanic Journal of Behavioural Sciences*, vol. 13, no. 2, pp. 193–208.

Rumbaut, RG 1997, 'The ties that bind: Immigration and Immigrant Families in the United States', in A Booth, A Crouter & N Landale (eds), *Immigration and the Family: Research and Policy on US Immigrants*, Lawrence Erlbaum Associates, Mahwah, NJ, pp. 3–46.

Ryan, S & Groza, V 2004, 'Romanian adoptees: a cross-national comparison', *International Social Work*, vol. 47, no. 1, pp. 53–79.

Scherman, R & Harre, N 2008, 'The ethnic identification of same-race children in intercountry adoption', *Adoption Quarterly*, vol. 11, no. 1, pp. 45–65.

Selman, P 2002, 'Intercountry adoption in the new millennium: the "quiet migration" revisited', *Population Research and Policy Review*, vol. 21, pp 205–25.

Selman, P 2009, 'The rise and fall of intercountry adoption in the 21st century', *International Social Work*, vol. 52, no. 5, pp. 575–94.

Selman, P 2012, 'The global decline of intercountry adoption: what lies ahead?', *Social Policy and Society*, vol. 11, no. 3, pp. 381–97.

Silverman, AR 1993, 'Outcomes of transracial adoption', *The Future of Children*, vol. 3, no. 1, pp. 104–18.

Smith, C & Carlson, BE 1997, 'Stress, coping, and resilience in children and youth', *Social Service Review*, vol. 71, no. 2, pp. 231–56.

Smolin, DM 2010, 'Abduction, Sale and Traffic in Children in the Context of Intercountry Adoption', Information Document No. 1 for the attention of the Special Commission of June 2010 on the practical operation of the Hague Convention of 29 May 1993 on Protection of Children and Co-operation in Respect of Intercountry Adoption, pp. 1–22.

United Nations 2009, *Child Adoption: Trends and Policies*, Department of Economic and Social Affairs, New York.

Wilkinson, HS 1995, 'Psycholegal process and issues in international adoption', *The American Journal of Family Therapy*, vol. 23, no. 2, pp. 173–83.

Verhulst, FC, Althaus, M & Versluis-den Bieman, HJM 1990, 'Problem behaviour in international adoptees: II Age at placement', *Journal of the American Academy of Child and Adolescent Psychiatry*, vol. 29, no. 1, pp. 104–11.

Versluis-den Bieman, HJM & Verhulst, FC 1995, 'Self-reported and parent reported problems in adolescent international adoptees', *Journal of Child Psychology and Psychiatry*, vol. 36, no. 8, pp. 1411–28.

Yoon, DP 2000, 'Causal modeling predicting psychological adjustment of Korean-born adolescent adoptees', *Journal of Human Behavior in the Social Environment*, vol. 3, no. 3–4, pp. 65–82.

13

Building a culturally diverse and responsive aged-care health workforce

Jennifer Martin

Introduction

Australians have one of the highest life expectancy rates in the world, ranking sixth among countries in the Organisation for Economic Co-operation and Development (OECD) (AIHW 2012). The life expectancy for Australian men is 79.5 years, only slightly lower than the 79.9 years recorded for males from the highest-ranking country, Switzerland. Australian women have a life expectancy of 84 years; likewise, only marginally lower than 84.6 for Japan, the highest-ranking country for females. Life expectancy projections for both Australian men and women have increased by 25 years over the past century. However, life expectancy for Aboriginal and Torres Strait Islander peoples is approximately 12 years lower than the general population (AIHW 2012).

Health is difficult to define, with wide-ranging definitions from a narrow physical focus on the absence of disease or infirmity to a social determinants model. For the past 60 years, the World Health Organization (WHO) has taken a holistic view of health that incorporates the biological, psychological and social. This broader view of health has guided policy and service development in Australia and includes, 'both physical and mental dimensions, within a context that includes genetic, cultural, socioeconomic and environmental determinants' (AIHW 2012, p. 2). This definition clearly links health and social work, with a strong association between poor health outcomes and social disadvantage.

Unlike in many other countries around the world, the non-Indigenous Australian-born population is fluent in only one language, English. Yet approximately

25 per cent of Australia's population aged over 65 years speaks a language other than English, with the majority of these people born overseas. This proportion is highest in Melbourne, with estimates of close to 40 per cent in general and 50 per cent in the northern suburbs where the study reported in this chapter was conducted. Migrant elderly are a significant and growing proportion of the Australian population. They have significant heath needs, yet their usage of aged-care services is low.

It is argued in this chapter that the problem of low utilisation of health services by elderly immigrants from culturally and linguistically diverse (CALD) backgrounds is best addressed by mainstream and ethno-specific service providers working in close collaboration. Key factors relevant to building a culturally diverse and responsive aged-care health workforce are examined. A case study highlights the benefits of ethno-specific service provision for older people from CALD backgrounds and the importance of cultural knowledge, language and skills in caring for older people. A positive attitude and commitment to client self-determination, cultural diversity and healthy ageing is essential.

Policy and practice context

The age profile of the Australian population is changing as the population is growing, ageing and living longer. It has been estimated by the federal Minister for Health that by 2050 more than one in 20 workers will be employed in aged care (Health Workforce Australia 2012a). The changing population profile and increased aged-care workforce has seen a rapid increase in health expenditure as a percentage of gross domestic product. This is within large-scale reforms of the health sector, with a rethinking of traditional roles of health professionals and their education and training requirements. Many of the new roles in the future will be in direct care as well as prevention to identify health and wellbeing issues early. A focus is on better alignment and coordination of services that are cognisant of new and emerging technologies, such as e-health, tele-heath and the use of avatars, as well as face-to-face practices. In addition to direct clinical work, this gives rise to new opportunities for social workers as systems designers and managers, consultants and application developers (Cormack 2012, cited in Health Workforce Australia 2012a).

There is a growing burden of chronic disease, workforce pressures and 'unacceptable inequities in health outcomes and access to services' (DOHA 2010a, p. 9) in Australia. Australia's ageing population means that a significant strain will be placed on the health budget as current fiscal spending on people aged 65 years and over is four times greater than on the rest of the population (Health Workforce Australia 2011). Health needs tend to become more complex as people age. A 2009 study of older Australians living in the community found that approximately half (49 per cent) of those aged 65 to 74 years had five or more chronic conditions. For those aged 85 years and over, this increased to 70 per cent (AIHW 2011). Priorities for strategic planning for sustainable health care into the future are wellness, prevention and primary health care. These are also priority areas identified by the WHO, as populations around the world are managing and planning for growing and ageing populations. The WHO slogan of 'good health adds life to years' sends a message of older people having active and productive lives. A focus is on the resourcefulness and roles of older people in their families and communities as opposed to the disease and deficits model of ageing (WHO 2012, p. 1).

Health care is a large sector of the world economy and can significantly impact on economic growth and development. Policy and economic development are inextricably linked as health financing policies directly impact on economic performance. Health policies are necessarily assessed on both health and economic outcomes. Ruger, Jamison and Bloom (2001, p. 19) identify four main areas that health policymakers must consider:

- health expenditure in relation to gross domestic product
- welfare gains from health improvements
- incentives for workforce development and changes in consumer behaviours
- the extent to which poverty is perpetuated or generated by health expenditure.

Attention is increasingly focused on the wellbeing of older people. However, inconsistent research findings show a simultaneous high life-satisfaction score alongside high suicide rates (Chong 2007). A recent study of older Australians found that the majority of respondents, 84 per cent, felt positive about their quality of life; however, the researchers lamented the lack of data available on cause of death and hence lack of analysis of mortality patterns, including suicide (AIHW 2012). A substantial proportion of older people are diagnosed with mental illness. In 2007, 8 per cent of older people living in the community were found to have a mental illness, and this figure increased for those in residential settings (ABS 2009).

The scarcity of reliable research on the health and wellbeing needs of older people from all backgrounds is concerning. The social work profession is well placed to make a significant contribution by including the 'voices' of older people in the design, delivery and evaluation of services (Powell 2007). Dominelli, Lorenz and Soyden (2001) argue that health care should be viewed within the context of social development, with strategies developed to assist minority ethnic elderly to age with care (p. 10). According to this view, social development is about 'putting people first', advocating for community-oriented models of practice. The strategies include mainstream and ethno-specific services working together and developing strong linkages.

For older people without health insurance, the high costs of treatment relative to income can mean lengthy delays for treatment on public hospital waiting lists and reduced medical options. The established link between poor health outcomes and poverty requires policies targeted specifically at addressing the health and economic needs of low-income earners. A study of older people in China found that high health expenditure was a major cause of poverty for those living in rural areas (Liu et al. 1998). Efforts are required to improve healthcare system infrastructure, accessibility, affordability and suitability. Health policies need to be attuned to demographic transitions, be responsive to changing age structures and provide opportunities for education and job creation. This approach can create economic growth at the same time as providing necessary services.

This gives rise to consideration of models and frameworks for service design and delivery of services for older people predominantly provided in mainstream settings. A Canadian hospital inpatient study at Mount Sinai Hospital (2001, p. 13) found that patients from non-Anglo backgrounds did not receive the 'same kind of care'. Workers from 'visible minority groups' also experienced discrimination. A key finding was the need to address systemic discrimination in the workplace. These findings were supported by a further Canadian hospital inpatient study by Ng et al. (2007), which highlighted the importance of providing culturally appropriate services in healthcare settings and the important leadership role of social workers in needs assessment and program development.

The health workforce in Australia

The Australian health workforce faces both challenges and opportunities, as major changes are occurring in the structure and financing of health services as well as new systems being implemented for performance reporting and accountability including an expansion of e-health (AIHW 2012). Heath Workforce Australia (HWA) was established in 2010 as an initiative of the Council of Australian Governments (COAG) to address the challenges of providing a skilled health workforce that meets the increased projected demands into the future. The *National Health Workforce Innovation and Reform Strategic Framework for Action 2011–2015* is a new approach to workforce development across the health and education sectors (Health Workforce Australia 2011). A social determinants model of population health and wellbeing views health broadly to include nutrition, housing, education, employment, family and community stability and safety. This approach necessarily broadens the definition of health to include a range of organisations and services not previously considered to be under the umbrella of health. The focus is on wellness, prevention and primary care and balancing the priorities of consumer and community needs with cost efficiency. It is about reconfiguring the health workforce and education in Australia to prepare and support this workforce.

Models of education traditionally provided by universities are not considered appropriate to meeting future health workforce demands. This claim is based on research conducted by Frank et al. (2010) of 20 international educational and professional leaders that identified numerous areas where professional education failed to meet health challenges. Brownie, Bahnisch and Thomas (2011a) argue that there is a disjuncture between professional education and practice models, as competencies are not considered to be well matched to changing population needs. This research finding is attributed to the tendency of various professions to act in isolation and in competition with each other. Brownie, Bahnisch and Thomas argue that shared competencies across health systems are crucial for meeting future challenges. Inter-professional education is considered essential:

> The path to the successful implementation of collaborative care involves inter-professional education, which is based on the clear articulation of the competencies that are essential to effective teamwork and the delivery of health care (Brownie, Bahnisch & Thomas 2011b, p. 22).

Health workforce planning is based on the premise that a paradigm shift is required that puts the needs of consumers and communities at the forefront rather than the interests of the professions (Health Workforce Australia 2012b). HWA's Strategic Framework is a national platform to guide health workforce planning in Australia into the future. It involves a 'whole of community approach' that includes all levels of government, the private sector, non-government organisations, health professionals, educators and trainers, regulation and accreditation bodies, and consumers working in collaboration with HWA. Priority areas identified are Indigenous health, primary health care, health promotion and illness prevention, and rural and remote health.

An emphasis is on changing organisational cultures supporting cultural competency in accordance with the Strategic Framework. This includes culture change to reduce the impact of 'professional silos' and fragmentation of the workforce, and recruitment of the 'right' people with the 'right' attitudes to older people and their needs and contemporary health care (Health Workforce Australia 2012b, p. 66). It is recommended that 'capacity enablers', such as new or emerging roles including generalist, supplementary, supporting and change-management roles, are required (Health Workforce Australia 2012b, p. 7).

A focus throughout is on the work culture of mainstream organisations to develop an efficient and competent workforce to perform effectively in cross-cultural situations. A guiding principle of the framework is that workforce issues must be addressed in 'ways that recognise Australia's social and cultural diversity and promote equity of access and outcomes across communities, geographic areas and age groups' (Health Workforce Australia 2011, p. 7). The concept of cultural safety, discussed in Chapter 8, is mentioned specifically in relation to Aboriginal and Torres Strait Islander communities. Evaluation is considered central to service and workforce development and innovation and all services are expected to have inbuilt mechanisms for monitoring, evaluating and progress reporting. An indicator of failure to reform the system will be that 'people from culturally and linguistically diverse backgrounds will not have services that meet their specific needs' (Health Workforce Australia 2011, p.6).

Responses to the needs of older people from CALD backgrounds

The *Aged Care Act 1997* (Cth) provides the regulatory framework for care principles and standards of care for older Australians. The federal government sets standards for the quality and delivery for aged-care services in both residential services and the community (Aged Care Australia 2010). Community services include:

- Home and Community Care (HACC)
- Community Aged Care Packages (CACP)
- Extended Aged Care at Home (EACH)
- Extended Aged Care at Home Dementia (EACHD) programs
- National Respite for Carer Program (NRCP).
  These programs must ensure that:
- access to the service is based on relative need
- well-managed, quality services are received
- information is provided about the service received and clients are consulted about any changes to that service
- the service is planned to meet individual needs (adapted from DOHA 2010b, p. 1).

A network of eight organisations has been established under the Partners in Culturally Appropriate Community Care Program (PICAC), one in each state and territory, to work together with aged-care homes, ethnic communities and the Department of Health and Ageing to identify and address the special needs of older people from CALD backgrounds (Aged Care Australia 2010). This initiative has resulted in the provision of cross-cultural training and information sessions. Ethnic communities have been encouraged to form partnerships with aged-care service providers in order to establish more culturally appropriate facilities.

The intention is to provide frail older people from ethnic communities better access to quality aged-care services. The program also aims to increase ethnic community participation in decision-making about aged-care services (Aged Care Australia 2010).

A number of studies of both residential and community services for older people have found that older people from CALD backgrounds have lower rates of service use than members of the general population, particularly those from new and emerging communities (Abraham 2012; DHS 2006; Howe 2006). Increasingly, however, the more established CALD communities have greater representation in use of aged-care services apart from meals services (DHS 2006). This is due to a range of diverse reasons, including difficulties for older people from CALD backgrounds understanding a complex system with limited or no knowledge of English, available services and how to access these.

It is widely acknowledged that the multifaceted Australian health system is difficult to navigate: 'This web of public and private providers, settings, participants and supporting mechanisms is nothing short of complex' (AIHW 2012, p. 17). Multiple service providers are located in a range of private and public settings. This is supported by various legislative, funding and regulatory arrangements, with responsibilities distributed across all three levels of federal, state/territory and local government, non-government organisations and individuals. For many older people from CALD backgrounds, particularly from new and emerging communities, navigating this service system on their own is too daunting, especially if they experience health issues and frailty. Some people may be frightened to access services due to language difficulties and/or past negative experiences with authorities, and require assistance from family or trusted members of the community. Extended or acute aged-care services are only sought as a last resort and it is usually for crisis management when there is a health emergency (Abraham 2012).

Specific issues facing older people

Worldwide, people are living longer due to the decline in infant mortality, the control of infectious diseases and improvements in nutrition and living standards. Ageing reflects trends in mortality, frequency of chronic disease and maintenance of autonomy. Attention to these independent, though related, variables will increase the proportion of the population surviving disease-free to an advanced age. Expected lifespan is likely to increase, alongside the number of years a person is disease-free. However, projections indicate that the number of years that an older person is expected to live with loss of independence and autonomy is also likely to increase. Cancer is a major health problem for older people, followed by cardiovascular disease and mental disorders, with a high correlation between physical health problems and mental disorders (AIHW 2012). Of specific importance to older people are disorders that affect hearing and vision, dental problems, incontinence (urine and faeces) and intellectual failure, particularly dementia.

One-third of those aged 65 years and over and three-quarters of those aged 75 years and over are taking medication on a regular basis. It is not unusual for an older person to be discharged from hospital on ten or more medications (Martin 2012). The elderly are a more diverse physiological group and are therefore much more prone to adverse reactions to drug therapy. The family is the greatest single source of support for older people. Loneliness is a key factor in compounding health problems, especially in elderly women. Healthcare workers have been criticised for their role in controlling access to services and for fostering a dependency view of older people, with policy and practices dominated by risk management.

Eric Erikson (1980) developed a concept of personality development linked with biological development over three decades ago that still remains relevant to social work practice today across all cultures. He argued that psychological and physical development were linked and identified stages of physical development and associated psychological tasks at each stage. The ages specified by Erikson for each developmental stage were an approximate guide, and allowed for wide variation according to individual differences with these stages overlapping. Erikson's final developmental stage was late adulthood, for those aged 60–65 years and over. He identified 'integrity' as a main developmental task, as well as 'living with dignity'. This requires having a sense of meaning and purpose in life as well as order. Integrity results in joy for living, in contrast to the despair that often develops in older people, particularly in Western industrialised countries, due to unresolved issues of loss and grief and loneliness. Issues of loss and grief are a particular issue for refugees and asylum seekers as well as older new immigrants who do not speak English and who are reliant upon younger family members.

A postmodern view of ageing focuses on living well in the community with an emphasis on:

- choice
- control
- coordination
- empowerment.

Assessment of older people requires consideration of hopes and dreams, and strengths and resources, in addition to needs and risk factors. Positive choices are highlighted in relation to the type and quality of care required. Older people who are also carers need to be seen as people with their own needs and desires and not purely as resources. The relationships developed between the worker, the older person and significant others are paramount. Assessment requires cultural knowledge and skills to inform decisions about the most appropriate actions. Initially, this may simply be deciding who to invite for a first meeting. A postmodern view challenges the notion of social workers as experts on culture. Expertise is based more on an understanding of the dynamic nature of culture. Workers are encouraged to discuss with the older person and those closest to them who is most appropriate to include in discussions and decisions about their health, wellbeing and cultural needs and requirements. Such an approach acknowledges the fluidity of culture and respects the diversity of practices within and between different cultural groups.

Dementia

Dementia is the third main cause of death in Australia (AIHW 2012). In 2011 it was estimated that 222 000 Australians (1 per cent) had dementia. It is projected that by 2031 this number will increase to over 464 000 (1.6 per cent) (AIHW 2012, p. 317). Research findings suggest these figures are, in fact, too low and that the prevalence of dementia may be much higher, but there is no national prevalence or incidence data readily available. There are no data subsets for diverse population groups including Aboriginal and Torres Strait Islander peoples and people from CALD backgrounds (Alzheimer's Disease International 2009; AIHW 2012; Anstey et al. 2010). While generally associated with the elderly, dementia is not a normal part of the ageing process. Many older people well advanced in years retain full intellectual functioning. Its occurrence is determined by genetic predisposition, family history and general health and wellbeing.

Dementia is common in older people but quite rare in middle-aged or young people. Dementia of the Alzheimer's type affects 6 per cent of people over 65 years in the Australian population. This percentage rises to 11 per cent for those aged over 75 years. It is estimated that half of all permanent residents in Australian aged-care facilities are diagnosed with dementia and have high care needs (AIHW 2011).

Dementia is a condition for which there is no known cure or medical treatment and which results in the gradual deterioration of memory, intellect and the ability for self-care (see box below).

Features of dementia

Presenting complaints

The person may complain of forgetfulness or feeling depressed but may be unaware of memory loss. Families ask for help:
- in early stages: because of failing memory, change in personality or behaviour
- in later stages: because of confusion, wandering, incontinence.

Poor hygiene in an older patient may indicate memory loss.

Diagnostic features
- decline in recent memory, thinking and judgment, orientation, language and social adjustment; often appear apathetic or uninterested, but may appear alert and appropriate despite poor memory
- loss of emotional control—may be easily upset (tearful, irritable)

Tests of memory and thinking include:
- ability to recall names of three common objects immediately and after three minutes
- ability to name the days of the week in reverse order.

(DOHA 2011)

The onset of dementia is slow and insidious and leads to major personality alteration, markedly affecting the individual's ability to continue to relate to the world around them. In advanced stages, the person affected will not recognise loved ones or even their own face in the mirror. It presents a social problem of considerable magnitude in countries such as Australia and China, which have an ageing demography. Dementia is difficult to diagnose and is a major challenge in terms of its management over often quite long periods.

CASE STUDY 13.1

BUILDING A CULTURALLY DIVERSE AGED-SERVICES WORKFORCE

In 2011 a study was conducted in a not-for-profit organisation with over two decades of experience in providing a broad range of services to support migrant and refugee communities in the northern suburbs of Melbourne. Over the past 12 years, this organisation has established a unique bilingual and ethnically diverse team of aged services staff, who provide in-home and centre-based care. The unique service model has focused on matching trained and experienced home support and centre-based staff with the language and cultural backgrounds of care recipients from established and emerging, ageing CALD communities.

Method

A case study design was adopted for the study, which used stratified sampling and a key indicators approach to ensure that the data collected was representative of the population studied. Interviews were conducted with 130 respondents: 64 clients from Chinese and Vietnamese backgrounds and 66 direct care staff. This sample size was representative of client population with a minimum of 5 per cent of service users and 50 per cent of direct care staff interviewed. Four focus groups were conducted: two with different groups of direct care staff, one with a Chinese community older person's group and one with members of a program activity group for older Vietnamese people that provided carer respite. All activities and services were conducted in either Chinese or Vietnamese. For the program activity group, all staff, including the bus driver who collected participants and the cook, spoke in Vietnamese to participants. There was no expectation to communicate in English. The research was conducted in English with interpreter translations and written transcription during the group meetings. This, however, was a limitation of the research.

The main research question was, 'What are the experiences of consumers and workers of bilingual, culturally matched, aged care services?' Focus group questions for both workers and clients focused on the questions of accessibility, capacity, appropriateness, responsiveness and effects on clients.

Findings

In the focus groups with workers and clients two dominant themes emerged:
- the interplay between accessibility, cultural appropriateness and responsiveness, and quality of care

■ how knowledge of language and culture enhanced workforce capacity and client satisfaction.

Main issues arising under each of these themes from the focus groups are discussed below, along with supporting comments from clients (C) and workers (W).

Accessibility, cultural appropriateness, responsiveness and quality of care

Cultural responsiveness was considered the key factor in the success of work with clients. Respondents identified functions and competencies related to biological, psychological and social needs common to the general ageing population. Effective practice was underpinned by personal qualities and attributes, competency and ethical standards of the workers. Personal qualities included honesty, genuine friendliness and warmth, being motivated and energetic, maintaining a positive and encouraging attitude, and having a sense of humour. This was within a relationship characterised by client self-determination and respect for privacy and confidentiality. Understanding and compassion for the clients and passion for the work were paramount.

Workers needed to be patient and persevere to fully understand their clients and recognise their changing needs. This required flexibility, adaptability and, at times, creativity, as demonstrated in the following quotes from the study:

> We remain positive—keeping them focused on what they still have. (W)
>
> Patience is important, as often there is a lot of repetition. I have heard the stories before but pretend I am listening for the first time. I can make references to the past that help people with the current situation. When we go to the shops together it can take five minutes to choose a loaf of bread. (W)

Direct practice skills in observation, non-verbal communication, listening, assertiveness and empathy were important:

> Older people can sometimes be seen as stubborn or set in their ways. It helps to understand where they are coming from. You need to take time to help them express how they feel. (W)
>
> Often you have to think of other ways of explaining things so they understand. For example some clients with dementia don't like talking. They may come in and watch me and I can ascertain quickly whether or not they want to converse or not. (W)

Cultural competence, a pleasant disposition and genuinely enjoying the work were considered essential. This required an honest, trustworthy and compassionate approach, combined with a sense of humour and positive outlook:

> We are a caring, competent, skilled, well-trained workforce—meeting all client needs happily—with good customer service. If they're happy we're happy! (W)
>
> I find the staff very good. They are very happy and helpful. I am so lucky. (C)
>
> A mature, experienced workforce and respectful relationships were significant:
>
> Respect for older people and generational differences are important. Most of us have/had aged parents and have an understanding of aged care. It is important to love and care for

them like a parent—to show that we care. Treat clients as we would like to be treated ourselves—keep them and us safe. (W)

They help me with things I can't do for myself, being patient and kind when I have good and
bad days. We share hobbies and talk about the grandchildren and go out to different places.
It helps me to forget my worries. (C)

Skills in direct care included personal care involving lifting, showering and dressing.
Assistance was provided with personal grooming for shaving, hair styling and make-up.
Workers helped with cleaning, cooking and shopping, and wellbeing activities including
reading, singing and dancing:

I make my clients feel comfortable, doing things together to keep them occupied. With one
client who has dementia and was not interested/motivated to do anything I used to sing
songs (old songs my mum taught me) while I worked. One day the client responded and
opened the door and started singing along with me. It was a really humbling experience. (W)

Personal qualities, attitudes and life experience were considered important. All workers
had extensive prior experience in performing the tasks required of them in cross-cultural
contexts, often with family members in their own homes. Knowledge gained from formal
education and training on the ageing process, diagnoses—dementia in particular—and
skills for responding to complex needs were useful. Workers used skills in problem-solving,
advocacy, conflict management, including managing difficult behaviours and stress management addressing issues of worker and client safety. Cross-cultural skills created opportunities for increased understandings, culturally appropriate care and culturally informed
interactions. Cross-cultural competency focused on knowledge of language and culture
employing a range of communication skills:

We provide a bridge between the generations—traditional ways and modern ways in
Australia. (W)

Language, culture, enhanced workforce capacity and client satisfaction

Knowledge of language and cultural beliefs and practices created shared understandings and put older people at ease, resulting in less likelihood of misunderstandings and
improved quality of care. Most clients did not speak English. Shared language and culture
made it easier for older people, carers and workers to communicate and to be specific in
getting clear messages across. This in turn promoted quality care:

They don't experience anxiety being with someone they can't communicate with. Own
language, own people. For example, at Easter I know the traditions, special food and religious
beliefs and customs. They are comfortable because they know I understand the beliefs. I
know how to address people according to different ages and relationships. The capacity to
trust is increased and you are treated almost like family. (W)

I might be watching television or listening to the radio in my own language and we can
discuss this together because we both understand. (C)

Shared language and culture meant that workers were able to provide quality care by meeting additional psychological, emotional and social needs while providing personal care in a manner that was respectful and comfortable for the client and family:

> You are giving clients their dignity by understanding and following their culture. (W)

Reminiscing on the past in a shared language was particularly important in meeting psychological and emotional needs of older clients and was a way of connecting with those with dementia:

> Older people like to reminisce about the older days. They ask what village my family came from. They want to talk about history and culture. We can relate to their stories and be more engaged. The client feels secure in the knowledge that we know their music, songs and dances. (W)

Direct care workers became important in their clients lives due to the amount of time spent with clients and the often personal nature of this care. Cultural understanding of body language was important particularly when clients found it hard to express themselves in words. This was particularly important for older people who were seen as increasingly reverting back to their first language and culture as they got older, particularly those suffering with dementia:

> If they can't communicate verbally you can follow the culture. Gestures mean different things in different cultures. We also know slang and more playful language. (W)
>
> I love my own language. I speak my language when I forget English. When the workers speak to me in my language I am so happy. It makes me feel important. (C)

Language and cultural understanding underpinned quality of care. This included cultural respect and understanding, and matching for gender and other cultural factors as required. It was much easier to communicate policies and procedures that workers are required to abide by and explanations of how the system works and the services available to clients and their families.

> Shared language and culture helps you figure out ways to connect with your client. It gives confidence to the carer/family members and opens up topics of conversation. It lays a foundation of respect and confidence in the care provided. (W)
>
> We can communicate better and I understand more. They understand what I need and can provide it straight away. They are like family to me. (C)

The ability to communicate in a shared language and listen to people's stories was a central component of the work.

> It is important to listen and to respect—really listen and respond because of shared language. Shared language makes it easier to calm clients down when they are agitated. (W)

Common language, cultural respect and understanding client needs were crucial:

> Listening to peoples' stories in a common language, sharing parts of their earlier lives is so important for understanding their culture and needs. (W)

> Being able to talk and listen in my own language is very important. I am not so lonely. (C)

Workers commented on the importance of language and culture for food preparation and social activities:

> When you are of the same culture you can cook what they want. You can play games and music in their own language. (W)

> They know where I like to shop for food and how it is to be prepared. They know how I like my home tasks to be done—ways to wash dishes and hygiene. (C)

Workers agreed that it was easier to build trust and for clients to talk about personal matters in their own language and this was important, particularly when they did not want to burden family members:

> There is more trust if you share the language. Of course this depends upon your attitude and how you present yourself as well as personality. (W)

> I feel more comfortable when I know the worker speaks my language and understands my culture. We can share stories and get to know and trust each other. (C)

Future directions

The bio-psychosocial model of health focusing on social determinants, wellbeing, prevention and primary care, adopted by the World Health Organization and the Australian Government for future aged-care service and workforce development, sits well with dominant paradigms in social work. In particular, the emphasis on the person in environment and the resourcefulness of older people maintaining an active role in the family and community is consistent with a social work strengths perspective. It resonates with Erikson's final developmental stage of 'integrity' and living a life with dignity, meaning and purpose. This is consistent with the positive view of ageing in social work critical theories. In particular, postmodern, anti-oppressive and anti-discriminatory, and feminist theories emphasise individual choice, control and empowerment.

Understanding and following a person's culture was considered a means of 'giving clients their dignity' by a worker in the case study. The central positioning of 'consumers' at the forefront of service development and delivery resonates with feminist notions of 'shared leadership' and 'consumer leadership' (Martin 2012). Dominelli, Lorenz and Soyden's (2001) social development model of 'putting people first' is consistent with notions of consumer leadership.

Social work services are important due to the strong link between poor health outcomes and social disadvantage. Social workers must not lose sight of marginalised and disadvantaged groups that have lower life expectancy, such as Indigenous Australians and members of CALD communities, who have lower access rates for health services and are vulnerable to discrimination in mainstream services. The low uptake of health services by people from CALD backgrounds demonstrates the need for a collaborative approach. Service providers in mainstream and ethno-specific services must work together across the aged and disability sector to prepare for an ageing CALD population. A main task is to establish a culturally responsive workforce to meet future needs and ensure services are culturally safe. Given the very personal nature of the care provided, complex needs and high levels of vulnerability, providing older people with choices and making them feel at ease and comfortable with services provided is crucial.

Social workers are required to balance consumer and community needs with cost efficiency. Issues of accessibility and affordability for all, particularly Indigenous people and older people from new and emerging communities who do not speak English, are main concerns for social workers. High costs of treatment, long waiting lists, delays in treatment and reduced medical options perpetuate discrimination and marginalisation of those from low income groups. The relationship between illness, health expenditure and poverty is an area requiring further study. More research is also needed on older people living in poverty and on mental illness and suicide.

The *National Health Workforce Innovation and Reform Strategic Framework for Action 2011–2015* focuses on the culture of mainstream organisations working effectively in cross-cultural situations. The study findings indicate the importance of ethno-specific service provision to older people by workers who speak their language and understand their culture. Dominelli, Lorenz and Soyden's (2001) social development model of caring for older people requires ethno-specific services and mainstream services to 'work together and develop strong linkages' for optimum outcomes. A multifaceted approach is required that recognises the complexities of the healthcare system and the needs of older people and promotes access to services by people from CALD backgrounds, particularly members of new and emerging communities.

The Strategic Framework also requires effective teamwork and increased models of multidisciplinary collaboration. The challenge is for disciplines to work collegially, rather than in competition with one another, and for educators to create new models of inter-professional education and multidisciplinary teamwork, while simultaneously providing the requisite knowledge for each profession. Universities need to closely consider the claim that educational models and competencies are not well matched to changing population needs. In recent years, Australian social work programs have been required by the professional accrediting body, the Australian Association of Social Workers, to include compulsory competencies in mental health, child protection, Indigenous studies and cross-cultural practice. This has reduced flexibility, with a crowded curriculum leaving little room for adaptability and responsiveness to population needs in other areas such as ageing. Educators are called upon to develop innovations in face-to-face practices as well as new technologies in e-health and tele-health and use of avatars to supplement learning experiences.

Recruitment of the 'right people with the right attitudes' is the cornerstone of Australian health workforce development in aged care, with this strongly supported by the study findings. This requires closer scrutiny and further development of selection processes in social work programs beyond academic performance and work experience to recruit people who genuinely like older people and want to work with them.

Changing population needs have created new and emerging roles for social work practice and workforce development in aged care. Better alignment and coordination of services is required to reduce complexities and difficulties in using the system and thereby improve access to services. Social workers are well placed to perform leadership roles in program development and needs assessment, especially in areas of high need such as dementia.

Conclusion

Building a culturally diverse and responsive aged-care health workforce requires a holistic view of health that incorporates biological, psychological, social and cultural factors. This holistic view is promoted and supported by the World Health Organization and underpins health policy and service development in Australia.

Social workers have an important role to play, given the strong association between poor health outcomes and disadvantage. The poor health outcomes and reduced life expectancy of Indigenous Australians are of particular concern, as is the under-representation of older people from CALD backgrounds using aged-care services. Discrepancies between high life-satisfaction scores, high levels of mental illness and unreliable data on suicide in the elderly require closer scrutiny and further research. The high costs of health care and reduced options for those on low incomes without private health insurance are concerning.

The large-scale reforms of the health sector in response to a growing and ageing population focus on wellness, prevention and primary health care within mainstream services. An emphasis is on developing the culture of mainstream organisations to work effectively in cross-cultural situations. It is argued in this chapter that the social development model of ethno-specific and mainstream services working together, and developing strong linkages, will result in optimum outcomes.

The study findings outlined in the case study above demonstrate the importance of cultural knowledge, language and skills in caring for older people from CALD backgrounds. This is underpinned by a positive attitude and commitment to client self-determination, cultural diversity and healthy ageing. Social work educators must prepare for this workforce expansion by creating opportunities for multidisciplinary teamwork. Increased content on the knowledge and skills required for working effectively with older people in cross-cultural contexts is required, including innovative use of technology. The challenge is to find space in the curriculum to be responsive to changing population and workforce needs.

An essential component is the recruitment of students and workers from diverse cultural and language backgrounds—especially those from Indigenous and new and emerging communities who have positive attitudes towards older people and a genuine desire to work with them. Empathy and respect are central to this work in providing a culturally and linguistically competent workforce to meet the needs of an ageing, multicultural, multilingual Australian population.

REFLECTIVE QUESTIONS

1   How can mainstream organisations develop a culture to provide an efficient and competent workforce to work effectively in cross-cultural situations?
2   How can mainstream and ethno-specific aged-care services work in the best interests of their clients to bring about improved health outcomes?
3   What are the roles of social workers in building a culturally diverse and responsive aged-care health workforce?

FURTHER READING

Chong, AM 2007, 'Promoting the psychosocial health of the elderly—the role of social workers', *Social Work in Health Care*, vol. 44, no. 1–2, pp. 91–109.
Dominelli, L, Lorenz, W & Soyden, H (eds) 2001, *Beyond Racial Divides: Ethnicities in Social Work Practice*, Ashgate, Aldershot.
Powell, J 2007, 'Promoting older people's voices—the contribution of social work to inter-disciplinary research', *Social Work in Health Care*, vol. 44, no. 1–2, pp. 111–26.
Williams, C & Graham, M 2012, 'Travelling hopefully', in C Williams & M Graham (eds), *Social Work in Europe: Race and Ethnic Relations*, Sage, London.

REFERENCES

Abraham, N 2012, 'What are the barriers for Somali and Assyrian Chaldean communities in accessing mainstream health and welfare services?', Masters thesis, RMIT University, Melbourne.
Aged Care Australia 2010, *Help Staying at Home: Services for Culturally and Linguistically Diverse People*, Department of Health and Ageing, Commonwealth of Australia, ACT.
Alzheimer's Disease International 2009, *World Alzheimer Report*, Alzheimer's Disease International, London.
Anstey, KA, Burns, RA, Birrell, CL, Steel, D, Kiely, KM & Luszcz, MA 2010, 'Estimates of probable dementia prevalence from population-based surveys compared with dementia prevalence estimates based on meta-analyses', *BMC Neurology*, vol. 10, no. 1, p. 62.

Australian Bureau of Statistics 2009, *National Survey of Mental Health and Wellbeing: Summary of Results, 2007*, cat. no. 4326.0, ABS, Canberra.

Australian Institute of Health and Welfare 2011, *Australia's Welfare 2011*, Australia's Welfare Series No. 10, cat. no. AUS 142, AIHW, ACT.

Australian Institute of Health and Welfare 2012, *Australia's Health 2012*, Australia's Health Series No. 13, cat. no. AUS 156, AIHW, ACT.

Brownie, S, Bahnisch, M & Thomas, J 2011a, *Competency-based Education and Competency-based Career Frameworks: Informing Australian Health Workforce Development*, Report by the National Health Workforce Research and Collaboration, University of Queensland Node of the Australian Health Workforce Institute and Health Workforce Australia, Adelaide.

Brownie, S, Bahnisch, M & Thomas, J 2011b, *Exploring the Literature: Competency-based Education and Training and Competency-based Career Frameworks*, Report by the National Health Workforce Research and Collaboration, University of Queensland Node of the Australian Health Workforce Institute and Health Workforce Australia, Adelaide.

Chong, AM 2007, 'Promoting the psychosocial health of the elderly—the role of social workers', *Social Work in Health Care*, vol. 44, no. 1–2, pp. 91–109.

Department of Health and Ageing 2010a, *Building a 21st Century Primary Healthcare System: Australia's First National Primary Health Care Strategy*, Commonwealth of Australia, ACT.

Department of Health and Ageing 2010b, *Aged Care Australia, Standards of Home Care Services*, Commonwealth of Australia, ACT.

Department of Health and Ageing 2011, *General Practice Programs to Improve Access and Outcomes in Mental Health*, Commonwealth of Australia, ACT.

Department of Human Services 2006, *Who Gets HAAC?*, Aged Care Branch, DHS, Victorian Government, Melbourne.

Dominelli, L, Lorenz, W & Soyden, H (eds) 2001, *Beyond Racial Divides: Ethnicities in Social Work Practice*, Ashgate, Aldershot.

Erikson, EH 1980, *Identity and Life Cycle*, WW Norton, New York.

Frank, J, Chen, Z, Bhutta, J, Cohen, N & Crisp, T 2010, 'Health professionals for a new century: transforming education to strengthen health systems in an interdependent world', *The Lancet*, vol. 376, no. 9756, pp. 1923–58.

Health Workforce Australia 2011, *National Health Workforce Innovation and Reform Strategic Framework for Action 2011–2015*, HWA, Adelaide.

Health Workforce Australia 2012a, *Health Workforce Insights*, Issue 4, HWA, Adelaide.

Health Workforce Australia 2012b, *Workforce Innovation: Caring for Older People Program, Final Report*, HWA, Adelaide.

Howe, A 2006, *Cultural Diversity, Ageing and HACC: Trends in Victoria in the Next 15 Years*, Department of Human Services, Victorian Government, Melbourne.

Liu, Y, Hu, S, Fu, W & Hsiao, WC 1998, 'Is community financing necessary and feasible for rural China?', in ML Barer, TE Getzen & GL Stoddart (eds), *Health, Health Care and Health Economics: Perspectives on Distribution*, Wiley, New York.

Martin, J 2012, *Mental Health Social Work*, Ginninderra Press, Adelaide.

Mount Sinai Hospital 2001, *Diversity and Human Rights in the Work Environment*, Diversity and Human Rights Office, Mt Sinai Hospital, Toronto.

Ng, J, Popova, S, Yau, M & Sulman, J 2007, 'Do culturally sensitive services for Chinese in-patients make a difference?', *Social Work in Health Care*, vol. 44, no. 3, pp. 129–43.

Powell, J 2007, 'Promoting older people's voices—the contribution of social work to inter-disciplinary research', *Social Work in Health Care*, vol. 44, no. 1–2, pp. 111–26.

Ruger, JP, Jamison, DT & Bloom, DE 2001, 'Health and the economy', in M Merson, R Black & A Mills (eds), *International Public Health: Diseases, Programs, Systems, and Policies*, Aspen, Gaithersburg, MD, pp. 617–66.

World Health Organization WHO, 2012, *Ageing and Life Course*, WHO Press, Geneva.

Index